CW00960176

Poverty, philanthropy and the state

Manchester University Press

Poverty, philanthropy and the state

Charities and the working classes in London, 1918–79

Katharine Bradley

Manchester University Press

Published by Manchester University Press
Altrincham Street, Manchester M1 7JA, UK
www.manchesteruniversitypress.co.uk

British Library Cataloguing-in-Publication Data is available

Library of Congress Cataloging-in-Publication Data is available

ISBN 978 1 7849 9368 9 *paperback*

First published by Manchester University Press in hardback 2009

This edition first published 2016

Printed by Lightning Source

For my parents, Frank and Annette

Contents

List of illustrations

All illustrations in this volume are reproduced with the permission
of the Barnett Research Centre at Toynbee Hall, London.

Preface

This book explores an area of recent British history that has not, until now, been rigorously examined by historians: the relationship between the voluntary sector and the state in the period 1918 to 1979.

The inter-war years and the period after the Second World War witnessed immense changes in the structure of the state and its relation to the individual. Since the introduction of the New Poor Law in 1834 the nature of British welfare had been in a state of flux. Although the apparatus of the nineteenth-century state was minimal, there was significant growth in local government responsibility for education, public health and housing. The long-standing traditions of mutualism and trade unionism formed part of the basis for the Liberal Party's Edwardian social reforms, which included a limited range of insurance-based schemes to help counter the impact of unemployment and sickness. These schemes were provided by the 'approved societies' which had grown out of larger friendly societies and mutual organisations. In the course of the inter-war period the complex interplay of state and charities continued as the role of local government continued to expand and voluntary or non-profit organisations adapted their work to suit the evolving frameworks and the new challenges posed by economic depression and long-term unemployment. Following the Second World War, the Labour governments of 1945–51 introduced a comprehensive welfare state and National Health Service that aimed to eradicate William Beveridge's 'five giants', Want, Ignorance, Idleness, Disease and Squalor. In this relatively short time social policy evolved from a model in which charities and similar bodies had been the main providers of some services and support with minimal state intervention to a model in which the state supported the needs of its citizens, and charities, as the 'voluntary sector', were the junior partner.

The university settlement movement, pioneered in east London in the 1880s, was at the heart of this reforming of welfare. Settlements such as Toynbee Hall, Oxford House or Blackfriars brought young university graduates to live and undertake social work in the poorer areas of cities, and to learn what it was to be less fortunate. For many 'settlers' it was a vivid and influential experience that helped to shape their future career. A number of those resident at settlements before the First World War would go on to become heavily involved in the reform of welfare, most famously William Beveridge and Clement Attlee. The settlement movement in turn was dependent for success on one particular group: the community in which it worked. Settlement activities were most effective when they responded to local needs and wants, and when they allowed local people to become involved in running these activities. Whilst the settlement movement may have been able to shape policy makers' views on welfare, its work was shaped by the community around it.

This book will explore these themes by looking at a number of the east and south-east London settlements, including Toynbee Hall, Oxford House, Bernhard Baron St George's Settlement, Canning Town Women's Settlement, Mansfield House University Settlement, Blackfriars Settlement and Fern Street Settlement. Although settlement houses could be found in towns and cities across the United Kingdom, the London settlements were among the oldest and most famous, and were well established in their communities by the period 1918–74. The ever-increasing complexity and development of the capital in the period also created specific challenges that the settlements had to address.

The book is therefore aimed at those interested in the historical development of British social policy, network theory, the shaping of ideas of citizenship, and the voluntary sector more generally.

Acknowledgements

I have become indebted to many people in the course of writing this book. It started life in 2002 when I took up a PhD studentship at the Centre for Contemporary British History at the Institute of Historical Research, University of London. My thanks must go first of all to Pat Thane, for her superb guidance, first through the supervision of my PhD and then later for mentoring me as a postdoctoral fellow. Without her wisdom and guidance this would have been a less rewarding exercise. I would also like to thank Sally Alexander and John Davies for examining the thesis in March 2006. The Leverhulme Trust funded my original PhD studentship, whilst an ESRC postdoctoral fellowship enabled me to undertake the additional research necessary to develop my thesis into this book. The University of Kent supported me through the coincidence of my first term in a lectureship and the completion of the manuscript. Thus thanks are due to my colleagues in the School of Social Policy, Sociology and Social Research at Kent, especially those at the Medway campus.

Other people have given me their support and encouragement along the way. Fiona Macintosh inspired me as an undergraduate to consider further study, and helped immensely in guiding me to my eventual research topic. Billie Melman gave much welcome encouragement and advice from the earliest days of my thesis, whilst Anna Davin introduced me to first to oral history and later to her own family connections with the settlement movement. Matthew Cragoe gave me much encouragement and good advice as I found my feet in academia, as did other colleagues at the University of Hertfordshire. Seth Koven and I have shared thoughts and tips on settlement archives over the years. Tim Wales has kindly shared his knowledge of West Ham and Daisy Parsons with me.

From 1999 until early 2007 I worked part-time as librarian/archivist at Toynbee Hall, one of the settlements discussed in this study. It was a great introduction to my research material and to others working in the field. My colleagues at Toynbee Hall are too many to mention individually but especial thanks must go to Jill Goldsworthy and Cynthia White, with whom I worked closely on the archives development project, as well as to Anne Grant, who volunteered her time to work with me in the archives.

I must thank the staffs of the various libraries and archives I have consulted in the course of preparing this study: Arike Oke of the Barnett Research Centre at Toynbee Hall, the British Film Institute, the British Library, the British Library of Political and Economic Science at the London School of Economics, Jane Bradley at the Worshipful Company of Goldsmiths' Library, Hackney Archives, Lambeth Archives Department, London Metropolitan Archives, the National Archives, the National Sound Archive, Nicholas Malton at the National Society for the Prevention of Cruelty to Children, Richard Durack and colleagues at Newham Local Studies and Archives, Royal London Hospital Museum and Archives, Malcolm Barr-Hamilton and colleagues at Tower Hamlets Local History Library, and the Women's Library.

I would like to thank Vanessa Chambers, John Clarke, Mark Crowley, Mark Freeman, Robyn Glessner, Helen Glew, Daniel Grey, Jane Hamlett, Yoichiro Horikoshi, Emma Jones, Jennifer Ledfors, James Lees, Liza Filby, Mary Clare Martin, Helen McCarthy, James Moore, Soyang Park, Ayako Towatari, Dave Wilson and Catherine Wright for their friendship and moral support. Nick Carn, Helen Corkin, Tracy Knight, Sithu Muang and Anna Ridgewell have provided much welcome distraction from historical matters over the years. Last but not least, many thanks must also go to my parents and my sister, Jane.

K.B.

List of abbreviations

BARS	British Association of Residential Settlements
BRC	Barnett Research Centre at Toynbee Hall
CCEL	Council of Citizens of East London
CCHF	Children's Country Holiday Fund
COS	Charity Organisation Society
CPAG	Child Poverty Action Group
CSV	Community Service Volunteers
CTWS	Canning Town Women's Settlement
GLC	Greater London Council
ICAA	Invalid Children's Aid Association
LAD	Lambeth Archives Department
LCC	London County Council
LMA	London Metropolitan Archives
LMHS	Lady Margaret Hall Settlement
MABYS	Metropolitan Association for the Befriending of Young Servants
MHUS	Mansfield House University Settlement
NACRO	National Association for the Care and Resettlement of Offenders
NADPAS	National Association of Discharged Prisoners' Aid Societies
PML	Poor Man's Lawyer
NLSA	Newham Local Studies and Archives
SWHCWS	South West Ham Children's Welfare Society
SWHHS	South West Ham Health Society
TNA	The National Archives, London
WUS	Women's University Settlement

Introduction

This book is a study of the settlement movement in London between 1918 and 1979, and the ways in which these charities interacted with the state and the communities around them. The study uses the settlements as a means of exploring a series of important dynamics in the history of British social policy, namely the evolutions of the mixed economy of welfare in the twentieth century. There have been many excellent histories of charities and the development of the British welfare state in the twentieth century, yet very few studies have addressed the changing relationship between voluntary organisations, their client groups and the state, especially in the period after 1945. These are vital questions that need to be addressed by historians, as they have a fundamental impact on the provision of welfare in Britain. These questions can be identified as follows: who decides what welfare services are needed and by whom; how they should be provided; who should provide them; and who should pay for them. The answers given to these questions by policy makers, politicians and voters over the years have varied.

The welfare state introduced by the Labour governments of 1945–51 made the state the main provider of welfare, and access to that welfare a right of British citizens, but it was not the only body concerned with the well-being of the nation. William Beveridge, the 'architect' of the welfare state, believed that voluntary action was an essential part of a modern democratic society, and never envisaged an all-encompassing state. Although it was often popularly believed that there was no longer a need for a 'voluntary sector' in the 1940s and 1950s, this was not the case. Whilst the welfare state provided a universal safety net for Britons, charities and voluntary organisations were able to provide the kinds of services that the state could not easily do. The continually tipping balance between voluntary organisations, commercial bodies and the state in the inter-war period has been well documented, as has the fondness on the part of both the

Conservatives in the 1980s and of New Labour in the 1990s and 2000s to place greater emphasis on the delivery of services by voluntary or non-governmental organisations. This book aims to fill this gap by extending the historical narrative beyond the inter-war period up to 1979 and the governments of Margaret Thatcher. An understanding of the complexity of this mixed economy of welfare and its development in the course of the twentieth century is important not only for historians but also for those who examine political processes, and social policy in particular.

The university settlements were set up in London from the mid-1880s onwards, and spread across the United Kingdom as well as North America, Europe and parts of Asia. They were a combination of mission, training school and community centre, bringing young university graduates to deprived areas of the capital and providing them with opportunities to develop skills and knowledge in a range of areas. Their other function was to serve as a centre for the community to congregate, as well as to access a range of social resources and activities. In turn, the young graduates and settlement staff became involved in local and national politics, as well as in various campaigns to extend the rights of working people. By the inter-war period, many settlements were working with local authorities on a wide range of projects, often in relation to health provision for women and young children, and in the Second World War they had an important role to play in co-ordinating relief efforts in heavily bombed areas of London. Although many areas of settlement work were taken over by the welfare state from the 1940s, they adapted their work accordingly to meet the emergent needs of their local communities – especially where these were not being or could not be met by the state. Thus the settlements are highly suitable for exploring the development of broader themes in British social policy history. This study also breaks new ground by examining the settlement movement beyond 1918: few serious studies have looked at the movement as a whole beyond the inter-war period, despite the importance of the work of these voluntary organisations both to their local communities and to the provision of social welfare more generally.

As this would suggest, the book is not an institutional history of the settlement movement, and neither does it seek to extensively survey the movement in London or elsewhere. Rather, it samples a number of London settlements: Toynbee Hall, Mansfield House, Canning Town Women's Settlement, Lady Margaret Hall Settlement, Blackfriars Settlement, Bernhard Baron Settlement, the Fern Street Settlement and Oxford House, as well as touching upon the Mary Ward

Settlement and Cambridge House as well as settlements outside London. I have drawn upon settlement and other archives, oral history testimonies, settlement workers' memoirs, newspaper articles, photographs and films, government reports and social surveys. This range of sources gives a flavour of the nature of archival holdings relating to the settlement movement. On the one hand, the settlements were involved in a widening range of activities and with an equally widening range of audiences in the course of the twentieth century: for example, Basil Henriques, warden of the Bernhard Baron Settlement and magistrate at the Inner London Juvenile Court, appeared in the Crown Film Unit docu-drama *Children on Trial*,[1] whilst cinema newsreel captured a flavour of such settlement activities as the visits of such dignitaries as Amelia Earhart, the female solo pilot, and the King and Queen.[2] By the 1950s it was not uncommon for television and radio news companies to visit settlements in order to record a snapshot of life there to fill a slot in the evening news round-up.[3] There is greater diversity of sources relating to settlements, but it is not always the case that such sources are readily accessible. Toynbee Hall's archives were catalogued, conserved and made easily available following a Heritage Lottery Fund grant in 2005. Whilst the archives are nonetheless rich and varied, there remain significant gaps: the settlement was bombed during the Second World War, and most of the papers of J. J. Mallon, warden of the settlement from 1919 to 1954, were destroyed. Although there are legal requirements regarding the retention of certain kinds of records, settlement staff have never been compelled to keep the kinds of sources that historians value: lists of club members and attendees of classes; the records of clinics and advice sessions; details of feedback on settlement activities from local people. It is often the case that settlement staff kept the sources that were important and meaningful to them in the course of their daily lives: annual reports, financial information, lists of residents and newsletters. In times of war, settlement staff seem quite reasonably to have abandoned assiduous record keeping in favour of coping with the needs of the community. Not all settlement records were kept at the settlements – some papers went home with the committee or staff member rather than necessarily being filed in series, photographs taken by individuals went home to be stored in their personal collections, whilst other items were kept as a keepsake once they no longer served a daily function. Such materials occasionally find their way back to the settlements: the Toynbee Hall ration book for 1939–45, detailing how many cups of tea and coffee were served through its canteen, among other things, returned when a friend of Doris Greening, the compiler of the record, gave it to the Barnett Research Centre for safe keeping.[4] Yet historians of the settlement movement can benefit from the increased and improved access to surviving archives through the various Heritage Lottery Fund projects to conserve the Aston-Mansfield and Toynbee Hall collections, the use of the Database of Archives of Non-governmental Organisations (DANGO), and the housing of many settlement archives in local studies libraries and archives.

The first question that this book will attempt to answer is how and why did the settlements, those very Victorian charities, survive beyond the First World War? Indeed, many settlements have survived into the twenty-first century. How did the evolution of the state and its responsibility for welfare impact upon them? To what extent were these charities willing – and able – to reframe their work and innovate? What were the consequences of these changes? How did they respond to changes in their local London communities, especially after the Second World War? Seeking answers to these questions is important, as the exploration of these issues helps to contribute to a better understanding of the complexity of British welfare services and their evolution in the course of the twentieth century. It can illuminate something of the changing nature of poverty and deprivation in the twentieth century, most notably the prevalence of relative poverty compounded by various forms of social and financial 'exclusion'. And it can also add to our understandings of the development of the concepts of citizenship, voluntarism and participation.

Using a range of settlement and other archives, this book explores these questions through various themes – health and well-being, citizenship, the law, immigration and community relations – tracing them from 1918 through to 1979. These themes do not encompass all settlement activities in the period, but they explore the issues that were of greatest importance to the settlements and the communities around them. Through examination of these themes this book takes apart the workings of the mixed economy of welfare, and explores both the changes and continuities. Chapter 1 is concerned with the historical contexts of the settlement movement. It looks at the roots of the settlement movement before tracing the major developments in British social policy which shape the political environment in which these organisations worked. It also explores the historiography of the settlement movement, charity and the development of the welfare state. Chapter 2 focuses on the changing demographics of the settlement movement, with particular reference to the changing ways in which women used settlements before 1950. Chapter 3 surveys work in relation to health and well-being, from Clara Grant's pioneering school clinic work with Margaret McMillan in Poplar to Kingsley Hall's work with the Philadelphia Association. Chapter 4 considers the role the concept of citizenship played in settlement activities – and the differences between the settlement conception of a 'good citizen' and what this meant for a member of the local community. The central theme of Chapter 5 is the relationship of the individual to the law. The first part of the chapter looks at breaking the law, from the settlements' work with juvenile offenders before the early 1950s to their later work with ex-offenders and probationers. The second part explores the development of civil legal aid and free legal advice, and the ways in which this operated as a social service for people negotiating the state in the 1960s and 1970s. The final chapter looks at the evolution of the East End from a predominantly Jewish to a Bangladeshi community, the work of the Council of Citizens of East London and its response to threats to both the Jewish and the Bangladeshi communities.

Notes

1   Jack Lee, dir. *Children on Trial* (United Kingdom: Home Office/Crown Film Unit, 1946).
2   ITN Source, 'Miss Earhart', footage of visit to Toynbee Hall, 25 June 1928, British Pathé BP25062873621; also ITN Source, 'King and Queen in the East End: their Majesties visit famous Toynbee Hall social centre, and the Queen's Hospital for Children', 28 November 1938, British Pathé, BGX407232377.
3   Barnett Research Centre at Toynbee Hall (hereafter BRC), TOY/DEP/3/3, Stepney Old People's Welfare, Organiser's Report, April 1959, regarding visit of Mrs Demlova from Hamburg Radio.
4   TOY/CEN/7/5, Doris Greening papers, ration book.

1

Historical contexts

The first two 'university settlements', Toynbee Hall and Oxford House, opened in the East End of London in 1884. In the course of the late nineteenth and early twentieth centuries, other 'settlements'[1] were established across London, other major British towns and cities, across Europe, Scandinavia, North America, Russia, India and Japan.[2] What these institutions had in common was a residential basis to their social work. Volunteers and paid staff lived in the poorer areas of cities, undertaking a range of social work activities and services for their local communities. Their programme varied, but there were many common features to their philosophy and approach.

The 'settlement movement' was an apt term for this network of charities. Movement was integral to the spread of the settlements across the globe. Young Americans on tours of Europe in the 1880s and 1890s typically included a visit to Toynbee Hall as part of their trip – some, such as Jane Addams and Robert A. Woods, established settlements on their return stateside.[3] Other young people made pilgrimages to the British settlements to gain inspiration for projects in their own countries, as was the case with Else Federn, the founder of the Ottakring settlement in Vienna.[4] Werner Picht, the German academic, stayed at Toynbee Hall from December 1911 to July 1912 in order to produce a study of the English settlement movement.[5] Those connected with the British settlements likewise visited other settlements around the globe. The founders of Toynbee Hall, Samuel and Henrietta Barnett, visited Jane Addams at Hull House as part of their world tour of the early 1890s.[6] The American settlements were the first to establish a national organisation in 1911,[7] followed by the British in 1920,[8] whilst the International Federation of Settlements had its origins in the International Conference of Settlements held at Toynbee Hall in 1922.[9] There were also various publications looking at the 'settlement movement', such as Will Reason's edited volume *University and Social Settlements* (1898), which surveyed the British settlements and presented essays on the nature of women's settlements as well as the movement's relationship to local administration and the trade unions.[10] From early in their development, the settlements believed that they had shared principles and values. This interplay was important, as it provided support and a sense of identity to newly founded settlements, and it remained so in the twentieth century.

There was a vast range of types of settlements in Britain alone: men's settlements, women's settlements, co-ed settlements, Jewish settlements,[11] educational settlements,[12] settlements with particular religious emphases, settlements set up by the Scout movement,[13] and more. Whilst the exchange of ideas across national and international networks was essential to the settlement movement, locality was even more important. The precise direction that a settlement took was shaped by the incidence of pockets of deprivation in a particular town or city, and the perceived needs of those areas. It was in turn shaped by such factors as existing networks of voluntary social workers, and also by the support services available through local and national government. The class structure of a particular town or city and the nature of its local government could have a direct impact on a settlement's involvement in local politics and networks,[14] whilst the extent to which women were involved in public life and the professions shaped their engagement with voluntary bodies.[15] Race also had a significant impact upon the ways in which individuals were both excluded from and engaged with the state and voluntary organisations. These dynamics shaped the founding of settlements; but they continued to impact upon the development of these institutions.

The British case

The British settlements are often treated by historians as a Victorian phenomenon. Indeed, the vast majority were established by 1901. The Victorian settlements were influenced by a number of trends in nineteenth-century society. They were firstly part of a much broader response to the early and rapid industrialisation and imperial expansion of Britain from the eighteenth century. British pre-eminence came with a price. The Victorian middle and upper classes lamented and idealised a lost rural past, often overlooking the reality of poverty in the countryside.[16] Cities and towns grew up rapidly, with areas of workers' housing often being poorly built, overcrowded and insanitary.[17] The Victorian middle and upper classes were also concerned with what they perceived to be the godlessness of the expanded industrial towns and cities, as Horace Mann's 1851 religious census appeared to suggest that the working classes had little interest in religion.[18] Although industrial areas were far from devoid of religious activity, the middle and upper classes were anxious about the nature of provision for worship available. The Church of England was slow to extend its presence in industrial areas, with significant gains being made by the Nonconformists and the Roman Catholics in the course of the nineteenth century.[19] Likewise, the Victorians did not approve of working-class social life revolving around the public house rather than the parish church.[20]

In the course of the nineteenth century these anxieties found expression in theological and political theories. During the 1830s the Oxford movement, or the 'Tractarians', led by John Henry Newman, sought to restore various Roman Catholic practices to the Church of England.[21] This created bitter tensions and divisions within the Church of England, leading to many Tractarian priests being forced to work in slum parishes, as there were few alternatives open to them. But their experience of serving the poor in this way influenced those concerned with social reform some decades later.[22] This notion of serving in the slums gained ground in the later nineteenth century. Thomas Hill Green, the Balliol philosopher, was a later advocate of extending opportunities for the working classes and for privileged young graduates to serve the poor, and was a decisive influence upon Arnold Toynbee and a number of other early settlement residents.[23] This sense of the importance of serving the poor in their environment was matched by increasing anxiety about the impact of industry, the city and modernity upon the working classes. This was a notable theme of the work of both William Morris and John Ruskin, the figure-heads of the Arts and Crafts movement, which aimed to restore the status of the artisan and the craftsman, and the supposedly lost link between the labourer and the products he created.[24] These two movements found common connection in the early settlement movement. Samuel Barnett's proposed 'settlement of university men' merged the impulse to serve those less fortunate with the concept that industrial urban life destroyed the soul.[25] At Toynbee Hall this was manifested in such projects as C. R. Ashbee's Guild of Handicraft (based at the settlement between 1887 and 1889), free musical concerts, art exhibitions and a wide range of classes in the liberal arts for adults.

Why London?

Why did the settlement movement originate in London, as opposed to any of the other British towns and cities? Nineteenth-century

London was by no means the poorest city in the country. But, unlike other cities, poverty in London was juxtaposed next to the immense wealth of the City of London and the seat of Parliament, a horrifying contrast. This also allowed the convenient construction of the 'East End' and the 'West End', following a similar typology to Benjamin Disraeli's 'two nations'. This image of two Londons, the London of the rich and the London of the poor, pervaded the language of charitable literature. The two were separate entities, which also corresponded with discourse that related poverty to ideas of depravity, as well as to imperialist views. Urban spectatorship emerged as an exciting and scintillating means for the middle and upper classes to explore this 'dark' labyrinth of poor London, and the resulting writing – George Gissing, W. T. Stead, Henry James – entrenched ideas about social divisions and expressed anxieties about society.[26] Such narratives encouraged contemporaries to conflate class with place, with the inference that movement outside these boundaries – workers marching on Trafalgar Square, middle-class women shopping in the West End – was ultimately an attack on social cohesion[27] and tantamount to 'matter out of place'.

It was also easy for the middle and upper classes to travel to the 'East End', should they wish to, either on foot or by the growing public transport network. This movement across boundaries for scintillation, entertainment and transgression was closely allied to the development of 'slumming', visiting the poorer districts ostensibly to give aid to the poor. Slumming was a complex phenomenon. Although individuals could visit the slums as a result of religious or other altruistic motives, the experience could be a means of indulging in or sublimating baser impulses. Seth Koven has pointed to the way in which early Toynbee Hall resident C. R. Ashbee was one of many to use club work as a means of accessing 'rough lads', to gain a thrill from being close to young working-class males.[28] Ian Horobin used his position as warden at Mansfield House from the early 1920s onwards for similar purposes, although he went further by indecently assaulting a number of boys over a period of around forty years.[29] Slumming was not just for the exploration of homosexual or paedophile desires. It allowed women the opportunity to enjoy life without the gendered or moral constraints that middle and upper-class families imposed upon young single women.[30] As late as the Second World War the experience of having spent some time in the East End or other deprived area could give a young middle-class person an air of authority about questions of political reform. In the film *Mrs Miniver* Mrs Miniver's eldest son, Vin, challenges the socialist views of Carol Beldon, the granddaughter of the local grandee. Yet Carol wins: Vin acquired his principles at university, whilst she gained her knowledge of the workings of the world after spending time at a settlement in the East End.[31]

But the relationship of slumming to early ethnography and the problem of matter out of place should not be ignored. Judith Walkowitz has examined the ways in which Henry Mayhew travelled through the urban landscape, detailing the characters he came across and mapping London 'tribes'.[32] This notion of 'tribes' of the London poor also intersected with anxieties about immigrant groups – the Irish, German, Italian and especially the Jewish communities who found a home in the capital.[33] The frisson attached to 'slumming' derived from the transgression of class, gendered and racial boundaries as women visited the homes of the poor on behalf of various charitable agencies and 'settlement residents' moved into deprived areas to establish themselves as the 'leaders' of the slums. Samuel Barnett saw the mission of the settlement movement as bringing leadership and culture to the slums,[34] assuming that there was not and could not be any 'native' manifestation of these qualities. Although some working-class households in the East End had the vote – and there were certainly ratepayers in the district – the settlements presented themselves as an implant of the civilised society of the West End.

The foundation of the settlement movement

In December 1883 Samuel Barnett, an East End curate, gave a talk at St John's College, Oxford, on the need for young men from the universities to live and undertake social work in deprived urban areas.[35] Barnett's proposals had been a long time in the making. Barnett and his wife, Henrietta, had met at the parish of St Mary's, Bryanston Square, in west London, where they were introduced by the prominent social reformer Octavia Hill. They learned their trade at St Mary's, becoming founding members of the Charity Organisation Society (COS) in the process. Following their marriage in 1873, Samuel Barnett was granted the living of St Jude's on Commercial Street, in Whitechapel. Henrietta and Samuel replicated many of the activities they were involved with at St Mary's – men's clubs, mothers' meetings, boys' clubs, adult education classes, COS visiting – whilst maintaining their parish duties.[36] Henrietta was also closely involved with the establishment of such innovative schemes as the Metropolitan Association for the Befriending of Young Servants (MABYS) and the Children's Country Holiday Fund (CCHF).[37] Samuel was consumed with the idea of reforming social work. He was impressed by the example of Arnold Toynbee, the young Oxford economist, who had spent his vacations working alongside the couple in the East End. Barnett believed that young men should come and live in areas like the East End to give something back to society; but also that they would learn something of what it was to be poor.[38] Barnett's proposals were given extra weight by the death of Toynbee in 1883. There was much grief expressed at the loss of a brilliant young man and a desire to continue his work.[39] There were other factors that focused the attention of the middle classes, namely a series of exposés of poverty in London, the most shocking of which was *The Bitter Cry of Outcast London*, by the Reverend Andrew Mearns.[40]

Toynbee Hall formally opened in January 1885.[41] It was not the first settlement to open: Oxford House in nearby Bethnal Green opened some months earlier. However, Toynbee Hall, as it came to be known, as a form of living memorial to Arnold Toynbee,[42] is generally seen as the first of the settlements.[43] Yet we should not view Toynbee Hall as either definitive of the settlement movement or the main influence upon other settlements and their development. Ultimately the key criterion by which a settlement could be defined as a settlement after 1945 rests upon the institution referring to itself in that way. Even in the nineteenth century there was a fine line between what was a 'settlement' and what was a 'mission'. Barnett defined a settlement as a place for 'men of education [to] settle in some industrial centre, and there undertake the duties which naturally arise'.[44] Residence for service and education was the fundamental definition of what a settlement was.[45] Until the 1970s settlements were defined through providing a residential base for voluntary and paid workers, with the latter forming an ever more important part of the daily life of settlements in the inter-war period.[46] Thus some settlements felt the need to change their name to 'community centre' or some such to reflect this. Religion became less overtly foregrounded in settlement aims and activities in the course of the twentieth century, but it would be a mistake to assume that it was any less of a powerful motivation.[47] Hugh McLeod has argued that, by the 1960s, new 'gods' had appeared in the form of Karl Marx, Wilhelm Reich, Herbert Marcuse and R. D. Laing.[48] Whilst these thinkers may have helped to inspire new directions in social work – Laing is examined in closer detail in Chapter 3 – it would be a mistake to overstate the 'end' of Christianity in volunteering and social work. Settlements always had several 'generations' of volunteers and paid workers whose ideas and motivations drew upon many sources – some embraced Laing, whilst others still conceived of their work in terms of giving service. Settlements have placed varying emphases during their lifetime on the importance of work inspired by religious belief and work designed to instil moral fibre or religious values in their audiences. The unchanging variable in defining a settlement has been their commitment to provide a variety of social services to a local community.

Toynbee Hall opened on the principle that residents from all religious and political affiliations would be welcome (as would local people of all persuasions and backgrounds), which enraged men connected with Keble College, Oxford. Oxford House was thus established as a High Church reaction to Toynbee Hall, providing similar fare but with a staunchly Anglican approach.[49] Although Oxford House was a response to Toynbee Hall, it was the first to open. Oxford House initially used the premises of the parish of St Andrew's in Bethnal Green along with a disused National School for residential accommodation.[50] But religious affiliation was not always based on such philosophical grounds. In other cases it functioned to bind an otherwise disparate group together and helped in recruiting volunteers and staff from feeder schools, colleges and religious institutions. It also helped the settlement in question to develop a distinct identity. The West Ham settlements, Mansfield House University Settlement and its sister settlement, the Canning Town Women's Settlement (CTWS), were founded in 1891 and 1892 respectively to function as Congregationalist institutions but, like many other Nonconformist bodies, had strong links with the local Labour Party and trade unions. In other circumstances, religious affiliation also equated with ethnic or cultural affiliations. The Oxford St George's Club in Stepney, founded in 1913 (known from 1930 as the Bernhard Baron Settlement) was a Jewish settlement.[51] Women's settlements also proliferated, such as Lady Margaret Hall Settlement in Lambeth and the Women's University Settlement in Southwark, both founded in 1887.[52] The Fern Street Settlement in Poplar was founded by Clara Grant, who based her settlement on the elementary school she ran.[53] The London settlements represented a diverse range of interests and approaches which evolved in the course of the nineteenth and twentieth centuries.

With the exception of Kingsley Hall and Fern Street, both founded in the early twentieth century, all the other settlements featured in this study were well established by 1901. The settlements underwent various evolutions before the First World War, as they found new challenges to tackle. Settlement programmes were effectively fixed by the First World War: men's settlements tended towards the provision of clubs and adult education, whilst women's settlements placed a greater emphasis on meeting the health needs of women and young children. Access to savings schemes and insurance clubs were common to all kinds of settlements, as was the provision of free legal advice through the Poor Man's Lawyer. This was pioneered at Mansfield House by Frank Tillyard, then a young lawyer living at the settlement, who gave the benefit of his legal knowledge *pro bono* in order to help out his working-class neighbours. Until 1939 the Poor Man's Lawyer scheme and similar bodies were the main providers of legal advice and support to the public in London and all major towns and cities.[54] The First World War seriously disrupted settlement life: male residents and settlement users were called up to serve; women were involved in war work and relief efforts. The war disrupted income flows to the settlements, and also the supply of volunteers and staff. But after the declaration of peace in 1918 the settlements largely set about restoring their pre-war programmes, as far as this was possible. The economic depressions of the 1920s and 1930s had a significant impact upon London working-class communities: CTWS provided a demob club for girls displaced from war work after the end of the war in 1918 who did not have new jobs to go to.[55] Mallon, warden of Toynbee Hall, became embroiled in brokering the 1926 General Strike,[56] whilst the settlement tried to minimise tension between striking dockers and the Cambridge undergraduates who were breaking the strike by driving buses and trains. The settlement was also opened up as a centre for the dockers to collect their strike pay, and brought in the music hall stars of the day to entertain the strikers.[57] Through its connections with the British Association of Residential Settlements (BARS) Toynbee Hall was also involved with the establishment of settlements on the new housing estates and in the 'Special Areas' hit hardest by the Slump of the 1930s and long-term unemployment, such as Bells Hill in Lanarkshire and Spennymoor in County Durham. They also worked with the National Council of Social Service to establish the Educational Settlements,[58] which had a remit to provide adult education to people in the Special Areas.[59]

The Second World War had a far greater impact on settlements as a result of the Blitz and the need to provide services and support a civilian population under attack. Toynbee Hall provided food for people in nearby air raid shelters, assisted those whose homes had been lost in the Blitz, provided cheap milk, entertainment in the shelters, as well as helping those who were injured or distressed to have a break from the pressures of war at Bottingdean, a house in Sussex lent to the settlement.[60] Clara Grant, warden of Fern Street in the heavily bombed London dockland, would leave her shelter after each raid to see how she and her settlement could be of assistance. Her co-workers also helped to keep up morale by sending parcels of books to local people serving in the Forces, as well as those working in the Demolition and Mortuary Squads.[61] Kingsley Hall continued to provide clubs for those young people who had not been evacuated, as well as running a school for evacuated children.[62] Lady Margaret Hall Settlement was involved with a range of services to the local community in Lambeth, including organising the evacuation of the elderly.[63] Oxford House gained a somewhat negative reputation in Bethnal Green for employing conscientious objectors, but nonetheless turned its clubhouses over to the community to provide refuge for air raid victims.[64] The settlements did what was needed, and largely they did it well.

Their challenge, after 1945, was to think carefully about what their role in a society with a strong welfare state should be. This was not a simple process. Those involved with fund raising often found it difficult to make their case persuasively and effectively in the 1940s and 1950s, faced with the popular assumption that poverty had 'gone away'.[65] Most found it necessary to change their work in accordance with the needs of the local community. In many working-class areas of London the process of clearing slums and building new council housing had a disruptive impact upon the community. Mary Ward Settlement found that its services came under greater pressure as newly built council housing greatly increased the local population,[66] whilst Fern Street found a need to support new families moving into Poplar as well as those elderly people who remained in the area.[67] Before the Second World War, Toynbee Hall had formed part of the fabric of the Jewish East End; by the early 1960s the Bangladeshi community in Aldgate was beginning to grow. From 1945 the settlements sought out or were found by new client groups: single mothers, Bangladeshis, former prisoners and the mentally ill. Some of this work was done solely by the voluntary sector; in other cases the settlements worked alongside the local authorities, the Home Office and the National Health Service. In some areas of work, such as free legal advice, the settlements had an important role to play in protecting and aiding the vulnerable in their dealings with the state. The phenomenon of the 'moving frontier of welfare', or the changing responsibilities of charities, local government and others for welfare in the 1920s and 1930s,[68] was just as evident after the Second World War. It may have been overshadowed by the welfare state, but, outside the provision of social security and mainstream health, the voluntary sector had the potential to be highly innovative and creative – if its projects were precariously financed. By looking at the settlement movement from 1918 through to 1979 this book will demonstrate the ways in which the mixed economy of welfare continued to operate on the ground.

Historicising the settlement movement

The final part of this chapter will look at the ways in which the settlement movement has been written about by historians and others. The historical narrative of the settlement movement has largely been dominated by discussion of Toynbee Hall. This has arisen in part from the Barnetts' successful portrayal of the settlement as a world-leading institution to their contemporaries, attracting not only British notables but visitors from all over the world to see its work. In addition to their own considerable output of writings on social problems, Samuel Barnett was honoured with a biography in 1902,[69] whilst *Toynbee Hall and the English Settlement Movement* by Werner Picht was published in English translation in 1914.[70] In 1918 Henrietta Barnett published her two-volume biography of her husband, *Canon Barnett: His Life, Work and Friends.*[71] Thus the 'historical' reputation of Toynbee Hall began. It was bolstered in the twentieth century through many of those prominent in public life having early connections with Toynbee Hall. In 1935 J. A. R. Pimlott produced a history of Toynbee Hall that celebrated its first fifty years – a confident book written at the apex of the settlement's achievements, especially useful for later historians in the way it drew upon the reflections of earlier residents and staff.[72] The centenary history produced by Asa Briggs and Anne Macartney in 1984 is strongest on the period before the Second World War, and does not properly historicise the post-1945 period, when the settlement movement faced some of its greatest challenges.[73] Toynbee Hall has also been the main focus of several doctoral theses, including Emily Klein Abel's 1969 study of the first thirty years of the settlement,[74] and was one of the main settlements examined in Seth Koven's work on the London settlements to 1914.[75]

Celebratory anniversary histories are in many cases the only historical studies of many settlements, varying in quality from an almost antiquarian collation of principal events and characters to a lively engagement with the rich history of the institution in question. Some of these texts are drawn on in this study, and, whatever their imperfections, they are an essential tool for those commencing work on a settlement archive.[76] Yet such histories, narrowly focused on particular institutions, potentially overlook the complex ways in which the settlements interacted with other charities, local and national government – and, of course, with local people. On the other hand, there have been other studies which look at the settlement movement as a whole and its relation to broader themes in British history. Seth Koven further examined the settlement movement in the context of urban exploration in the nineteenth century, and particularly the erotic dynamics of 'slumming', mentioned earlier.[77] Nigel Scotland retained a focus on the London settlement movement in his survey of settlements and missions in the Victorian period, which looked in particular detail at the function of religion in the founding and running of these institutions.[78] Martha Vicinus's work explored the meanings and impacts of women's settlements as a form of female space in the nineteenth century,[79] whilst Katharine Bentley Beauman's study of the women's settlement movement verges on the antiquarian, but puts important flesh on the bones of women's experiences at settlements until the 1960s.[80] Not all studies have focused exclusively on the London settlements: Jennifer Harrow surveyed the settlement movement in England to 1939,[81] whilst Mark Freeman's work has examined the Educational Settlement movement before the Second World War.[82] Other important studies of settlements outside of London include Michael Rose's work on the Manchester Settlement,[83] and Hilda Jenning's work on the history of the Bristol University Settlement.[84] Although many previous studies of the settlement movement have concentrated upon the Victorian and Edwardian periods, with some venturing into the inter-war period, the movement demands to be studied over the *longue durée*, so that we can fully document and understand the changes wrought in British social policy from the First World War through to the 1970s. This book adds to the historiography of the settlement movement by providing a sustained analysis of settlements in London after 1918, and especially by breaking new ground in looking at the period after 1945. Others – notably Jennings – have taken a longer view in their studies of settlements, but this study will look in greater depth at the networks, parallels and contrasts that existed between these geographically proximate charities.

The first school of thinking about the history of charities and their relation to the welfare state adopted a Whiggish approach to the problem. Commentators such as Madeleine Rooff and Elizabeth Macadam focused positively on the ways in which voluntary activity had contributed to the continual expansion of welfare services, and especially on the growing interaction of the state and charitable bodies.[85] This 'welfare escalator' school of thought privileged the centrality of the state within the welfare mix, and thus interpreted the expansion of state welfare in terms of a linear trend towards its inevitable and ultimately Beveridgean outcome. By the 1970s and 1980s these understandings came under attack from revisionist historians – at the same time that the welfare state itself was severely hit by the economic consequences of the OPEC oil crisis and then by the policies of Margaret

Thatcher's governments of 1979 onwards. Historians including Pat
Thane and Jane Lewis turned their attention to exploring the complexity of the mixed economy of welfare, and problematising the
notion of the 'welfare escalator'.[86] Frank Prochaska examined the role
of philanthropy and voluntary action in the nineteenth century,
with particular emphasis on its importance for women of all classes
and exploring its social, political and economic functions.[87] Discussion
of philanthropy and the welfare state was also connected with the
dissection of the theory of 'consensus' in social policy after 1945, or the
contention that both Labour and the Conservatives were in general
agreement about the need to uphold welfare and health provision.
In 1990 the second issue of the newly launched journal *Twentieth
Century British History* consisted of three articles on the subject of
the mixed economy of welfare, conflict and consensus: Webster on the
National Health Service, Lowe on the impact of the Second World War
on the foundation of the welfare state, and Finlayson on the 'moving frontier' of welfare in the inter-war period.[88] These and other
studies collectively argued that, whilst charities, mutual and philanthropic bodies had always worked with the state in some form or
other, there was far from a smooth or indeed inevitable progression
towards a welfare state. Finlayson's expression, the 'moving frontier'
of welfare, neatly encapsulates the ways in which the mixed economy
of welfare was in flux: although local government took on increasing
responsibility for welfare and related services, it did not follow that
charities were automatically excluded from service provision or that
specific roles and responsibilities were not subject to intense and
ongoing negotiation between interested parties. These patterns continued into the 'classic' welfare state of 1945–75, as can be seen in the
complexities of funding and providing services for the elderly[89] and
the debates around the Seebohm report of 1968.[90] It was also a fallacy
that the two major political parties were in accord over welfare and
social security – although they were in tacit agreement over the need
to maintain the welfare state, their aims and approaches differed
greatly.[91] Thus historians have demonstrated that the development of
British welfare was not a linear evolution but a complex process of
negotiation and mediation at all levels.

Other important areas of research include the resurgence of interest
in the question of citizenship and civil society. T. H. Marshall's writings on citizenship and social policy were highly influential from the
1950s onwards in the light of the newly established welfare state,[92]
but fresh impetus was given to the field through the work of Pierre
Bourdieu and Jürgen Habermas. Habermas is particularly associated

with the theory of the 'public sphere', or the salons and discussion groups that fostered the debate of social issues and led to the formation of societies to take action against them.[93] Bourdieu, on the other hand, discussed social capital, or the resources that an individual or association can draw upon in order to build and maintain productive networks with others.[94] Other theorists have contributed to these debates, such as Jane Jacobs,[95] Richard Sennett[96] and Robert Putnam.[97] All these discussions explore 'public' forms of human interaction, and specifically the ways in which individuals will work together for the development of the public good and their own interests within it. All suggest that democracy requires active participation on the part of citizens, but there remain real issues about the operation of power and participation. Such debates are fundamental for an understanding of the operations of citizenship and volunteering before, within and beyond the welfare state. John Garrard's study of democratisation in Britain found that participation in civil society – so joining friendly societies and the like – was a means by which working people could gain some autonomy from their employers and landowners, and that these groups acted as a means by which Britons could be inducted into the political system. But Garrard also found the particular development of civil society in Britain allowed its elites to be involved in this process and to see some of their behaviour and values replicated within it.[98] David G. Green argues that, by drastically reducing the powers of the friendly societies, the welfare state has reduced both citizens' liberties and their willingness to participate in civil society.[99] M. J. D. Roberts has also examined the work of voluntary associations and their function within the public sphere of tackling what they perceived to be threats to moral and social order.[100] Thus the achievement of the public or social good is dependent upon people acting collectively, with the tacit approval of elites; but there is also an assumption that the provision of public goods through taxation and right has a deleterious impact upon society in other ways. Volunteering has potent functions which it would be unwise to dismiss as the meddling of do-gooders.

It would appear that volunteering and voluntarism in their various forms are essential to British civil society and its mixed economy of welfare in its various forms. Although volunteering has acquired popular semantic associations with activities undertaken to improve the welfare of others, it is not exclusively concerned with them.[101] For people of all backgrounds, participation in civil society has been a means of ensuring the protection of their interests and needs, yet the nature of this and the extent of this participation have evolved over time. In the course of the twentieth century – and, as will be seen here, in the example of the settlement movement – volunteers became less central to the work of charities. To qualify this, volunteers remained import-ant in such duties as acting as trustees and honorary treasurers, but paid staff came to predominate by the inter-war period. Whilst some staff, especially those involved in the management of charities or areas of work, enjoyed ongoing salaries, it became increasingly common for staff to be employed on short-term contracts connected with dedicated projects. This trend was connected with the diversification of settlement funds from the inter-war period, especially after 1945 (see Appendix). Whereas, in the nineteenth century, volunteers were at the heart of charities like the settlements, they were often relegated to a secondary role by the inter-war period. Whilst the 1960s marked a high point in the development of new charities and pressure groups to cater for those failed by the welfare state,[102] volunteering came to be seen as a means of channelling the energies of young people safely.[103] However, volunteers in late twentieth and early twenty-first-century Britain are stereotypically seen as white middle-aged and middle-class females – although research has disproved this. Yet there are still powerful ob-stacles to volunteering. Britons from black and minority ethnic back-grounds are as active as volunteers from all other backgrounds, but they often feel excluded from white-dominated, established charities.[104]

It is also essential to consider the work of economists and social policy specialists, who have placed the voluntary sector under increas-ing scrutiny from the 1970s onwards. Although commonly used in the United Kingdom, the phrase 'voluntary sector' is problematic as a descriptor for philanthropic activity. Whilst many philanthropic bod-ies rely upon voluntary labour in order to carry out their activities, it does not follow that all do. 'Voluntary sector' also connotes a universe in which there are other discrete yet complementary sectors alongside it. Finlayson notes that the phrase gained currency in the 1940s as con-temporaries sought to make sense of the relationship between private or for-profit providers of welfare, charitable or philanthropic bodies and the 'welfare state'.[105] In this way the phrase gained meaning in terms of how charitable or philanthropic bodies worked to provide personal social or other welfare services in the context of state-provided welfare and the operation of the various 'sectors'. Thus the term does not adequately cover those areas of philanthropic endeavour which do not explicitly provide such services, despite its common use. The alternative, 'charities', is likewise a problematic term, given the vagaries of the law relating to charities. The Charities Commission and an array of English and Welsh, Scottish and Irish laws provide legal definitions of a 'charity' and codes of behaviour to which charities should adhere. However, those organisations whose work is both philanthropic and political are excluded from being classified as 'charities'. In the United States the term 'nonprofit sector' is used, which circumvents some of the problems mentioned above – yet it still directs the attention towards those philanthropic activities which have counterparts in or dealings with other 'sectors'.

The work of researchers investigating the case of the non-profit sector in the United States has led to some interesting concepts concerning how the sector operates. Weisbrod's work on the US nonprofit sector argues that charities and similar bodies are the providers of public goods; they provide the services that are necessary but which are not profitable.[106] Weisbrod also explored the notion of 'failure': when the state and private for-profit bodies are unable or unwilling to provide public goods, the voluntary or nonprofit sector fills the gap.[107] Mixed economies of welfare emerge where there are failures of the voluntary sector. Salamon identified instances of the voluntary or nonprofit sector failing, and argued that partnerships with the state or other parties helped to ensure the provision of a particular service.[108] Although Weisbrod and Salamon are more concerned with the United States, aspects of their theories in relation to the United Kingdom have been discussed at length by Kendall and Knapp.[109] More recently, social policy specialists have reconfigured their discussion to focus on the concept of risk within welfare states, and failure thus joins debates about the ways in which individuals, organisations and governments manage risks such as unemployment, illness and old age.[110] These theories have resonance with historical studies of the development of the mixed economy of welfare, adding an international and economic dimension to our understanding of the topic.

This book therefore draws upon existing theories of the mixed economy of British welfare, but also with concepts of 'failure' in a critical manner as a means of exploring the question of how and why the settlement movement survived beyond the First World War and its subsequent negotiation of the welfare state after 1945. It will argue, following Salamon and others, that the mixed economy of welfare after 1945 was subject to a series of 'failures', but that these failures are more complex than the theories may initially suggest. Whilst the economic theories surrounding failure and the provision of public goods are important, they potentially overlook the realities of the human factor in shaping the concatenations of welfare provision. As will be seen at various points in the course of this book, individuals and organisations alike desperately attempt to impose an arrangement that suits their view of the situation, but are unable to overcome or persuade the more powerful state or funding body to do so. It will further suggest that increased state involvement in welfare had broader implications for charities, in terms of encouraging patterns of paid semi-professional or professional employment as well as the move towards short-term funded projects vulnerable to the withdrawal of funding. These developments also changed the ways in which people entered upon careers in the charitable sector and their motives for becoming involved in volunteering. It is vital for historians, economists and social policy specialists to locate the analysis of the settlement movement within the broader economies of welfare, the better to understand it and the evolution of charities more generally.

Notes

1 'Settlement' will be the generic term used to refer to these institutions in this study, apart from such instances as where the institution refers to itself as a 'university settlement', 'residential settlement', 'educational settlement' or, less commonly in the United Kingdom, 'settlement house'.
2 For details of settlements affiliated to the International Federation of Settlements, see www.ifsnetwork.org. For details of British settlements, consult the British Association of Settlements and Social Action Centres, www.bassac.org (December 2007).
3 Jane Addams described her visits to Toynbee Hall and the formative experiences that led to her founding Hull House in Chicago in her 1910 memoir, *Twenty Years at Hull-House* (repr. 1990, ed. J. Hurt, Urbana IL: Prairie State and University of Illinois Press). See also A. Kennedy, 'The settlement heritage', in *National Conference of Social Work*, ed. International Federation of Settlements (International Federation of Settlements, 1953). Mention of Stanton Coit, founder of the Neighbourhood Guilds, can be found in J. A. R. Pimlott, *Toynbee Hall: Fifty Years of Social Reform* (London: Dent, 1935), p. 253. Excellent resources for the US settlement movement are D. M. Barbuto, *The American Settlement Movement: A Bibliography* (Westport CT: Greenwood, 1999), and *American Settlement Houses and Progressive Social Reform: An Encyclopedia of the American Settlement Movement* (Phoenix AZ: Oryx, 1999).
4 See E. Malleier, 'Making the world a better place: welfare and politics, welfare as politics? Activities of Jewish women in Vienna before 1938', *Aschkenas* 16:1 (2007); *Das Ottakringer Settlement. Zur Geschichte eines frühen internationalen Sozialprojekts* (Vienna: Verband der Wiener Volksbildung, 2005); *Jüdische Frauen in Wien 1816–1938. Wohlfarht, Mädchenbildung, Frauenarbeit* (Vienna: Mandelbaum, 2003).
5 W. Picht, *Toynbee Hall and the English Settlement Movement*, trans. L. A. Cowell (London: Bell, 1914); K. Bradley, 'Database of Toynbee Hall Residents, 1884–1940' (London: Barnett Research Centre at Toynbee Hall, 2005).

6   H. Barnett, *Canon Barnett: His Life, Work and Friends*, 2 vols (London: John Murray, 1918) II, pp. 30–2.
7   J. Trolander, 'Microfilm review: Archives of the settlement movement: the National Federation of Settlements and Successors, 1899–1958', *Journal of American History* 79:4 (1993).
8   British Association of Residential Settlements, *The British Association of Residential Settlements: Report, 1935–1938* (London: BARS, 1938).
9   Pimlott, *Toynbee Hall*, p. 255.
10 W. Reason (ed.) *University and Social Settlements* (London: Methuen, 1898), especially P. Alden, 'Settlements in relation to local administration', M. Sewell and E. G. Powell, 'Women's settlements in England', and A. Sherwell, 'Settlements and the labour movement'.
11 For an account of the establishment of the Oxford St George/Bernhard Baron settlement in east London, see B. L. Q. Henriques, *The Indiscretions of a Warden* (London: Methuen, 1937).
12 M. Freeman, ' "No finer school than a settlement": the development of the educational settlement movement', *History of Education* 31:3 (2002); J. S. Davies and M. Freeman, 'Education for citizenship: the Joseph Rowntree Charitable Trust and the educational settlement movement', *History of Education* 32:3 (2003).
13 The Scout settlement, Roland House, was located on Stepney Green, in east London.
14 See K. Bradley, 'Creating local elites: the university settlement movement, national elites and citizenship in east London, 1884–1940', in S. Couperus, C. Smit and D. J. Wolffram (eds) *In Control of the City: Local Elites and the Dynamics of Urban Politics, 1800–1960* (Leuven: Peeters, 2007).
15 See S. Koven and S. Michel, 'Womanly duties: maternalist politics and the origins of welfare states in France, Germany, Great Britain and the United States, 1870–1939', *American Historical Review* 95:4 (1990).
16 R. Treble, 'The Victorian picture of the country', in G. E. Mingay (ed.) *The Rural Idyll* (London: Routledge, 1989).
17 Particularly evocative accounts can be found in F. Engels, *The Condition of the Working Class in England*, trans. W. O. Henderson and W. H. Chaloner (Oxford: Blackwell, 1971). H. Gavin, *Sanitary Ramblings, being Sketches and Illustrations of Bethnal Green, a Type of the Condition of the Metropolis and other Large Towns* (repr. London: Frank Cass, 1971).
18 H. McLeod, *Religion and the Working Class in Nineteenth Century Britain* (London: Macmillan, 1984), pp. 13, 57.
19 See especially McLeod, *Class and Religion in the late Victorian City* (London: Croom Helm, 1974); *Religion and the Working Class in Nineteenth Century Britain*.
20 H. Cunningham, *Leisure in the Industrial Revolution, 1780–1880* (London: Croom Helm, 1980), pp. 84, 91.
21 I. Ker, 'Newman, John Henry (1801–1890)', in H. C. G. Matthew and B. Harrison (eds) *Oxford Dictionary of National Biography* (Oxford: Oxford University Press, 2004, 2007).

22 N. Scotland, *Squires in the Slums: Settlements and Mission Settlements in late Victorian Britain* (London: I. B. Tauris, 2007), p. 23.

23 A. Vincent, 'Green, Thomas Hill (1836–1882)', in Matthew and Harrison, *Oxford Dictionary of National Biography*.

24 T. Hilton, *John Ruskin* (London: Yale University Press, 2002). F. McCarthy, *William Morris: A Life for our Time* (London: Faber & Faber, 1994), p. xv.

25 S. A. Barnett, 'The ideal city', in H. E. Meller (ed.) *The Ideal City* (Leicester: Leicester University Press, 1979); 'University settlements', *Nineteenth Century*, December 1895, p. 1023.

26 J. R. Walkowitz, *City of Dreadful Delight: Narratives of Sexual Danger in late Victorian London* (London: Virago, 2000), pp. 16–17.

27 *Ibid.*, pp. 40–1.

28 See S. Koven, 'From rough lads to hooligans: boy life, national culture and social reform', in A. Parker *et al.* (eds) *Nationalisms and Sexualities* (London: Routledge, 1991); *Slumming: Sexual and Social Politics in Victorian London* (Princeton NJ: Princeton University Press, 2005).

29 T. Stamp, *Stamp Album* (London: Bloomsbury, 1987), pp. 126–7. Also 'Sir Ian Horobin sentenced to four years' imprisonment', *The Times*, Wednesday 18 July 1962, p. 9.

30 M. Vicinus, *Independent Women: Work and Community for Single Women, 1850–1920* (London: Virago, 1985), p. 220.

31 W. Wyler (dir.) *Mrs Miniver* (United States: MGM Studios, 1942).

32 Walkowitz, *City of Dreadful Delight*, p. 19.

33 J. White, *London in the Nineteenth Century: 'a human awful wonder of God'* (London: Jonathan Cape, 2007).

34 Barnett, 'University settlements', p. 1022.

35 H. Barnett, *Canon Barnett* I, p. 310.

36 Pimlott, *Toynbee Hall*, p. 16.

37 S. Koven, 'Barnett, Samuel Augustus (1844–1913)' and 'Barnett, Dame Henrietta Octavia Weston (1851–1936)', in Matthew and Harrison, *Oxford Dictionary of National Biography*; 'Henrietta Barnett, 1851–1936: the (auto)biography of a late Victorian marriage', in P. Mandler, S. Pedersen and J. Clive (eds) *After the Victorians: Private Conscience and Public Duty in Modern Britain. Essays in Memory of John Clive* (London and New York: Routledge, 1994).

38 Barnett, *Canon Barnett* I, p. 307; A. Kadish, 'Toynbee, Arnold (1852–1883)', in Matthew and Harrison, *Oxford Dictionary of National Biography*.

39 Kadish, 'Toynbee, Arnold (1852–1883)'.

40 A. Briggs and A. Macartney, *Toynbee Hall: The First Hundred Years* (London: Routledge, 1984), p. 2.

41 *Ibid.*, p. 1.

42 Barnett, *Canon Barnett* I, pp. 308–13.

43 Kennedy, 'The settlement heritage'.

44 Barnett, *Canon Barnett* II, p. 24.

45 Scotland, *Squires in the Slums*, p. 16.

46 J. Harrow, 'The Development of the University Settlements in England, 1884–1939' (PhD dissertation, University of London, 1987).
47 See Koven, *Slumming*, pp. 228–81, for a thorough discussion of the religious motivations of male settlement residents at Oxford House and Toynbee Hall; likewise Vicinus, *Independent Women*.
48 H. McLeod, *The Religious Crisis of the 1960s* (Oxford: Oxford University Press, 2007), p. 243.
49 Barnett, *Canon Barnett* II, p. 29.
50 Oxford House, *The Oxford House in Bethnal Green, 1884–1948* (London: Brakell, 1948), pp. 10–11.
51 See Henriques, *The Indiscretions of a Warden*.
52 See K. B. Beauman, *Women and the Settlement Movement* (London: Radcliffe, 1996); Vicinus, *Independent Women*.
53 See C. E. Grant, *From 'Me' to 'We': Forty Years on Bow Common* (London: Fern Street Settlement, 1940).
54 See J. Mervyn Jones, *Free Legal Advice in England and Wales* (Oxford: Slatter & Rose, 1940).
55 Newham Local Studies and Archives, Canning Town Women's Settlement, Executive Committee minutes, 27 May 1921.
56 Toynbee Hall, *The Universities' Settlement in East London: Report, 1962–1963* (London: Toynbee Hall, 1963), p. 7.
57 Pimlott, *Toynbee Hall*, pp. 212–13.
58 *Ibid.*, pp. 240–1.
59 See Freeman, 'No finer school than a settlement'; M. Freeman, 'The magic lantern and the cinema: adult schools, educational settlements and secularisation in Britain, c. 1900–1950', *Quaker Studies*, 11 (2007).
60 Briggs and Macartney, *Toynbee Hall*, pp. 125–6.
61 R. Beer and C. A. Pickard, *Eighty Years on Bow Common* (London: Fern Street Settlement, 1987), p. 12.
62 Kingsley Hall and Children's House, *Report, 1943–1944* (London: Kingsley Hall and Children's House, 1944), pp. 3, 6.
63 Lambeth Archives Department, Lady Margaret Hall Archives, IV/183/3/2, Correspondence, including job descriptions and applications for domestic employees, 1930–1951, Letter from Miss Cameron to Miss E. Hepworth, 31 July 1941.
64 Oxford House, *The Oxford House in Bethnal Green, 1884–1948*, 96, 102.
65 J. S. Eagles, 'Major Lionel Ellis', in Toynbee Hall, *Toynbee Report, 1970* (London: Toynbee Hall, 1970), p. 32.
66 Mary Ward Settlement, *Annual Report for the Year ended 31st August 1959* (London: Mary Ward Settlement, 1959), p. 4.
67 Beer and Pickard, *Eighty Years on Bow Common*, p. 18.
68 Geoffrey Finlayson, 'A moving frontier: voluntarism and the state in British social welfare, 1911–1949', *Twentieth Century British History* 1:2 (1990).
69 W. F. Aitken, *Canon Barnett, Warden of Toynbee Hall: His Mission and its Relation to Social Movements* (London: Partridge, 1902).

70 Picht, *Toynbee Hall.*

71 Barnett, *Canon Barnett.*

72 Pimlott, *Toynbee Hall.*

73 Briggs and Macartney, *Toynbee Hall.*

74 E. Klein Abel, 'Canon Barnett and the first Thirty Years of Toynbee Hall' (PhD dissertation, University of London, 1969).

75 S. Koven, 'Culture and Poverty: The London Settlement House Movement, 1870–1914' (PhD dissertation, Harvard University, 1987).

76 M. Ashworth, *Oxford House in Bethnal Green, 1884–1984* (London: Oxford House, 1984); G. Barrett, *Blackfriars Settlement: A Short History* (London: Blackfriars Settlement, 1985); M. Daunt, *By Peaceful Means: The Story of Time and Talents, 1887–1987* (London: Time and Talents Association, 1989); K. Bradley, *Bringing People Together: Bede House Association, Bermondsey and Rotherhithe, 1938–2003* (London: Bede House Association, 2004); J. Glasby, *Poverty and Opportunity: One Hundred Years of the Birmingham Settlement* (Studley: Brewin, 1999).

77 Koven, *Slumming: Sexual and Social Politics in Victorian London*, 'From rough lads to hooligans', 'Culture and poverty'.

78 Scotland, *Squires in the Slums.*

79 Vicinus, *Independent Women.*

80 Beauman, *Women and the Settlement Movement.*

81 Harrow, 'The Development of the University Settlements in England, 1884–1939'.

82 M. Freeman, 'The provincial social survey in Edwardian Britain', *Historical Research* 75 (2002).

83 M. E. Rose and A. Woods, *Everything went on at the Round House: A Hundred Years of the Manchester University Settlement* (Manchester: Manchester University Press, 1995).

84 H. Jennings, *University Settlement Bristol: Sixty Years of Change, 1911–1971* (Bristol: University Settlement Bristol Community Association, 1971).

85 See M. Rooff, *A Hundred Years of Family Welfare: A study of the Family Welfare Association (formerly Charity Organisation Society), 1869–1969* (London: Michael Joseph, 1972); *Voluntary Societies and Social Policy* (London: Routledge & Kegan Paul, 1957); E. Macadam, *The New Philanthropy: A Study of the Relations between the Statutory and Voluntary Services* (London: Allen & Unwin, 1934); also B. B. Gilbert, *The Evolution of National Insurance in Great Britain: The Origins of the Welfare State* (London: Michael Joseph, 1966); M. Bruce, *The Coming of the Welfare State* (London: Batsford, 1961), also H. Llewellyn Smith, *The Borderland between Public and Voluntary Action in the Social Services* (London: Oxford University Press, 1937).

86 See P. Thane, *Foundations of the Welfare State* (London: Longman, 2nd edn 1996); (ed.) *The Origins of British Social Policy* (London: Croom Helm, 1978); J. Lewis, *Women and Social Action in Victorian and Edwardian England* (London: Edward Elgar, 1991).

87 F. Prochaska, *Women and Philanthropy in Nineteenth Century England* (Oxford: Clarendon Press, 1980); *The Voluntary Impulse: Philanthropy in Modern Britain* (London: Faber & Faber, 1988), 'Philanthropy', in F. M. L. Thompson (ed.) *The Cambridge Social History of Britain, 1750–1950*, pp. 357–93 (Cambridge: Cambridge University Press, 1990).

88 C. Webster, 'Conflict and consensus: explaining the British health service'; R. Lowe, 'The Second World War, consensus and the foundation of the welfare state'; G. Finlayson, 'A moving frontier: voluntarism and the state in British social welfare, 1911–1949', all in *Twentieth Century British History* 1:2 (1990).

89 See especially R. Means and R. Smith, *From Poor Law to Community Care: The Development of Welfare Services for Elderly People, 1939–1971* (Bristol: Policy Press, 1998).

90 See P. Townsend *et al.*, *The Fifth Social Service: A Critical Analysis of the Seebohm Proposals* (London: Fabian Society, 1970).

91 Thane, *Foundations of the Welfare State*, p. 290. For a more positive view of consensus, see D. Fraser, *The Evolution of the British Welfare State: A History of Social Policy since the Industrial Revolution* (Basingstoke: Palgrave, 2003).

92 T. H. Marshall and T. Bottomore, *Citizenship and Social Class* (London: Pluto, 1992).

93 J. Habermas, *The Structural Transformation of the Public Sphere: An Inquiry into a Category of Bourgeois Society*, trans. T. Burger and F. Lawrence (Cambridge: Cambridge University Press, 1989).

94 P. Bourdieu, *Outline of a Theory of Practice*, trans. R. Nice (Cambridge: Cambridge University Press, 1977).

95 J. Jacobs, *The Death and Life of Great American Cities* (New York: Random House, 1961).

96 R. Sennett, *Respect in an Age of Inequality* (Harmondsworth: Penguin, 2003).

97 R. Putnam, *Bowling Alone: The Collapse and Revival of American Community* (New York: Simon & Schuster, 2000).

98 J. Garrard, *Democratisation in Britain: Elites, Civil Society and Reform since 1800* (Basingstoke: Palgrave, 2002).

99 D. G. Green, *Reinventing Civil Society: The Rediscovery of Welfare without Politics* (London: IEA, 1993).

100 M. J. D. Roberts, *Making English Morals: Voluntary Association and Moral Reform in England, 1787–1886* (Cambridge: Cambridge University Press).

101 N. Deakin, *In Search of Civil Society* (Basingstoke: Palgrave, 2001).

102 H. Curtis and M. Sanderson, *The Unsung Sixties: Memoirs of Social Innovation* (London: Whiting & Birch, 2004).

103 J. Sheard, 'From Lady Bountiful to active citizen: volunteering and the voluntary sector', in J. Davis Smith, C. Rochester and R. Hedley (eds) *An Introduction to the Voluntary Sector* (London: Routledge, 1995).

104 *Ibid.*, p. 121.

105 G. Finlayson, *Citizen, State and Social Welfare in Britain, 1830–1990* (Oxford: Clarendon Press, 1994), p. 287.

106 B. A. Weisbrod, *The Nonprofit Economy* (Cambridge MA: Harvard University Press, 1988).

107 B. A. Weisbrod, *The Voluntary Nonprofit Sector: An Economic Analysis* (Lexington MA: Lexington Books, 1977).

108 See L. M. Salamon in W. W. Powell (ed.) *The Nonprofit Sector: A Research Handbook* (New Haven CT: Yale University Press, 1987). Also discussion of Salamon, Weisbrod and others in J. Kendall, *The Volun-w*), esp. pp. 1–4.

109 Kendall, *The Voluntary Sector*; J. Kendall and M. Knapp, *The Voluntary Sector in the United Kingdom* (Manchester: Manchester University Press, 1996); J. Kendall and M. Knapp, 'The United Kingdom', in L. M. Salamon and H. K. Anheier (eds) *Defining the Nonprofit Sector: A Cross-national Analysis* (Manchester: Manchester University Press, 1997).

110 See P. Taylor-Gooby and J. Zinn (eds) *Risk in Social Science* (Oxford: Oxford University Press, 2006).

2

Living, working and volunteering
at the university settlements, 1918–50

Through the settlements in London it was possible for residents, volunteers and employees to experience a diverse range of social work activities and to come into contact with people from all backgrounds. There was no one 'settlement experience' that could be distilled; likewise the expectations of what this experience should entail could vary widely between the volunteers and staff of a settlement, as well as between settlements in London and elsewhere. Memoirs of life at the settlements often portrayed the experience as an enriching one that either led to or supported an individual's choice to enter upon a career in social work. Yet the experience could also be overwhelming, stressful, frightening and bewildering in equal measure. This was in turn affected by the point in the life cycle at which the resident or staff member joined the settlement and their particular relationship to it, as well as other factors such as their gender, marital status and their relative class background.

Motives for joining a settlement could be complex: it was a means of expressing religious views and working out a vocation; it could be driven by a desire for political action; it could provide the resident or staff member with a place to live as well as to work. By the inter-war period a stay at a settlement had been used by many male residents as a starting point for a successful political and administrative career: William Beveridge, resident at Toynbee Hall between 1903 and 1905, left the settlement to work as a journalist before joining the civil service. In 1919, at the age of thirty-nine, he became one of the youngest people to be appointed a Permanent Secretary, at the Ministry of Food. Beveridge went on to become Director of the London School of Economics in 1919, then Master of University College, Oxford, in 1937, before (reluctantly) beginning the *Report into Social Insurance and Allied Services* of 1942 which laid the blueprint for the welfare state.[1] Gaining in renown by the inter-war period was Clement Attlee, another Toynbee Hall alumnus, who began his political career in east

London local politics, before serving as MP for Limehouse between 1922 and 1950. He gained experience in Ramsay MacDonald's cabinets in the 1920s, before assuming the Labour leadership after the resignation of George Lansbury in 1935. In 1945 Attlee led the Labour Party to a landslide victory in the general election; the subsequent governments established the welfare state, along with the National Health Service and an extensive programme of nationalisation.[2] Beveridge and Attlee were the most prominent of the settlement residents; there were many others who enjoyed a high degree of success in their chosen field, such as the educationalist Cyril Jackson,[3] the civil servant William Braithwaite[4] and the politician Percy Alden.[5] The settlements often traded upon their links with these higher echelons as proving their influence in the political and administrative spheres, but as Jennifer Harrow found, and will be discussed later, their ability to influence politicians and policy makers was ultimately limited.[6] Yet these individuals were at one extreme end of a continuum of experiences and outcomes. There were many other types of experience at settlements which deserve sustained attention from historians and which further illuminate such trends as the development of paid staff over volunteers and the emergence of project workers.

The leaders of the settlement movement

The experience of those 'leading' the settlement movement – wardens, head workers and the like – differed greatly from that of the newer volunteer or staff member in our period. The majority of the inter-war leaders trained before the First World War, with relatively few younger people gaining a foothold in settlement management before the Second World War. This was the case until the 1970s. The leaders of the inter-war period – characters such as Mallon at Toynbee Hall and Henriques at Bernhard Baron Settlement – were well-connected individuals, with years of social work experience to draw upon. This group also tended to leave the greatest number of papers and published accounts of their experiences behind, which provide useful insight into the motivation of those who went on to prominence in the movement, if little necessarily into those who left after a short while or who did not reach similar levels of renown.

J. J. Mallon (1874–1961) was writing his autobiography when it was destroyed in the bombing of Toynbee Hall in 1941. Mallon was reportedly devastated by the loss of the manuscript, and failed to return to it in peacetime,[7] yet a reconstruction of his life is possible through the extant papers of Toynbee Hall and his occasional appearance in other memoirs. Mallon was an unusual choice for warden of Toynbee Hall. First, he was not a graduate. He was born in 1875 in Manchester, the son of Irish migrants, and left school at fourteen to take up an apprenticeship to support his family following the death of his father.[8] Mallon's route to the trade unions came through the settlement movement as he enthusiastically took up evening classes and debating at the Ancoats Settlement in Manchester, where he also took up the role of Secretary to the Associates.[9] The Associates group was founded in 1898, and was drawn from the body of local helpers at the settlement. They organised social events and cultural activities, went out into the countryside as well as getting involved in campaigns for women's suffrage and against sweated labour.[10] Mallon found his vocation with the last of those activities.

The campaigns against sweated labour animated the entire spectrum of social reformers. In 1906 Mallon was appointed the Secretary of the National League to Establish a Minimum Wage,[11] where he worked alongside Mary Macarthur, the leader of the Women's Trade Union League and founder of the National Federation of Women Workers.[12] Following the Trades Board Act of 1909, he sat on the first thirteen of the Trades Boards, before being called upon by the government in the First World War to broker industrial disputes.[13]

1 Toynbee Hall after the air raid of 10 May 1941

2 External view of the gatehouse and warden's lodge at
Toynbee Hall before the bombing in 1941

Mallon was also a founding member of the Romney Street group,[14] a luncheon club for the discussion of political issues, among his many other connections. Mallon served on the Whitley report into industrial relations of 1917, as well as the Royal Commission on Licensing Laws (1929–31)[15] and Ramsay MacDonald's Economic Advisory Council. He was a member of the Aliens Deportation Advisory Committee and the Industrial Council and was a juvenile court magistrate. During the General Strike, Mallon was a member of a deputation to the government asking them to enter into conciliation with the strikers.[16] Frederick Marquis, later known as Lord Woolton, was a friend of his from his Manchester days,[17] which led to Mallon advising on entertainment in air raid shelters during the Second World War.[18] Mallon was also a Governor of the BBC from 1937 to 1939 and from 1941 to 1946.[19]

Mallon was able to energise the settlement in its post-war crisis of the early 1920s,[20] and to steer the organisation into fresh directions, notably in regard to the development of drama and music and the hosting of the Inner London Juvenile Court at the settlement between 1929 and 1954. Mallon also managed the correspondence that came into the settlement, suggesting projects that could be passed on to settlement residents. He was an 'expert', a person to be called upon, yet his experience of direct social work appears to have been minimal. From his earliest days as Secretary of the Associates' Union at Ancoats, Mallon was an organiser and a networker. Coming from a lobbyist background, Mallon was something of an exception among other settlement workers. As a result of his previous background he was adept at putting his settlement in the public – and policy – eye, and particularly adroit at publicising it through after-dinner speeches, popular journal articles and radio broadcasts. Mallon's reputation as a Poo-bah[21] of social work and reform drew upon and was reflected by Toynbee Hall.

Basil Henriques (1890–1961) was a far more 'typical' settlement leader than Mallon. Henriques was born into an affluent London Jewish family and attended Harrow before going up to Oxford. At university Henriques was introduced to new ways of thinking that would change his ideas about his future career. His history tutor, Kenneth Leys, nurtured his interest in religious reform, and introduced him to the settlement movement.[22] Henriques also read Alexander Paterson's *Across the Bridges*,[23] a book that found an eager audience among young Oxford students keen to find themselves in the world. Paterson, the Borstal reformer and member of the Prison Commission, began his career in the Oxford and Bermondsey Mission in south London,[24] and *Across the Bridges* is an evocative account of his time there. In the 1910s the mission ran several small clubs, each attracting around eighty to a hundred boys from the impoverished area around London Bridge and Tower Bridge.[25] Paterson's book inspired many of his readers, including Henriques, to volunteer in the slums. Henriques wrote:

> I felt that Bermondsey needed *me*, but I felt still more that I needed Bermondsey. I simply must learn first-hand of their hardships and handicaps. I must discover for myself the virtues that enable them to live so nobly under such conditions . . . I felt I must make that struggle. I must cross that bridge.[26]

His enthusiastic reading did not, however, prepare him for his first experience of the club:

Of all the impressions of that first night the most extraordinary was that these 'slum boys of the lower classes' should speak to me as though I were their equal. I, who until now had scarcely even spoken to anyone who had not had an education like my own or who had not mixed in the same kind of circle, unless it was to my batman or butler, was just accepted as an equal by these boys. It seems very silly now, but nothing seemed more odd to me that night than that.[27]

Henriques was struck by the readiness of the boys to welcome him as a member of the group. The 'slum boys' who attended this club were probably far more tolerant on first impressions of a naive young graduate than the 'unclubbable' delinquents of the streets – possibly as they were by now accustomed to the presence of awkward upper middle-class young men at their clubs. Henriques still had to build up a rapport with the boys, by joining in their activities and slowly winning their confidence.[28] He was struck by the absence of similar clubs for Jewish boys, and mulled over the possibility of establishing one himself.[29] Although there was a proliferation of youth clubs in Stepney, none was specifically run by or for Jews, apart from the Jewish Boy Scout troop at Toynbee Hall from 1913.[30] When Henriques came into an inheritance upon the death of his father he was able to put his plan into action.[31] His first step, in October 1913, was to join Toynbee Hall as a resident.[32] He remained there until April 1914, although he was not especially happy at the settlement, finding his fellow residents too 'scientific' or stuffy. He used his time there to gain experience in a variety of areas of social work, but it was mainly a convenient base for him whilst he set up his own settlement.[33]

Henriques opened the Oxford and St George's in the East Jewish Boys' Club on Betts Street in 1914, shortly before he was called up for service in the First World War. He was assisted at the club by a range of helpers, including Rose Loewe, whom he married in 1916.[34] The club grew rapidly during the course of the inter-war years. In 1930 the club was renamed the Bernhard Baron St George's Settlement, following a donation of £65,000 from Baron, a tobacco dealer and philanthropist,[35] which enabled the settlement to move to new, purpose-built accommodation. By the early 1930s the settlement buildings were home to a range of clubs for boys, girls and adults, as well as an infant welfare centre, a children's playground, a roller-skating rink, a dispensary, a sun ray treatment room, a canteen, a library, a model electric train room, a boxing-cum-dancing hall, handicraft rooms and a floodlit football pitch on the roof, not to mention offices for probation officers and a synagogue.[36] The settlement offered a range of welfare and leisure services catering for local people from the cradle

to the grave – literally, as Henriques was also an advocate of settlements being a point for accessing friendly and burial societies.[37]

Henriques was extremely active in the interests both of his settlement and the wider community. He became a Justice of the Peace in
1924 at the age of thirty-three, was the chairman of the committee of
the Norwood Orphanage for Jewish children, a manager of three local
schools, was a Visiting Guardian of the Jewish Board of Guardians,
and was on the House Committee of the London Hospital. In 1925
he was appointed a Juvenile Court magistrate.[38] Henriques was also
one of the earlier and most prominent members of the National
Association of Boys' Clubs (NABC), founded in 1924.[39] Like his fellow
magistrates at the East London Juvenile Court, Miriam Moses[40] and
J. J. Mallon,[41] his interest in the local community was wide-ranging,
and brought him into contact with people from a variety of backgrounds. His thinking and approach to social work were multilateral,
a matter of personally knowing who to recommend to whom. Like
Mallon and many others, he straddled the divide between the voluntary
sector and the state through his portfolio of interests. But what of
others involved in the settlement movement in this period?

Lady Margaret Hall Settlement

Lady Margaret Hall Settlement (LMHS) was founded in 1887 on
Kennington Road in Lambeth, south-east London. LMHS drew its
inspiration from Women's University (later Blackfriars) Settlement in
Southwark, and recruited, at least initially, from the women's colleges
at Oxford, Cambridge and London. It was not dissimilar to other
women's settlements through organising a programme of clubs for
children and young people, children's country holidays, work with disabled children and their families. It helped to establish the School
of Sociology that later became part of the London School of Economics,
and by the inter-war period was well established as a place for social
workers to train. It expanded its activities across various sites in the
Lambeth area, and ventured into new areas, such as free legal advice,
after the First World War.[42]

The 'traditional' narrative of institutional settlement histories focuses
on the pioneers, the senior and most prominent members of staff or
volunteers in the settlements who were responsible for the foundation and development of the institution's policies and activities –
characters such as Samuel and Henrietta Barnett of Toynbee Hall,[43] or
the novelist and commentator Mrs Humphrey Ward of the Passmore
Edwards Settlement in St Pancras, central London.[44] Although prominent,

such characters formed part of a complex network of staff and volunteers at settlements. Relatively few settlement residents – especially
women's settlement residents – were able to commit to full-time volunteering. Some paid their rent through independent means, whilst
a patchwork of scholarships, grants and employment kept the rest
in residence. An increase in short-term project funding, especially
from the 1920s onwards, provided new opportunities for women: it
also reflected structural changes beginning to occur in the voluntary
world.

Yet there was another, equally important, category of staff working
in settlements: the domestic staff. In both men's and women's settlements, large domestic staffs were employed in order to maintain an
environment similar to that enjoyed by students at Oxbridge colleges.
Settlement residents were typically housed in bed-sitting rooms and
ate their meals together in communal dining rooms. Domestic staff
oversaw the cleaning of rooms and linens, the availability of hot water
for washing, and the preparation of meals, thereby facilitating the
residents' voluntary social work. At the most basic level, the domestic
staff played an essential role in managing the settlement on a daily
basis, but this relationship changed in the course of the inter-war period,
in parallel with the gradual decline in domestic service. It was also
the case, as will be seen here and later, the line between 'domestic'
and 'settlement' resident or staff was often blurred.

The LMHS wages book for the period 1916 to 1941[45] provides an
insight into the dynamics of the relationship between domestic and
settlement staff. In October 1916 there was a small body of waged
domestic staff consisting of a 'Boy', Mrs Crowther and a dustman,
alongside ten salaried members of staff. Waged staff were invariably
domestic or similar staff, whilst salaried staff could include those in
social work professions, administrators and the more senior domestic
staff, such as bursars, whose role at settlements often included the
collection of rent and other monies from residents as well as the
management of the 'household'. The balance of waged to salaried staff
in October 1916 appears to have been anomalous, possibly on account
of the availability of domestic staff during the war, as by April 1919
the staffing had reverted to what would be its main pattern through
to 1941. In April 1919 the settlement listed a cook, a parlour maid, a
house parlour maid, three housemaids and a kitchen maid as its basic
domestic staff.[46] From 1920 onwards, charwomen were also employed
by the settlement on an *ad hoc* basis, with other temporary domestic
staff such as odd job men, window cleaners and the somewhat catch-
all role of 'man' and sewing women.[47]

Before the financial year 1923–24 payments made to salaried staff were ascribed to the person's name, rather than recording the expenditure on their role, so it is not always clear who undertook which duties. After the change in accounting procedure it is possible to gain insight into the changes that were occurring. In that year the salaried staff comprised the warden and her sub-warden, the secretary of the Invalid Children's Aid Association (ICAA), the bursar, a paid worker (categorised as clerical staff) and a portress.[48] From the later 1920s into the 1930s, the settlement's clubs – the Salamanca and the Duke of Clarence – were able to employ paid workers (rather than relying on volunteers), and this was dutifully recorded, alongside payments for the leaders of the Unemployment Club from 1932.[49] As the recession bit harder in 1933–34 an additional worker for the Duke of Clarence was offered board and lodging in lieu of a salary, although a general settlement worker took a salary in 1934–35. By 1938 the staff of the settlement thus comprised the core staff of the warden, sub-warden and bursar, along with a training secretary, two workers for the Duke of Clarence, an ICAA worker, a general settlement worker (now on a board and lodging basis), the Misses Ross and Pilsky (roles not stated), Miss Crossman (the Cowley estate worker) and a part-time typist. The domestic staff based in the main settlement house remained at their 1919 levels, being joined by odd job men, window cleaners and cleaners attached to the various clubs and satellites. What was emerging just before the Second World War was a salaried staff not employed as individuals performing a number of unspecified roles, but increasingly recruiting women to particular paid posts. The posts in turn were more tightly focused in their scope, fulfilling specific needs for running clubs or dealing with the increasing number of social work students training at the settlement.[50] On the domestic staff, it is noticeable that the 'traditional', live-in roles such as house parlour maid were still important, but that 'dailies' such as the various cleaners and odd job men were gaining ground.

The build-up to the Second World War accelerated these trends. The staff as a whole was scaled back in the course of 1939, with the domestic staff largely and then entirely absent by the end of 1942. The sub-warden role was vacant by 1941, as was the role of training secretary, but the bursar was joined by a financial secretary.[51] Club leader roles continued throughout the war, alongside the newer post of Cowley estate worker, whose role was to support the community of this newly built LCC estate on the Brixton Road. When the settlement opened a nursery in the 1940–41 financial year, a matron, assistant matron, nursery assistants and teachers were employed.[52] Whilst these records suggest a growing trend towards more professional and specialised roles within charities, they do not offer much insight into the kinds of people who applied for the roles or their motivation for entering into employment at settlements. More can be gleaned through an analysis of the employee correspondence files for 1930–51, which coincide in part with the wage records mentioned above.

The Crossman sisters began a long acquaintance with LMHS in early 1930, when Miss W. Crossman joined the settlement firstly to cover a holiday absence. In May 1930 she was offered the post of assistant at the Duke of Clarence club, and then was appointed assistant club worker in late 1933. In December 1934 she tendered her resignation for the following August, as she was engaged to be married. The marriage was indefinitely postponed in the spring of 1935, and Crossman remained at LMHS, becoming the Cowley Estate worker in 1937.[53] She remained at the settlement during the Second World War, working with bombed out families and also in leading the local Air Raid Patrol unit.[54]

Twenty-six years old at the time of her appointment, Crossman had been educated at the Chelsea College of Physical Education, before becoming an assistant at the West Chelsea Girls' Club. In 1927, aged twenty-three, she joined the Milk Street Girls' Club in Bath, where she taught gymnastics, crafts, swimming and arranged outings, along with running Guide and Scout groups, and visiting families. She also supplemented her work by attending lectures in social science at the University of Liverpool, near her parents' home.[55] According to the annual report of the Milk Street Girls' Club for 1929, Crossman had been successful in building up the work of the club, from introducing a house system to train the girls in leadership to bringing twelve Guides to camp at her parents' house in Crosby. The report also noted that Crossman was a paid employee,[56] not a volunteer, a significant point, as will now be seen. In a reference given to the LMHS warden, Mrs Fish, the president of the club, wife of the Archdeacon of Bath and major figure in the philanthropic endeavours of that city, noted an earlier instance of marriage being postponed on account of Crossman's fiancé's poor health.[57] Crossman was by all accounts an exceptionally able worker, as testimonies from her former employers demonstrated – but she evidently worked in order to keep herself whilst waiting to be married. It is not clear whether the fiancé mentioned in 1930 was the same as the fiancé of 1935. These incidents must have been bitterly disappointing, also possibly rewarding for a woman who clearly enjoyed working with young people and yet was prepared to give up her work on marriage. Despite these personal disappointments Crossman thrived at LMHS, as several glowing testimonies demonstrated:

she is a woman of independent character and would like now a more
senior position, for which she is well fitted. She has a delightful sense
of humour [. . .] She is most businesslike and reliable in every way [. . .]
she has been a stimulating and inspiring leader in A.R.P. and other
forms of war work [. . .] She has shown great courage and resourceful-
ness in emergencies.'[58]

This is a tantalising glimpse into the ways in which women negotiated the 'marriage bar', even in such female-dominated professions
as social work. Her feelings about the broken engagements and the
opportunity to remain in her work are lost from the historical record,
but nevertheless she appears to have found satisfaction in her later
work. Yet, if her wedding had come about, would a woman like
Crossman have been happy to withdraw from active social work to
become a committee leader like Mrs Fish? Did women use social work
careers as a means of finding suitable husbands, or as an appropriate
way to pass the time whilst saving up to marry?

Miss Crossman was joined by her sister, Jean, in the early 1940s.
Jean helped with her sister's air raid patrol duties on the Cowley estate
alongside working as the settlement secretary, although she soon left
in order to take up duties with the ATS. Jean remained in residence
at LMHS whilst in the Auxiliary Territorial Service, and used her stay
at the settlement and her informal work on the estate with her sister
to assist her application for a grant to train as a hospital almoner in
the later 1940s.[59] Jean appears to have approached her career in a
very different manner from that of her sister. The elder Crossman had
attended a training college before gaining employment in a girls' club,
building up her experience in each post in order to gain promotion.
Yet Jean was on the verge of a career in social work through starting
out as an administrative worker, and helping her sister out. Arguably,
the war disrupted young people's opportunities to enter full-time college training, but Jean had nevertheless used a non-social work post
and training to gain the skills she needed in order to acquire her grant
for almoner training. This was not an uncommon method of entry, as
the case of Beryl Arnold demonstrated.

Beryl Arnold worked as the bursar's live-in assistant at the settlement in 1948, having recently completed her studies at Godolphin
and Latymer Girls' School in Hammersmith, west London. Beryl had
hoped to gain a place at the women-only Bedford College to study
social sciences on account of her work at LMHS but was unsuccessful. Instead she used her experience as a basis for gaining a post as
an assistant librarian. Again, the crossover here between the domestic
and the administrative is blurred – to replace Beryl, the settlement

had contacted the National Institute of Home Helps. When this proved fruitless, they decided to try the Girls' Friendly Society magazine[60] – although whether to recruit leaders such as Crossman (who had lived in the Girls' Friendly Society hostel in Bath) or to recruit members is unclear. What this case and the case of Miss W. Crossman suggest is that where families were unable or unwilling to support young women financially in full-time volunteering or training that did not attract a grant, then settlements provided an ideal alternative for thwarted ambitions. Where young women could work as residential staff it meant that they could earn money to support themselves and their families whilst also relieving pressure on space at home and gaining some independence. This was also indicative of the broader trends in the voluntary sector, with increasing importance being placed on paid staff rather than volunteers.

These were not advantages exclusively for women in their early careers. Elizabeth Knowles, the Hut Social Worker in 1949, had begun her career as a music teacher, qualifying in 1925 at the Trinity College of Music in London. In 1934 she changed direction, taking up training at the Talbot Settlement, the Dockhead Club and St Francis' House in south-east London. Between 1936 and 1938 she was able to take up a club and social work post at St Luke's in Eltham, south-east London, gaining her club leaders' certificate before emigrating to South Africa from 1938 to 1948. In Grahamstown she took up a residential post caring for children in need of care or protection and difficult girls, whilst also completing her BA in Social Science at Rhodes University College.[61] Likewise, Isabel Shaw, working at the Barton Hill Settlement in Bristol, had trained as a secretary, largely working in business, before moving to the settlement in 1944. Shaw was making a lateral career move by moving into social work organisations, but her administrative skills had been put to good use by Barton Hill in putting her in charge of their Home for Mothers and Babies. Shaw may not have had much experience in direct social work, but her ability to manage the paperwork and administration of such a home was a skill much in demand at settlements.[62]

Other women were keen to join the settlements as a means of serving the country during the Second World War. Elizabeth Hepworth worked as a librarian at the Bodleian Library in Oxford during the early part of the war, but as her male colleagues left for the civil service or to work as shelter wardens Hepworth was galvanised into action. She applied to LMHS because she was 'fed up because I do not consider [the librarian post] work of really urgent national importance, have got the authorities to say they are willing to release me for war work and will guarantee my job for me after the war, and am now looking for something really useful to do'.[63] Miss Cameron, then warden of the settlement, gave Hepworth a flavour of what was needed: general secretarial work to keep up with the additional paperwork in wartime, but also helping to co-ordinate an evacuation bureau for older people, and maintaining a library and educational service to people in the shelters. Extra bodies were needed, Cameron argued, as during the war 'the Settlements therefore become a kind of first line for meeting the needs, physical and mental, of the people of London in this very badly bombed neighbourhood'.[64]

And settlement work was certainly exciting during the war. Winnie Davin accepted a post at Bristol University Settlement between 1941 and 1943 whilst her husband, Dan, was serving with the Second New Zealand Expeditionary Force.[65] The job provided her and her small child with somewhere to live, and there were plenty of interesting activities to get involved in: 'Infant Welfare Centres, Play Centres, Children's Library, Clubs for Boys + Girls, After-care Works, Crafts + Domestic Subjects, Drama, Housing Estate Work etc'. She was also able to work on establishing and later running the Home for Mothers and Babies (which Isabel Shaw later ran), as well as getting involved in the preliminary research for the Beveridge report.[66] As Hilda Jennings observed of her volunteer, she took the post 'because it offered Air raids and an opportunity to pioneer in meeting new wartime needs', while other correspondents offered only 'a safe and comfortable home'.[67] The settlements also welcomed those fleeing Nazi rule. Else Federn, the warden of the Ottakring Jewish women's settlement in Vienna, also joined Winnie Davin at the Bristol Settlement.[68] What was important to the settlement was the skills such women brought to the post – and in this way, women out of their twenties had much to offer. And like the younger women who used settlements as a half-way house between the family home and their possible marital home, for older single women or those temporarily separated from their husband a job at a settlement provided money, a home and company – and, in some cases, excitement and fresh challenges.

The improvised nature of women's entry into social work professions here is striking, demonstrating how settlements like LMHS were both destinations and starting points, with women arriving at the settlements as students or trainees, moving on to other institutions to gain experience. It also highlights the relative fluidity between so-called 'domestic' posts, such as bursar, and the more purely 'social work' posts during a period in which short-term contract funding for projects was beginning to establish itself. Although professional training in social work, teaching and nursing was readily available, this partly reflects the inability of some women to access it on a full-time basis and their need to finance entry to their chosen career in other ways, certainly before the introduction of the mandatory grant for university studies by the Attlee governments. It also suggests that women's strategies for entering social work through the university settlements encompassed a variety of motivations aside from a desire to help others: somewhere cost-effective, respectable and safe to live whilst working and training. These were considerations that could apply at various points in women's lives for a variety of reasons, the kinds of reasons not included in *curricula vitae* or application letters, about which in many cases we can only speculate – disappointment in marriage, loss of a potential husband in the previous war, need to leave the parental home, or to find a home and work after marital break-down or the death of a spouse. But if this was the case at a women's settlement, how did women at men's settlements fare?

Toynbee Hall

Despite its association with male residents and staff such as Clement Attlee and William Beveridge, Toynbee Hall had an active cadre of women volunteers and staff, many of whose commitment to the settlement was of longer standing than that of the male residents. Henrietta Barnett, the wife of the Reverend Samuel Barnett, the vicar of St Jude's church in Commercial Street, Whitechapel, had a strong network of women volunteers who helped with parish duties and social work, a project which ran alongside her husband's work at the neigh-bouring settlement.[69] When the Barnetts left the settlement in 1906 women's involvement in the settlement continued. Before the First World War several of the male residents lobbied for the introduc-tion of a women's residential element, following the successful co-educational experiments of settlements in North America. An opportunity to develop this area of work arose in 1915, when the settlement uprooted its residential element to Poplar, farther east among the London docks, and opened a women's settlement alongside the men's.[70] But neither the women's nor the men's settlement in Poplar was able to survive its early years, and folded, with some embar-rassment, in 1917.[71]

Women were not formally readmitted as residents at Toynbee Hall until the 1960s. Despite the disappointment of the Poplar experiment, women continued to play a number of key, if overlooked, roles in the work of the settlement. Margaret Kendall undertook a variety of roles, from bursar to secretary, managing the settlement's property and making sure that the considerable programme of adult education classes ran smoothly. But her work was not confined to that. Kendall was an active and enthusiastic Girl Guider. With help from the settlement cook, Mrs Reardon, she was able to start a Brownie pack in 1919. As the girls grew older, they began to clamour for a Girl Guide patrol, which Kendall provided by 1925. Her activity was not limited to catering for girls in the immediate locality, as she built up Guiding at the settlement to the point where, in 1934, Toynbee Hall housed the east London headquarters of the Girl Guide Association.[72] Kendall remained at the settlement until 1949, when she left to pursue a career in nursing.[73] Nevertheless, the pattern of facilitating the development of a social work/caring career first through an administrative post held true of Margaret Kendall.

It was not just women from the lower middle and middle classes who contributed to the life of the settlement. In 1913 a Mrs Rosetta Reardon joined the staff of Toynbee Hall as cook, whilst her husband became the settlement's porter. She remained heavily involved with the settlement until shortly before her death in 1963.[74] She moved from being cook to the warden's housekeeper,[75] later to helping to run the older people's luncheon club.[76] She became fundamental to the life of the settlement, facilitating its everyday running and providing a sense of stability and friendship to the residents and staff. She was also the longest-serving member of staff, clocking up fifty years and embedding herself in the life of the settlement. In an obituary notice, she was described thus:

> Mrs Reardon was an unfailing source of information, reminiscence and wit; never an ex-Resident, from no matter how far back, re-visited Toynbee Hall without visiting Mrs Reardon, and being greeted and remembered by her, and she seemed to have known all the old people from their schooldays onwards. When failing health made it necessary for her to give up her work in the luncheon club, it was with the greatest reluctance that she did so, although most people would feel that retirement at 78 is not a sign of laziness. Right up until the day of her sudden last illness she kept her lively interest in Toynbee and all its doings, and with her passing a real and vital link between past and present has been broken.[77]

As mentioned earlier, Mrs Reardon was responsible for rounding up the first cohort of Brownies, drawing upon her friendships with local people.[78] The Reardon family, by design or accident, were closely involved in the life of the settlement. The Reardons' son, 'Johnnie', went on to become a prominent local Labour councillor, before becoming Mayor of Stepney in 1957, when a point of pride for him was to attend the opening of a public garden at the settlement where he had grown up.[79] Rosetta Reardon provides a different model of women's lives at settlements. Unlike many of the unmarried women at women's settlements, Rosetta Reardon's family life was incontrovertibly bound up in the life of Toynbee Hall. And her 'family' came to include the many young men who spent time at the settlement at the beginning of their post-university careers. If some women went to settlements to escape from or to relieve pressure on their biological families, or to find spiritual families or communities of kindred souls, then Rosetta Reardon literally integrated her family with the settlement itself.

The residents themselves also had wives and in some cases children living with them. J. J. Mallon lived in a flat over the main Commercial Street entrance to the settlement with his wife, Stella, the daughter of A. G. Gardiner, the editor of the left-wing *Daily News* paper.[80] When E. St John Catchpool returned to Toynbee Hall after the First World War as sub-warden to Mallon, he brought his wife, Ruth, with him in tenements at the rear of the campus. Ruth, a qualified doctor, threw herself into work with mother-and-baby clinics whilst 'Catch' was at Toynbee.[81] There were other women living on site: Edith Ramsay, head of the LCC Stepney Women's Evening Institute, Stepney borough councillor and prominent unofficial social worker, lived for many years in tenements to the rear of the campus. Ramsay also played a vital and active part in the management of the settlement through acting as a trustee.[82] This cadre of women around the settlement has largely escaped the historical record, but their contribution to the life of the charity was by no means insignificant or unimportant. When commissioned to collect data on the cost of living in east London for the Ministry of Labour in 1936, Mallon's task force included two men in a team of nine. Of the seven women who volunteered to collect the data, one was Edith Ramsay, whilst another was Stella Mallon; Alice Lascelles, the daughter of Edward Lascelles, a friend of Mallon and a regular visitor to the settlement, was also drawn in. The wives of two Toynbee Hall residents, Mrs Stewart and Mrs E. P. Hitchcock, were likewise recruited. All formed part of a community of 'Toynbee women' who carried out such occasional 'women's work' as collecting data.[83]

The settlement was also home to a variety of welfare organisations, such as the Invalid Children's Aid Association and the Children's Country Holiday Fund, which, whilst not part of the settlement proper, provided opportunities for women to become involved in the daily work of Toynbee Hall. Hosting other organisations had long been a characteristic of the settlement, from Samuel Barnett's granting of space for trade union and friendly society meetings, and by the inter-war period this hosting had expanded to include the charities mentioned above, as well as the Inner London Juvenile Court and branches of public services such as the insurance department of the Ministry of Health.[84] During the Second World War the profile of women at Toynbee increased. Female probation officers working alongside the Inner London Juvenile Court moved into the residents' flats;[85] women undertook work for the Ministry of Food in the lecture hall,[86] whilst keeping up the welfare services that were ever more urgent. Skilled social workers of both genders were required to help process the many refugees from Europe who arrived before the fall of France; more still were needed for helping to co-ordinate waves of evacuee children from the East End.[87] In this way, women who had skills in other areas of work – managing hostels or working as secretaries – had a vital role to play, as finding and reuniting family members and in many other ways helping people to rebuild their lives in the midst of the devastation of the Blitz became one of the main functions of settlements, as Edith Ramsay found.[88]

After the declaration of peace in 1945, Toynbee Hall reverted to type with the return of male residents. Yet, as one resident from the 1950s

3 J. J. Mallon and Toynbee Hall residents around the dinner table, *c.* 1930s

4 A. E. Morgan, residents and guests having their evening meal at
Toynbee Hall, *c.* 1950s

recalled, the male residents were on some level aware that they no
longer fitted in the world of social work, that theirs was an outmoded
pursuit.[89] This was part of a growing unease and confusion at
Toynbee Hall and doubtless other settlements about what their role
should be in the post-war world of the welfare state, a debate played
out in private and not so private conversations as well as in vehicles
such as the *Warden's Letter*, distributed to residents, staff, volunteers
and interested parties.[90] Yet mixed residence was a distinctive feature
of the wardenship of Walter Birmingham in the 1960s, and it was
accompanied by other fresh approaches to residential volunteering,
notably the provision of accommodation for young people 'at risk' and
the support of new groups such as Community Service Volunteers.[91]
Whilst women had always had an important role to play at the settlement, it was not always publicly acknowledged, let alone celebrated,
until well into the post-war era. Although there were single women
like Edith Ramsay and Margaret Kendall connected with the settlement, the women attached to Toynbee Hall in this period were often
married to men with connections with the settlement. In many ways,
what little we know of their activities through the survival of files on
the nutrition research project may provide answers to some of the questions posed by such cases as that of Miss Crossman, who did not cross

the 'marriage bar' and thereby leave her work behind. Perhaps those who did abandon a career in social work – or other areas – took advantage of opportunities to do bits of research or to help out with clubs and clinics as a means of keeping in touch with friends and colleagues, of staying challenged and contributing something back to society. Whilst elements of these patterns persisted into the 1950s and beyond, the ways in which women used the settlements changed fundamentally after the Second World War. Settlement life remained highly gendered: men were more likely to become the wardens of women's settlements than women were to take up the same role at male settlements. But more women were in residence at settlements of all types after the war, as the expansion of social work training and funding for university courses made such educational programmes somewhat more accessible. Settlements continued to be places where social work students could undertake placements, whilst initiatives such as the Community Service Volunteers working in conjunction with the settlements introduced a broader spectrum of residents.[92] Whilst there were more women – and indeed people from all social backgrounds – involved in settlement life from the 1960s onwards, few were able to break the 'glass ceiling' into settlement management, despite the diversification of routes into social work and settlements.

Notes

1 J. Harris, 'Beveridge, William Henry, Baron Beveridge (1879–1963)', in H. C. G. Matthew and B. Harrison (eds) *Oxford Dictionary of National Biography* (Oxford: Oxford University Press, 2004). See also N. Timmins, *The Five Giants: A Biography of the Welfare State* (London: HarperCollins, 2001).

2 See R. C. Whiting, 'Attlee, Clement Richard (1883–1967)', in Matthew and Harrison, *Oxford Dictionary of National Biography*, also K. Harris, *Attlee* (London: Weidenfeld & Nicolson, 1982); R. D. Pearce, *Attlee* (London: Longman, 1997).

3 R. Blair, 'Jackson, Sir Cyril (1863–1924),' in Matthew and Harrison, *Oxford Dictionary of National Biography*.

4 W. Braithwaite, *Lloyd George's Ambulance Wagon: being the Memoirs of William J. Braithwaite, 1911–1912* (Bath: Chivers, 1970).

5 M. C. Curthoys and T. Wales, 'Alden, Sir Percy (1865–1944)', in Matthew and Harrison, *Oxford Dictionary of National Biography*.

6 J. Harrow, 'The Development of the University Settlements in England, 1884–1939' (PhD dissertation, University of London, 1987), p. 637.

7 A. Briggs, 'Mallon, James Joseph (1874–1961)', in Matthew and Harrison, *Oxford Dictionary of National Biography*.

8 *Ibid.*

9   M. E. Rose and A. Woods, *Everything Went on at the Round House: A Hundred Years of the Manchester University Settlement* (Manchester: Manchester University Press, 1995), p. 68.

10 *Ibid.*, p. 67.

11 A. Briggs and A. Macartney, *Toynbee Hall: The First Hundred Years* (London: Routledge, 1984), p. 93.

12 A. V. John, 'Macarthur, Mary Reid (1880–1921)', in Matthew and Harrison, *Oxford Dictionary of National Biography*.

13 Briggs and Macartney, *Toynbee Hall*, p. 94.

14 J. M. Lee, 'The Romney Street group: its origins and influence, 1916–1922', *Twentieth Century British History* 18: 1 (2007).

15 J. A. R. Pimlott, *Toynbee Hall: Fifty Years of Social Reform* (London: Dent, 1935), p. 208.

16 Barnett Research Centre at Toynbee Hall, TOY/SPE/1, Annual Reports (hereafter TOY/SPE/1), *The Universities' Settlement in East London: Report, 1962–1963*, p. 7.

17 Rose and Woods, *Everything went on at the Round House*, p. 68.

18 TOY/SPE/1, *Annual Report, 1938–1946*.

19 Briggs and Macartney, *Toynbee Hall*, p. 121.

20 *Ibid.*, p. 94.

21 Pimlott, *Toynbee Hall*.

22 S. McCabe, 'Henriques, Sir Basil Lucas Quixano (1890–1961)', in Matthew and Harrison, *Oxford Dictionary of National Biography*, B. L. Q. Henriques, *The Indiscretions of a Warden* (London: Methuen, 1937), pp. 17–23.

23 A. Paterson, *Across the Bridges, or, Life by the South London Riverside* (London: Edward Arnold, 1911).

24 V. Bailey, *Delinquency and Citizenship: Reclaiming the Young Offender, 1914–1948* (Oxford: Clarendon Press, 1987), p. 2.

25 Henriques, *The Indiscretions of a Warden*, p. 24.

26 *Ibid.*, p. 21.

27 *Ibid.*, p. 25.

28 *Ibid.*, pp. 26–7.

29 *Ibid.*, p. 29.

30 Briggs and Macartney, *Toynbee Hall*, p. 79.

31 Henriques, *The Indiscretions of a Warden*, p. 29.

32 *Ibid.*, p. 35.

33 *Ibid.*, pp. 38–46.

34 McCabe, 'Henriques, Sir Basil Lucas Quixano (1890–1961)'.

35 A. E. Watkin and C. Clark, 'Baron, Bernhard (1850–1929)', in Matthew and Harrison, *Oxford Dictionary of National Biography*.

36 Henriques, *The Indiscretions of a Warden*, pp. 195–6.

37 B. L. Q. Henriques, *Club Leadership* (London: Humphrey Milford, 1933), p. 244.

38 L. L. Loewe, *Basil Henriques: A Portrait, based on his Diaries, Letters and Speeches and collated by his Widow, Rose Henriques* (London: Routledge & Kegan Paul, 1976), p. 71.

39 Henriques, *The Indiscretions of a Warden*, p. 277.
40 Miriam Moses (1884–1965) was a noted Stepney politician and social activist. She became a JP in 1922, and was the first female mayor of Stepney, in 1931. Among other activities, she was the co-founder of the Brady Girls' Club (1935). See S. Kadish, 'Moses, Miriam (1884–1965)', in Matthew and Harrison, *Oxford Dictionary of National Biography*.
41 Briggs, 'Mallon, James Joseph (1874–1961)'.
42 See Lady Margaret Hall Settlement, 'Summary: Brief History of the Settlement since 1887', www.lmhs.org.uk/about.php (accessed 2 August 2007).
43 For an account of the lives of the Barnetts, see Henrietta Barnett, *Canon Barnett: His Life, Work and Friends* (2 vols, London: John Murray, 1918).
44 For Mary Ward, see J. Sutherland, 'Ward, Mary Augusta (Mrs Humphry Ward) (1851–1920)', in Matthew and Harrison, *Oxford Dictionary of National Biography*.
45 Lambeth Archives Department (hereafter LAD), IV183/3/1, Wages Book (with details of servants).
46 LAD, IV183/3/1, April 1919.
47 LAD, IV183/3/1, April 1920–21, April 1921–22, October 1922–23.
48 LAD, IV183/3/1, October 1923–24.
49 LAD, IV183/3/1, October 1928–29 and October 1932–33.
50 Lady Margaret Hall Settlement, 'Summary: Brief History'.
51 LAD, IV183/3/1, October 1938–39 and October 1939–40; financial secretary, October 1940–41.
52 LAD, IV183/3/1, October 1940–41 and October 1941–42.
53 LAD, IV183/3/2, Correspondence, including job descriptions and applications for domestic employees, 1930–52; Miss Crossman, staff file, 1930–38.
54 LAD, IV183/3/2, Testimonial for Miss W. Crossman, 19 February 1942.
55 LAD, IV183/3/2, Letter from Crossman to Miss Butler, 7 March 1930.
56 LAD, IV183/3/2, Milk Street Girls' Club report, September 1928 to September 1929.
57 LAD, IV183/3/2, Letter from Mrs Fish to Warden, 10 March 1930.
58 LAD, IV183/3/1, Letter to Miss Warren, of the National Council of Girls' Clubs, 1 March 1937'; Testimonial for Miss W. Crossman, 19 February 1942.
59 LAD, IV183/3/2, Testimonial for Jean Crossman, 14 September 1946, and Letter to Miss H. Ross, Further Education and Training Grant Department, Ministry of Labour, 22 August 1947.
60 LAD, IV183/3/2, Arnold's form of application for residence; Letter to Mrs Mattinson *re* Beryl Arnold, 21 February 1949.
61 LAD, IV183/3/2, Staff file/c.v. for Elizabeth Knowles, 1949, Hut Social Worker.
62 LAD, IV183/3/2, Letter to Miss W. H. Hogg from Isabel Shaw (Barton Hill), 8 July 1946.
63 LAD, IV183/3/2, Letter from E. Hepworth to Miss Cameron, 22 June 1940, and Letter from E. Hepworth to Miss Cameron, 28 July 1941.

64 LAD, IV183, Letter Miss Cameron to E Hepworth, 31 July 1941.
65 A. Davin, 'Community, life-cycle, diaspora: a daughter's view', in B. Brookes and D. Page (eds) *Communities of Women: Historical Perspectives* (Dunedin NZ: University of Otago Press, 2002), p. 21.
66 *Ibid.*, pp. 22–3.
67 H. Jennings, *University Settlement Bristol: Sixty Years of Change, 1911–1971* (Bristol: University Settlement Bristol Community Association, 1971), p. 33.
68 *Ibid.*, p. 33. See also E. Malleier, *Das Ottakringer Settlement. Zur Geschichte eines frühen internationalen Sozialprojekts* (Vienna: Verband der Wiener Volksbildung, 2005).
69 S. Koven, 'Henrietta Barnett, 1851–1936: the (auto)biography of a late Victorian marriage', in P. Mandler, S. Pedersen and J. Clive (eds) *After the Victorians: Private Conscience and Public Duty in Modern Britain: Essays in Memory of John Clive* (London and New York: Routledge, 1994), p. 44.
70 Pimlott, *Toynbee Hall*, pp. 194–6.
71 TOY/SPE/1, *Toynbee Hall Annual Report, 1916–1919*, pp. 9–10.
72 Pimlott, *Toynbee Hall*, pp. 250–1.
73 BRC, TOY/CEN/8/5, Park House Papers, Letter, Margaret Kendall to F. W. McNulty, 18 August 1949.
74 TOY/SPE/1, *The Universities Settlement in East London: Report, 1963–1964*, p. 12.
75 Briggs and Macartney, *Toynbee Hall*, p. 126.
76 TOY/SPE/1, *Report, 1963–1964*, p. 12.
77 *Ibid.*
78 Pimlott, *Toynbee Hall*, pp. 250–1.
79 Toynbee Hall, *Warden's Letter* (London: Toynbee Hall, 1955–59), No. 6, August 1957, pp. 1–2.
80 Briggs, 'Mallon, James Joseph (1874–1961)'.
81 E. St John Catchpool, *Candles in the Darkness* (London: Bannisdale, 1966), pp. 115–16.
82 B. Sokoloff, *Edith and Stepney. The Life of Edith Ramsay: Sixty Years of Education, Politics and Social Change* (London: Stepney Books, 1987).
83 BRC, TOY/CEN/2/2/6.
84 Pimlott, *Toynbee Hall*, p. 241.
85 Briggs and Macartney, *Toynbee Hall*, p. 128.
86 BRC, Image Bank, 'Wartime use of lecture hall by Ministry of Food'.
87 Briggs and Macartney, *Toynbee Hall*, p. 126.
88 Sokoloff, *Edith and Stepney*, p. 105.
89 Tony Lynes, interviewed by Niamh Dillon, Pioneers in Social Welfare and Charitable Work series, F16969, tape 4, side B (London: National Sound Archive, 2005).
90 See esp. Toynbee Hall, *Warden's Letter*, October 1955 (1) and March 1956 (2).
91 See Briggs and Macartney, *Toynbee Hall*. Also Elizabeth Hoodless, interviewed by Louise Brody, Pioneers in Social Welfare and Charitable Work series, F18454, tape 4, side A (London: National Sound Archive, 2006).
92 TOY/SPE/1, *Toynbee Hall Report, 1973*, pp. 6–7.

3

Health

Before the National Health Service was established in 1948, settlements were important providers of health care and allied services in urban working-class communities. Such work had its roots in the public health movement of the nineteenth century and concern about the well-being of the poor, such as Engels's evocative account of slums in Manchester.[1] The settlement movement of the nineteenth century itself engaged with the poor living conditions of working-class districts through local government activism, such as membership of Sanitary Committees and writing letters to local newspapers about conditions.[2] The health of children within the urban environment attracted especial attention. For example, the Children's Country Holiday Fund (CCHF) was one of Henrietta Barnett's many social projects of the 1880s and enjoyed close co-operation with the settlements into the 1980s and beyond. The CCHF began taking poorly children to the countryside to recuperate, but this was soon extended to give all eligible children a break from the deleterious urban environment.[3] Concern was also expressed about the quality of working-class parenting, from fears of overcrowding leading to incest to the need to inculcate middle-class ideals of family life.[4] This concern was not just about the immediate welfare of impoverished London children; it also fed into discourse from the 1880s onwards about the degeneration of the nation, and great anxiety over the 'racial health' of Great Britain, from its declining population and the poor physique of men who enlisted in the Boer War.[5]

A related concern throughout the nineteenth century was the question of rational recreation, or the provision of suitable spaces for wholesome and constructive entertainment in an attempt to improve the intellectual, moral and physical health of the working classes.[6] Octavia Hill, connected with Women's University Settlement, and Henrietta Barnett, of Toynbee Hall, were also part of the movement to increase public spaces so that the working classes could enjoy fresh air and the space to roam around freely.[7] The latter were also engaged with the provision of free Sunday afternoon musical concerts and a range of classes, lectures and debates for adults in conjunction with the University Extension Movement, the Workers' Educational Association, the Board of Education and the London County Council, as well as under their own auspices.[8] Thus settlement health work did not operate within a vacuum; rather, it took place within a general mushrooming of voluntary health work and a growing relationship between charity workers and local government administration.[9] This chapter will focus upon the ways in which the settlements worked to try to improve the health of their local communities, as well as their social and psychological well-being.

Settlement health work was undertaken in highly gendered ways. Many women's settlements were heavily active in providing health-care services, whilst men's settlements concentrated on allied services such as insurance clubs and first aid training. This bias was entrenched by the 1890s, by which time it was common for most women's settlements to provide district nursing services and CCHF breaks as a general minimum.[10] More exceptional cases included Canning Town Women's Settlement (CTWS) and the Women's University Settlement (WUS), which branched out into hospital and dispensary provision.[11] Work with disabled children was also a common feature of the settlements. WUS worked closely with the Invalid Children's Aid Association (ICAA),[12] whilst branches of the same organisation were active at Lady Margaret Hall and Toynbee Hall into the inter-war period.[13] From 1895 CTWS ran schools for disabled children[14] in addition to working with the Invalid and Crippled Children's Society (ICCS), whilst Mary Ward established a similar school at Passmore Edwards Settlement in 1899.[15] WUS also provided workshop space and apprenticeships for disabled boys in order for them to learn a trade to support themselves in later life.[16] Infant welfare provision was extensive, and was boosted by the Maternity and Child Welfare Act of 1918. Infant welfare clinics could be found at other settlements, including WUS,[17] and the range of services offered by settlements expanded to include child guidance and nutrition clinics at Bishop Creighton House and sunlight treatment at Cambridge House by 1938.[18]

Although sharing out and sick benefit clubs were common to both men's and women's settlements,[19] there was a greater preponderance of hospital Saturday collections and other friendly society savings schemes at men's settlements. Some, like the Mansfield House Hospital Saturday Fund, were for the benefit of settlement club members.[20] Another model could be found at Toynbee Hall, where they hosted a local branch of the insurance department of the Ministry of Health, allowing local people to access this state service in their neighbour-hood.[21] The settlement also granted space for friendly societies to meet.[22] This provision had its roots in the temperance work of the settlements. Trade unions and friendly societies had traditionally met in public houses;[23] by offering friendly societies alongside 'dry' men's clubs and other activities, settlements hoped to provide further reasons for working men to resist the temptations of the pub.[24]

This gender division also reflected the fact that, following the 1911 National Insurance Act, men, women and children had varying access to health care provided by the state. The 1911 Act required all workers earning less than £160 a year to insure themselves against illness through an 'approved society', a friendly society 'approved' by the government.[25] Whilst this meant that a greater number of men had recourse to medical services through approved society health insurance, it did not extend to their children or wives, aside from a maternity benefit. Women who were employed in an insurable occupation were eligible to pay into such schemes in their own right,[26] but those who did not work or were employed in non-insurable occupations were vulnerable. However, the Maternity and Child Welfare Act of 1918 required local authorities to make provision for the health of mothers and their young children.[27] As mentioned above, this Act enabled settlements to extend their work with mothers and babies; it also helped them to further develop working relations in local government and with other charitable or political interest groups.

The Second World War disrupted these trends. Settlements of all types were involved in local war planning before the declaration of hostilities in 1939, and later had a vital role to play in helping with the relief effort, as seen in the previous chapter. Settlements became involved with evacuating children, the elderly and the distressed from London. Some settlement staff found themselves advising and working with the government, such as Mallon's work on feeding and entertainment in air raid shelters.[28] After the war, growth of the National Health Service in tandem with reconstruction and slum clearance created new challenges for the settlements. Whilst they abandoned much, if not all, of their earlier healthcare work, they gradually refocused their efforts to concentrate upon the welfare needs and 'well-being' of needy groups, namely the elderly, single-parent families, families with disabled children, and other families at risk of social exclusion. There were also experiments with assisting those with mental health issues, such as the Philadelphia Association therapeutic community at Kingsley Hall in the late 1960s and the

Grendon Prison outpost at Toynbee Hall. This chapter will analyse the evolution of settlement healthcare work away from the offering of medical services through to the provision of support to vulnerable members of the community, and their changing relations with funders and local authorities.

Clara Grant and health in Poplar

Clara Grant, warden of the Fern Street Settlement in Poplar, was an untypical settlement leader, basing her activities on the two schools she ran in the area, Devons Road and Fern Street. Yet through Grant it is possible to gain insight into the health and welfare issues that concerned settlement and other social workers before the First World War, and how these subsequently shaped inter-war approaches to those problems. For Grant, the crux of social problems lay in medical deficiencies, broadly understood. Grant realised that educational efforts were wasted on empty stomachs, and so ran a scheme at the Devons Road school which offered a simple breakfast for fifty infants each day throughout the year, as well as evening meals for her schoolchildren and their parents.[29] Grant managed a ticket scheme to provide children who had suffered from rickets and other debilitating illnesses with milk and eggs,[30] and also employed a nurse to monitor the health of her pupils.[31] However, the apogee of her medical work lay in helping Margaret McMillan to run a famous experimental school clinic out of the Devons Road school.[32]

The Devons Road school clinic was set up in 1908, and took advantage of provision under the 1907 School Medical Inspections Act. It was funded by the American soap magnate and philanthropist Joseph Fels[33] and run by McMillan under the aegis of the Metropolitan District of the Independent Labour Party Committee for the Physical Welfare of Children,[34] with the blessing of the London County Council.[35] The majority of the clinic patients came from Devons Road school, which made following up cases easier for the doctors and the settlement nurse seconded to the clinic; children also lost less school time in attending hospital appointments.[36] Grant recalled that the school clinics were educational for the doctors and dentists in more ways than one:

> Our doctors could always talk simply to the mothers, except one stranger who, when a mother said: ''E's very fussy with 'is food,' replied, 'Oh, he's fastidious, is he?' 'No, 'e ain't, 'e's fussy.' It was also interesting to hear a school dentist talking to mothers ascend from 'deciduous' to 'temporary' and thence to 'milk' teeth.[37]

Over a two-year period the clinic treated 450 children from a school of 1,000 pupils, with the cases of 201 children written up in a report by Reginald Tribe in *School Hygiene* in May 1911. Tribe commented in this article that the experience of the clinics had provided him and fellow medics with an insight into the common health problems of children from poorer homes:[38] anaemia and debility; ear diseases; throat and nose conditions; tuberculosis.[39] He commented that:

> Perhaps the chief lesson is the great value of a School Clinic in co-operating with all the work done for the child, the country holiday, the home conditions of poverty, the choice of a career on leaving school, the need for feeding the necessitous, and the relation of physical fitness to educational efficiency. The practical needs of the moment may call for the equipment of Clinics that serve a whole group of schools; but the ultimate ideal is the establishment of a clinical room in every school.[40]

For Tribe, the experience of working at the clinic confirmed the need to treat the physical manifestations of child poverty in a holistic manner, as part of the general educative effort of an elementary school. The school clinic at Devons Road proved unfeasible to operate in the longer term,[41] but it was a seedbed for McMillan's clinic and camp school projects in Deptford,[42] and Fern Street medical provision continued until 1924, when an LCC treatment centre was opened in Bow.[43]

Aside from its significance to McMillan's later work, this short-lived clinic demonstrated the potential for schools – and settlements – to tackle the greater problems of poverty through attempting to ameliorate the health of children and young people through the schools they were compelled to attend. It also illuminated the need for health care to be readily accessible, as children were more likely to attend if seeing a nurse for follow-up appointments did not mean a special trip to a large hospital. It was also vital, as Grant noted, for medical professionals to communicate with their patients and their parents in language they understood. This concept of understanding the local community on its own terms was central to Grant's view of the role of a settlement, and here it was applied to the practicalities of improving health in a deprived area of east London. The nature of state provision for elementary education underwent rapid evolution in the later nineteenth century, following the introduction of compulsory elementary education under the 1870 Forster Act. Parents were still required to contribute to school fees until 1891, when the state paid school fees up to 10s per head. The Balfour Education Act of 1902 created local education authorities, and thus brought the responsibility for funding and managing schools into the remit of local government.[44] The local education authority was establishing itself as a body for the administration of schooling: yet it did not effectively deal with some of the obstacles to learning, such as intense poverty and malnutrition in a particularly deprived community, such as the docks. Thus Grant's experiments with funding from private bodies enabled her and others to explore the possibility of combating the ill effects of poverty through school meals and medical inspections and to use this as a basis for subsequent campaigns. These experiments were successful in that the 1906 School Meals Act required local authorities to provide meals for students, although problems would continue throughout the twentieth and twenty-first centuries with reconciling quality of food with authority budgets. Clara Grant provides a case of a settlement social worker exploiting contacts within the volunteering world, political activists and her paid position within a rapidly evolving area of state and local government activity. This relationship would continue to be played out in the course of the inter-war period, as the following case study of West Ham will demonstrate.

Infants and mothers

The majority of women's settlements had some form of health provision for mothers and small children. This was a more general staple of women's voluntary work. It ranged from the provision of mothers' meetings and schools for mothers (and fathers) to infant welfare clinics and trips out of London, and brought together state and voluntary provision. Such work straddled altruistic impulses to help needy families as well as ideas about supporting the nation's imperial destiny. It also arose from the particular frameworks for providing medical care in the capital before the establishment of the National Health Service in 1948.

Prior to 1948 the voluntary sector and the state through the Poor Law had been the main providers of health care. The Poor Law made provision for workhouse or stand-alone infirmaries, whilst voluntary hospitals were funded through a combination of philanthropic donations and contributory mutual aid schemes. As Virginia Berridge has pointed out, the state had a long tradition of intervening in public health. This was heightened by pressure from social researchers such as Booth and Rowntree, the eugenics movement and the labour movement to improve standards of working-class health. Local government became increasingly involved in the provision of aspects of health care, such as the school meals mentioned in the previous section, although much of the funding for health care was derived from friendly societies and other forms of mutual provision. As Berridge also emphasises, the contribution of friendly societies to the funding of health care also meant that a strong local element in health provision and administration was retained until the 1930s and 1940s.[45] The 1911 National Health Insurance Act built upon these mutual traditions to provide health care for workers, but still left gaps which were catered for by local authorities and voluntary providers. The Maternity and Child Welfare Act of 1918 was an example of this as an attempt to improve maternal and infant mortality rates through the education of mothers and clinic supervision. It was administered by local authorities, although there were considerable variations in how the Act was administered by authorities and the role of voluntary health organisations within that provision, as Lara Marks found.[46] Increasing concern about the uneven and specialist provision of voluntary hospitals, especially in London, and interest in social medicine led to further changes in the funding structure of hospitals and other health care providers. Notably, the 1929 Local Government Act enabled authorities to provide general hospitals paid for by the rates.[47]

These developments had important consequences for voluntary providers of health care in the course of the inter-war period. The increased role of local government in health care provided more opportunities for charitable bodies to apply for funding for specific projects, but it also meant that such bodies had to undertake work which fitted the criteria of the London County Council or the local borough council. The LCC in particular had specific ideas about the voluntary provision of health care, and used its powers as a funding and statutory body to direct activities.[48]

The Canning Town Women's Settlement Hospital and the South West Ham Health Society

Although settlements provided a wide variety of clinics, Canning Town Women's Settlement was the only one to provide a full-scale hospital, when it took over the local medical mission in 1892.[49] The CTWS Hospital was devoted to the needs of women and children, providing free medical advice along with out-patient services and home visiting.[50] By 1918 it also offered minor and major surgery and ran a dispensary which was used by 600 patients a week. Yet by the early 1920s it was causing the settlement to run into financial difficulty, and its survival was threatened. As one of the hospital doctors put it, the settlement had arrived in Canning Town intending to address the religious and social needs of the community:

the social including *mind* and body. In the early days, the need of the body had been very urgent, but ... the work of a Hospital was now so specialised that it was no longer possible for the settlement to undertake it.[51]

But the settlement was reluctant to abandon its work in relation to the hospital, despite also competing with the other hospitals for women and children that had opened in the area since the 1890s, namely the Queen Mary Hospital for Women and Children in Plaistow and the St Mary's Hospital in West Ham Lane, Stratford.[52]

Were the problems faced by the women in Canning Town unique? Until the 1970s historians such as David Owen tended to see the inter-war period as a bleak time for voluntary hospitals, as they were hit by a drop in voluntary subscriptions and donations in the aftermath of the First World War.[53] However, research by Steven Cherry and by Martin Gorsky, John Mohan and Martin Powell has suggested that this was not the case.[54] Rather than facing a shortfall in income, the voluntary hospitals experienced diversification in their sources of funding.[55] So why did the CTWS find it difficult to raise funds for its hospital?

The CTWS Hospital ran into problems with the King Edward's Hospital Fund from 1915. This caused major difficulties, as the King's Fund was one of the main funders of voluntary hospitals in London in this period.[56] The Fund was unhappy with the financial manage-ment of the hospital, and a series of additional, emergency applica-tions for funds by the hospital did not improve matters.[57] Visitors from the King's Fund were further antagonised by an incident in which they arrived for an inspection, to be allegedly ignored and then later insulted by the hospital staff.[58] The CTWS Hospital had little altern-ative other than to look at other sources of funding and to consider changing the scope of the medical work accordingly: to chase the available funding rather than obtaining funding for the most press-ing needs. The executive committee of the settlement explored the possibility of holding flag days or bazaars to raise additional funds,[59] before concluding, wisely, that funds might be better secured from grants created by the Maternity and Child Welfare Act.[60] But the hospital's debts were beginning to impinge upon other areas of the settlement's work. By November 1919 the warden, Mrs Parker Crane, was com-plaining that her staff were working to raise funds for the hospital and neglecting to raise money for its other areas of work.[61] Within weeks the settlement had resolved to abandon its hospital project, but with the proviso that the hospital should be maintained as a going concern whilst the settlement approached other bodies such as medical schools to take it over.[62] In 1922 the hospital was put up for sale, and was bought by the Invalid and Crippled Children's Society. In the course of 1923 it reopened as a children's hospital, and continued as such until the reorganisation of health services in West Ham after 1947.[63]

The desire of the settlement to continue to run the hospital was noble in principle, but it was far beyond its financial and organisational capabilities by the inter-war years. Obtaining financial support for the hospital was one of the major issues faced by the settlement, but it was also a case of not irrationally duplicating work being carried out elsewhere by others: especially those with access to better resources and greater expertise. This was not a problem exclusive to charities involved in the provision of medical or health care, but one which affected charitable bodies in all arenas.

Although CTWS were forced to abandon the hospital, this was not the end of its involvement in health care. Rather, the cessation of the hospital project marked a phase in which the settlement and Mansfield House occupied themselves with public health campaigning. The South West Ham Health Society and Infant Welfare Centre (SWHHS) was founded before 1918; whilst it was independent of both the West Ham settlements, it was dominated by their staff and volunteers. The warden of Mansfield House was appointed *ex officio* as Chair, whilst the warden of CTWS was likewise an *ex officio* member of the committee. The Society drew on all manner of local expertise, from the CTWS's Invalid Kitchen and its branch of the Invalid Children's Society, the local Charity Organisation Society, the Baptist Tabernacle, the School for Mothers, the Salvation Army, the Co-operative Society, representatives of local churches and the medical profession and the borough council, including the mayor.[64] The aim of the SWHHS was to promote the health and welfare of mothers and children in the South West Ham area.[65] It worked towards this in a number of ways, from providing an infant welfare clinic and School for Mothers, as well as ante- and postnatal services, pioneering new developments in health care, to lobbying the borough council on health matters. It was a pressure and action group promoting the rights of the needy, and it especially worked to meet the needs of women and children after 1918. Like many other groups, it joined the rush to secure money from the new stream of funding made available under the Maternity and Child Welfare Act, and it tailored its work to suit what could and would be funded by local government.

Much of its work involved the implementation of the Maternity and Child Welfare Act after 1918. Lara Marks has compared the ways in which Labour- and Conservative-led London boroughs implemented this Act, demonstrating a link between Labour councils and greater engagement with its requirements.[66] Although West Ham was a Labour borough and was generally not unsympathetic to the cause of working-class women and their young children, that did not mean that the South West Ham Health Society had an easy task in securing the facilities it needed. Shortly before the Act was passed, the Society led a campaign to establish a day nursery in West Ham for mothers working in munitions.[67] A conference on the subject in March 1918 led to a delegation being sent to the borough Public Health Committee to state their case, although the matter was passed on to the Medical Officer of Health.[68] Additional support came with the inclusion in the Maternity and Child Welfare Act of a clause allowing such facilities to be funded by the Local Government Board, thereby removing an obstacle to opening such a nursery.[69] The National Union of Women's Suffrage Societies and the Women's Co-operative Guild joined the campaign in the autumn of 1918, and a second conference was held, which resolved to push the borough of West Ham to implement all the requirements of the Act.[70] A small nursery was started at Lees Hall shortly afterwards, which was overseen by the SWHHS welfare sub-committee.[71] Even with support and close links, negotiation and persistence were required.

But the Society was also responsive to emergent needs, and increasingly paid attention to the need to provide affordable dentistry to local people. Such basic dental hygiene as having a toothbrush for each member was well beyond the means of the poorest East End families. Clara Grant recalled families in the area around Fern Street where an uncle might share his toothbrush with nieces and nephews – such was the luxury of owning a toothbrush.[72] This problem was not limited to the East End. Before dental services were available under the NHS, the cost of treatment could be prohibitive, even for relatively affluent workers, let alone for those without savings or insurance which covered dentistry. The SWHHS campaign reflected the findings of the Dawson and Lawrence reports of the 1920s and the campaigns of the British Medical Association in the 1930s to address these issues of access to ancillary health services, especially for young people.[73]

In 1921 the Society explored the possibility of providing dental care to mothers and children under five through its infant welfare clinic. It liaised with infant welfare clinics in north Islington, North Kensington and Willesden to find out more about the cost of equipment and running a dental clinic itself.[74] The Society found that a dental clinic was beyond its means,[75] so it attempted, unsuccessfully, to persuade the borough council to allow the women from the clinic to use its services.[76] The problem re-emerged in the 1930s, but with a better solution. The Fairbairn Club at nearby Mansfield House University Settlement enlisted the *pro bono* services of a dentist for its members, and this was extended to the clinic mothers.[77] Dental care continued to be an issue of concern for the Society through to the later 1940s, as they discovered that boys and girls aged fourteen to eighteen and who had left school often had difficulty accessing dental services, whereas younger children were more likely to be able to see a dentist through their school or by being young enough to benefit under the Maternity and Child Welfare Act.[78] The question of access to dental care was one the SWHHS was unable to solve before the introduction of NHS dental services, but its concern was shared by many others involved in health care provision.

As the National Health Service established itself, the role and purpose of the South West Ham Health Society evolved. In the late 1940s and early 1950s it concentrated its efforts on co-ordinating its infant welfare and antenatal provision with that of the local government health committees, which part-funded them at the time.[79] Its work continued until 1953, when the Society appears, from the extant minutes, to have been wound down. In 1960 it was re-established as the South West Ham Children's Welfare Society, which concentrated on providing for the social needs of disabled children.[80] The work of the CTWS Hospital and the SWHHS should be seen as operating along a continuum from the 1890s to the 1950s and beyond. There was a general degree of consistency in its approach, from identifying medical needs among women and children, and finding the means to address them – although the work was increasingly shaped by the availability of public and philanthropic funding. It was not always a smooth or successful process, as the financial difficulties of the hospital suggest, but there is nevertheless an enduring pattern of adaptation and negotiation with funding bodies and authorities. This pattern helped to ensure the provision of medical services to some of the neediest groups, whilst also offering opportunities for settlement workers to build up networks with other charities and to establish their presence in local government.

Toynbee Hall and nutrition research

One of the biggest debates of the inter-war period focused upon nutrition and malnutrition. Recruitment for the Boer War had revealed the importance of good nutrition for the health of individuals and the nation as a whole. Improving maternal, infant and child nutrition had been an important area of public health programmes since the start of the twentieth century, and there was concern whether or not rates of maternal morbidity and health more generally were improving as a result. In addition to the impact of public health programmes, attention also focused in the 1930s on those families who suffered from the effects of long-term unemployment and life on Public Assistance. Researchers sought to reconcile the needs of the public budget and family purse by finding the minimum amount at which a family could be adequately and healthily fed. Interest in this area was fuelled by Seebohm Rowntree's calculations of family budgets, particularly in *The Human Needs of Labour*, an updated version of which was published in 1937.[81] Contemporaries were especially divided over the issue of whether or not such public health programmes had a positive impact upon national health, as indeed are historians such as Charles Webster and Jay Winter. Webster argued that although national averages appeared to improve in the course of the inter-war period, there were still significant regional health inequalities.[82] Winter, on the other hand, argued that infant and maternal mortality were affected not by economic performance but rather by the care given to women during pregnancy and the practices of the medical profession.[83]

Toynbee Hall attempted to enter the nutrition debates in the mid-1930s. The motive for commencing the nutrition project is unclear, but it seems that a combination of the British Association of Residential Settlements (BARS) members' own projects, their own participation in or assistance with other organisations' work on nutrition, and politicians' interest in the matter were powerful stimuli. Mallon himself had explored similar aspects of poverty in *Poverty Today and Yesterday* (1930), which he co-wrote with Edward Lascelles.[84] Although *Poverty Today and Yesterday* was essentially a general introduction to the problems of poverty for the lay reader rather than a detailed analysis, Mallon tackled, as he had in an earlier piece on women's wages, the issue of working-class expenditure.[85] Like Rowntree in his later studies, Mallon was sympathetic to the notion that the working classes should have a living wage, i.e. an income should provide for more than the basic needs.

In the spring and summer of 1936 Mallon and Hodgkinson began to seek advice – and, most important, funding – for a research project into nutrition. One of Mallon's first ports of call was Sir David Munro, then head of the Medical Research Council. Mallon proposed that Toynbee Hall and its affiliates could produce a detailed and comprehensive study of poverty in the east London area.[86] Mallon also asked David Hughes, a settlement resident involved with the project, to find a suitable physician to advise them. One of Hughes's first steps was to contact Professor Edward Provan Cathcart, of Glasgow University, for advice on the project, with whom he corresponded during September 1936.[87] Cathcart was an eminent nutritionist who had carried out many studies of nutrition and health in urban areas and of the health of infantrymen in the First World War. In 1936 he chaired the Department of Health for Scotland's Committee on Scottish Health Services, which advocated a national health policy. Its recommendation was that improvement in diet was necessary to promote better health.[88] During the 1930s medical researchers were developing knowledge of how nutrition was essential to health, although their findings were not well known. Cathcart suggested that data on dietary conditions might not be easily available or particularly reliable, but he did suggest that the Toynbee Hall project might concentrate upon household management, including the consumption of gas, coal, beer and cigarettes, as these had not been widely investigated.[89] Hughes commented to Hodgkinson that Cathcart had remarked 'that the collecting of information about dietary conditions is a woman's job'.[90] This phrase is ambiguous in both Hughes's letter to Hodgkinson and in the original from Cathcart, as it is not clear from the context whether Cathcart is praising women researchers or being derogatory. Women had the best access to other women through their work as health visitors. Margery Spring Rice's health survey, *Working Class Wives* (1939),[91] had used exclusively female expertise in collecting data. Whether offhand or intentional, the comment had results. When commissioned to collect data on the cost of living in east London for the Ministry of Labour in 1936, Mallon's task force included two men in a team of nine.[92] Of the seven women who volunteered to collect the data, one – Edith Ramsay – was a noted social worker resident in a Toynbee-owned block of flats; Alice Lascelles was the daughter of Edward Lascelles, Mallon's collaborator on his *Poverty* book; Mallon's wife, Stella, was drawn in, as were the wives of a Toynbee Hall resident and a member of Council respectively, Mrs Stewart and Mrs E. P. Hitchcock. All formed part of a community of 'Toynbee women' who carried out such 'women's work' as collecting data. As will be seen, Mallon also included women's settlement staff in his team of researchers. Although women were not full residents of the settlement at this point, Mallon was still keen to use their expertise to strengthen the project.

Around the same time, in late 1936, Mallon and Hodgkinson began collecting data on the price of food in east London on behalf of Seebohm Rowntree.[93] The data, which were collected from CTWS, the

LCC Public Assistance Committee, the Bishopsgate Unemployment Assistance Board, St Hilda's East and St Margaret's House,[94] were used by Rowntree in *The Human Needs of Labour*.[95] Again, they followed Cathcart's advice about using women to collect data about domestic matters. Mallon and Hodgkinson were given a questionnaire which they forwarded to their colleagues at the other settlements. It asked for information about expenditure on a range of basic foodstuffs, from bread and potatoes to scrap beef and scrag end of mutton. Their collaborators used a variety of techniques for eliciting results. At CTWS, Catherine Towers passed the list on to a local woman who was renowned for being a shrewd shopper; the Public Assistance Committee based its list on outdoor relief scales: 'the prices which they quoted were obtained from shops where relief coupons are exchanged for goods'.[96] The PAC figures were therefore based on the amounts claimants could realistically expect to receive. St Margaret's House consulted its mothers' club. G. T. Kelly, the warden, wrote:

> They are seventy quite typical poorer East End housewives and they were quite unanimous in their replies. Practically every one replied without a moment's hesitation. One felt anew how much even 1/2d means to them and how expert they are in their job of buying in spite of the criticisms of the other experts.[97]

Gertrude May Truscott, the deaconess of St Hilda's East, got her statistics from the Women's Fellowship:

> There were forty-eight members present. All of them live in this neighbourhood and I kept a special ear open for the remarks of two of the very poorest who were sitting in the front row just beside my feet.
> I hope that the result is what Seebohm Rowntree requires. It seemed to me to be more satisfactory than for us to go out and look at prices without knowing whether the women would actually buy at those prices.[98]

F. G. Clarke, the district officer, and his assistant, Williams, of the Bishopsgate Unemployment Assistance Board, decided to research the prices for themselves, visiting Shoreditch, Bethnal Green and the local street markets, as they had no official data to use.

The women attending the Fellowship provided Truscott with detailed information, including the availability of cheaper, imported alternatives for breast of mutton, minced beef and shin beef. Their comments on the use of certain items, like oatmeal, and how items were normally purchased give a greater insight into working-class household budgets than the official figures provided by the LCC Public Assistance Committee. They frequently provided price ranges for certain items, and gave not general figures for 'luxury' items like jam but made distinctions between 'standard' plum jam and 'best' plum jam. This suggests that women would balance their food budget against the family's needs in a particular week and, in a good week, perhaps opt for the slightly better cut of meat or for British produce. In a harder week they would purchase cheaper alternatives. This suggests that many women were careful and shrewd shoppers, with intimate knowledge of the best places to get foodstuffs at suitable prices – the standard market price was not necessarily the price at which they bought. This was one of the requirements stipulated by Tennant to Mallon and Hodgkinson. They asked their data collectors to bear in mind that 'it will therefore be necessary to obtain prices from the kind of local shop with which the wife of such a workman [on low wages] would trade'.[99]

During the week of the survey Peter Tennant of the British Association for Labour Legislation (BALL) wrote to Mallon and Hodgkinson inviting them to join a committee to promote the findings of a survey into nutrition BALL was to undertake. Tennant hoped that the survey would examine the medical and physical impact of malnutrition, as well as its social aspects, evidence of malnutrition, its consequences for maternal and infant mortality, experiments in distressed areas, schools, the role of the housewife, the role of agriculture, distribution, transport and economic policy, the psychological aspects of malnutrition and, finally, the international dimension.[100] It was to be a wide-ranging and demanding study, and it would require publicity – and action – to justify the pains taken. May Tennant, Peter's mother, and the first woman factory inspector in England, as well as an acquaintance of Mallon's from the Trades Boards days,[101] undertook to write to Mallon, an old friend of hers, on 19 November 1936 to solicit his help.[102] Mallon could not help directly, given his own commitments, but he suggested that Hodgkinson might do so instead. Mallon wrote, 'He has the merit of . . . having already had to do with certain enquiries with nutritional aspects in this part of London.'[103] At this point the letters relating to the BALL survey dry up until the early months of 1937, when there was an exchange of letters between Mallon, Viscount Astor and Lord Strabolgi about Rowntree's book.

In December 1936 and January 1937 there was a flurry of interest in nutrition from other BARS members. Eric Mawson wrote to Mallon to comment that the BARS executive was discussing the possibility of malnutrition as a conference topic, and had been in touch with the Ministry of Health to obtain a questionnaire; and that a Dietetics Study Group at Durham House Settlement was ready to commence nutrition research.[104] In late January 1937 Grace Drysdale, of the Edinburgh University Settlement, enquired about the survey at Toynbee Hall, expressing interest in pursuing her own. Hodgkinson replied that the Toynbee Hall research project had not settled on any particular line of enquiry, and – presumably following Cathcart's advice of the previous autumn – was trying to avoid duplicating other studies. Hodgkinson commented in his letter that 'the difficulty about Nutrition is that no one quite knows what it all means and certainly none of the experts can agree on any standard of measure for the problem'.[105] His letter suggested that Toynbee was interested in pursuing research into the consumption of milk. Drysdale noted that she was about to start a survey of sixty families in the Craigmillar area of Edinburgh.[106] R. H. Wyatt, warden of the University Settlement in Manchester, also enquired about progress at Toynbee, as his settlement was about to survey 500 families in the Ancoats slum clearance area.[107] Toynbee Hall had stimulated interest in the field, yet its own research into nutrition did not take place, for reasons that remain unknown.

From March 1937 the paper trail dwindles. Peter Tennant wrote to Hodgkinson enclosing the minutes of the BALL Nutrition Enquiry Committee. This meeting, on 15 March 1937, had established two further committees: a political committee, which included the Archbishop of York, Field Marshal Lord Milne, Lord Passfield (as Sidney Webb was to become), Lady Hall, two Members of Parliament, Hodgkinson, Duncan Sandys and H. J. Tennant; and a scientific committee, which included Eleanor Rathbone, Dr M'Gonigle, the Medical Officer of Health for Stockton on Tees and the author of a major report on adult nutrition among slum and modern housing dwellers,[108] Professor Stapledon and Mrs Neville Smith of the Women's Institute. Beveridge and Lord Astor were added to lend weight to the survey. Thereafter any Toynbee Hall influence waned, and no further letters survive between Hodgkinson, Mallon and Tennant.

Lord Astor, whose connection with the settlement movement included founding (and financing) the Virginia House Settlement in Plymouth and also the Astor Institute, had entered into discussion with Mallon on how best to organise a debate on the report of the Advisory Committee on Nutrition to the Ministry of Health,[109] and to conscript a Labour peer to debate this with Astor. Astor wrote:

> Too many of my Tory Peers are concerned in keeping up the price of food for the benefit of agriculture and indirectly landowners to be useful in a Nutrition debate and cheaper food.
>
> When we have a debate, Labour Peers fail us if the price of food is being pushed up by a Marketing Board or Scheme. They think that

anything called National Planning must be sound even if it leads to dear food.

Rowntree's book – *Human Needs of Labour* – brings out that people of this country should have cheap food. Do try and get some Labour Peer to talk intelligently.[110]

Toynbee Hall did not, as far as the records show, undertake its own research project, but Mallon, Hodgkinson, Hughes and their colleagues at the women's settlements in particular attempted to contribute to a national debate. Food had become a key area of interest for social reformers at a time when understanding of the relationship between poverty, poor diet and ill health was expanding. It was not just that people could not afford 'luxuries' such as spectacles or fillings in their teeth, or even panel doctors, but that an impoverished diet could create problems which required much attention.

Whilst the letters between Mallon, Hodgkinson and others are interesting, the richest material on this issue is the questionnaires from the women's settlements, the scribbled notes recording the women's comments on the food items and the weekly budgets, the asides that show the reality of feeding a family on a limited budget. The middle-class women investigators extracted valuable information by stepping beyond the limits of the questionnaire and engaging in dialogue with their subjects about their lives. All the women involved in the survey were talented and able in their own right, and Mallon allowed them the opportunity to undertake this work. They contributed to understanding the women they worked for and lived with as neighbours. These female (and male) researchers shopped in the same markets as the women whose lives they were investigating. The warden of St Hilda's listened to what the women had to say about the lists presented to them; Catherine Towers of CTWS gave the list to a women's club member. The researchers tried their best to empathise with the women whose daily lives and shopping habits they were investigating. They collected data that engaged with national concerns, but, apart from some brief-lived discussions with politicians and major players in the debate, they were unable to influence policy more broadly. Although the nutrition research projects failed to reach people in this way, other settlement projects – such as the drafting of the Hire Purchase Act, discussed in Chapter 5 – had more success in this regard.

The Oxford House Country Schools

If neither Toynbee Hall nor Oxford House had concerned themselves with the health and welfare of women and children to any great extent

before 1939, the Second World War changed that relationship dramatically. The impact of evacuation and the Blitz forced both settlements
to enter into new forms of work – the provision of homes for respite
and evacuation.

The government began planning for evacuation as war with
Germany became increasingly likely. On 1 September 1939 the order
to Evacuate Forthwith was given, and over the next three days 1.5
million people were moved as part of the government's evacuation
scheme, according to figures given by Richard Titmuss in his account
of evacuation and social services in the Second World War, *Problems
of Social Policy* (1950). This figure included children and their mothers,
the disabled, those in Public Assistance institutions, children in borstals
and remand homes, as well as civil servants. Those who were in hospital but could complete their treatment at home were released, as were
some 5,600 prisoners. There was also extensive private movement of
universities, schools, nursing homes and charities, as well as of individuals. According to Titmuss, the government never knew the precise extent of private evacuation, but the Ministry of Health in 1944
estimated that 2 million people had made their own arrangements
in this early part of the war.[111] It was a massive displacement of the
civilian population: families dispatching children often did not have
time or sufficient funds to arrange new clothes and shoes,[112] whilst
receiving areas had not given thought to the most efficient or pleasant
way of distributing children, their parents and teachers to suitable digs.[113]

Although evacuation is included in many general accounts of the
war, the historiography of evacuation is surprisingly limited, given
the popularity of the topic. Evacuation has been seen as one of the
key agents of social change – as well as conflict – through bringing
people of different backgrounds together. Angus Calder noted how
some hosts or potential host families looked upon their charges as
'vermin',[114] whilst others reported 'horror' stories of children being told
by their parents to defecate in a corner of the room rather than on the
carpet.[115] These were clearly tensions that had the power to disrupt
the orderly conduct of the war on the home front, as well as to make
life for the individuals concerned unpleasant on all sides. Yet academic research specifically on the evacuation remains scarce, although
there has been some recent research in the field of psychology which
has looked at the phenomenon as a means of exploring attachment
styles in adults. In 2006 John Rusby used research with 900 wartime
evacuees from Kent as a basis for a study investigating the impact of
childhood evacuation in later life. He concluded that whilst evacuation
itself did not cause problems for all evacuees, some former evacuees

still repeated the experience of being separated from their parents as teenagers in their attachment to others in later life.[116] From the historical perspective, Travis Crosby has explored the social history of the evacuation, looking at the perceptions of the relationship between host and evacuee, the incidence of tensions over racial and class difference, and the disputes between local and national government on the ways in which evacuation should be administered.[117] Robyn Glessner analysed the experiences of the *Kindertransport*, those Jewish or non-Aryan children evacuated from Nazi Europe, exploring the ways in which these children were received by their host families and the tensions inside the relationship.[118] However, as two of the most recent researchers of evacuation – Glessner and Rusby – have found, since the 1980s the majority of historical work concentrating upon the evacuation has taken the form of oral history and popular memoirs.[119] Although some of these stories may not have the polish of academic history, they are still of great use. Micro-histories – such as Ted Enever's account of how he and his parents left Canning Town for a private evacuation in Bedfordshire following a severe raid on London on 7 September 1940[120] – allow us to understand the complexity of the evacuee experience. It was not confined to children from the slums, although this is an abiding image of the 'evacuee'.[121] There is clearly a psychological or therapeutic point to these oral history projects, as well as to the work of the Evacuees' Reunion Association, whose aims are to link up former evacuees, to provide them with support and counselling as well as to educate the public about the evacuation.[122] Remembering the experiences of evacuation can be a way in which former evacuees can relate the experience to their children and grandchildren, and engage them with their 'family history' of the Second World War. Certainly those who were evacuated were often too small or too far away to be a part of the 'Myth of the Blitz', as explored and exploded by Angus Calder,[123] which means that they are part neither of the narrative of 'banding together' nor of its converse. The narrative has undercurrents of parental abandonment and the mixed fortunes of the children in securing a friendly family. The unfriendly family forms part of this discourse as a force to be reckoned with and then won over, as in Nina Bawden's *Carrie's War*. Some former evacuees talk happily of life in the countryside, whilst others complain of harsh hosts and homesickness. But what of those children who were too 'difficult' for this arrangement?

Evacuation attracted the attention of researchers from all disciplines, and several studies of children's experience of wartime evacuation were undertaken during the war. One of the larger studies was the Cambridge Evacuation Survey, which compared experience of middle-class children from Tottenham with that of working-class children from Islington.[124] The children in the Cambridge survey were far from the poorest, and most were happy with their host families, yet problems still emerged. Tensions were a major theme of the Cambridge surveyors. They found that older housewives had trouble coping with boisterous youngsters,[125] whilst growing boys often ate more than their temporary parents were allocated. The researchers noted that:

> In two of these [cases with 'problem children'] the foster mothers were of the complaining type who could not help finding fault, though in both cases they had pleasant, intelligent girls billeted with them; in the other case the children were overcrowded and uncomfortable and had evidently been taken in with the idea of making all that was possible out of them financially.[126]

The Fabian Society likewise commissioned a general report on what would be the first wave of evacuation in 1939–40.[127] Other studies during the war itself included the government's Shakespeare Committee report on conditions in reception areas,[128] and the Ministry of Health undertook a survey of hostels for 'difficult' children.[129] Post-war treatment of the subject included a report on London children in Oxford by Barnett House, which praised the efforts of foster mothers and pointed out the connections between unsuccessful billets and desperately unhappy children. They also noted that many of the London children had enjoyed their time in Oxford, wandering around both country and colleges.[130] Richard Titmuss wrote on evacuation in *Problems of Social Policy*.[131] The topic inspired a number of PhD theses and journal articles.[132] The research projects demonstrate that there was keen interest among academics, civil servants, politicians and those involved in organising the evacuation on the ground in dealing with so-called difficult children, many of whose problems stemmed from their pre-war lives. Interest in exploring why children failed to respond to evacuation – as well as its potentially positive impacts upon those who came from more chaotic homes – indirectly led to the Oxford House Country Schools project.

Although researchers were concerned with the impact of evacuation on all children, they were especially interested in the question of 'difficult' children. It was a genuine problem for those in the reception areas, who had to arbitrate between irate foster parents, scared and homesick children and their parents in the attempt to find a solution. Being 'difficult' encompassed a wide range of phenomena, from the varying views of parents and host families on what constituted 'good' behaviour to anxious children who wet or soiled their bed and clothing to those children who displayed significant psychological disturbances. There was a public outcry over the issue of 'bad' children, some of it greatly exaggerated, but nonetheless the Ministry of Health was compelled to find an alternative means of looking after children who could not or would not cope with normal billeting and hurriedly instigated a system of hostels.[133] By mid-1941, 10,000 children were living in 660 rapidly assembled hostels.[134] These children were a small proportion of the total evacuated, but they were the greatest source of anxiety. Those whose problems extended beyond disagreement about standards of behaviour or cleanliness attracted psychiatrists' attention. The pre-eminent post-war child psychologists D. W. Winnicott and John Bowlby[135] both worked with 'difficult' children in hostels and used the experience as a means of developing theories about childhood attachment and the importance of primary carers.[136] Winnicott in particular applied his findings from wartime hostel work to recommendations for the peacetime management of hostels for such children and their use in preventing juvenile delinquency.[137] During the war and into the later 1940s the view was that evacuation had the potential to provide the solution to peacetime problems of juvenile delinquency and familial unhappiness. Hostels provided a safe environment for children to develop secure attachments with adults, to access psychiatrists and to enjoy a stable, regulated schedule.

Before 1939 Oxford House had not concerned itself with the health and welfare of women and children to any great extent, but this changed on the outbreak of war. Settlements were involved in evacuation, acting either as a staging post for government operations or as one of the many 'private' providers of evacuation. They were in a good position to do this – the settlements were a central focus for all kinds of activities in neighbourhoods, including the provision of information and advice through Citizens' Advice Bureaux and the other welfare organisations that they hosted. The impact of evacuation and the Blitz forced Oxford House and other settlements to enter into new forms of work – the provision of homes for respite and evacuation. Toynbee Hall had the loan of a house at Midhurst, in Sussex, for the duration of the war which was used to provide east Londoners with a break from the stresses of bombing raids and waiting to hear about relatives,[138] whilst Oxford House developed the Country Schools programme. They were not the only ones to experiment with residential care for children: Kingsley Hall ran a similar wartime project, Kingsley Hall School, in Sarratt, Hertfordshire, as a boarding school for evacuated young east Londoners, supported by the Duke of Bedford and the Save the Children fund.[139] The Oxford House Country Schools were funded through a combination of parental contributions on a sliding scale of 5s to 9s per week, although financial support was also received from the London County Council and the Board of Education. The British War Relief Society of the United States donated a total of £17,000, along with gifts in kind, with further support from the Newby Trust and the Worshipful Company of Goldsmiths.[140]

The author of *Citizens in Readiness*, an account of Oxford House's wartime experiment with Country Schools, openly admitted that, prior to 1939, the male residents of that settlement showed little interest in training in social work. In the author's view, the call-up for national service removed such men from the settlement, and drew full-time social workers in their place. These full-time social workers were untrained and inexperienced; many were male conscientious objectors looking for an alternative way to spend the war.[141] But it was not merely a case of expelling one sort of volunteer and bringing in another – there were other influences at work. Prior to the war Oxford House had been used by graduates and others preparing for the Anglican priesthood, and their interests had largely extended to providing clubs for men and boys. However, shortly before the outbreak of war, Guy Clutton-Brock took up the wardenship of the settlement. Clutton-Brock was quite a departure for the settlement – although a religious man, he had a totally different approach to social work. As the first Principal Probation Officer to be appointed in the Inner London area he was in the vanguard of juvenile court reform. As a probation officer he had been particularly concerned with the welfare of young people in borstals and other institutions. He had been an advocate of using hostels as a means of restoring errant young people back to 'good ways':

> There is a need for life in a community with other boys or men, where some social lessons may be learned, and where a more concentrated attention is possible on his peculiar weakness, or where some of the externals of discipline may be brought to bear to induce that self-discipline which has failed to develop; and yet he may be fit to go daily to work and so avoid the dangers of a completely institutional life. In such a case a hostel is a suitable compromise.[142]

So, to Clutton-Brock's mind, communal living was a way of reaching out to young people and bringing them back within 'normal' society. Such hostels were a mainstay of juvenile court provision, providing accommodation for the remanded and those subject to residential orders;

some, like the John Benn Hostel attached to Toynbee Hall, were also open to any young people who wished to live there. The combination of a fresh batch of residents and the professional experience of Clutton-Brock paved the way for their experiments with the Country Schools.

The settlement had a variety of emergent needs to deal with as hostilities began in earnest in 1940. Oxford House opened a nursery to help women in war work, and it provided basic accommodation for those who had been bombed out of their houses.[143] It was later registered as an Emergency Rest and Feeding Centre, and functioned as a point for evacuation from the East End.[144] The settlement also used its network of contacts to provide private billeting in the countryside for its friends and neighbours as far as this was possible. One of those tasked with finding billets stumbled across an empty house in mid-Wales, Parc Llwydiarth, and a new venture began in the autumn of 1940.[145]

Parc Llwydiarth was initially used as a hostel which took people of all ages, from the elderly to small children, largely to give them respite and relief from the bombing in London.[146] In early 1941 a further house, Plas Dolanog, was taken over to be used by children aged three to thirteen. However, problems arose over sending the London children to the local school. Not only did their arrival swell the numbers beyond its normal capacity, but they did not speak Welsh, the school's primary language. Neither the Welsh nor the London children were being effectively educated, so the settlement had to act. The solution was to move the adults out of Parc Llwydiarth and open it as a boarding school.[147] The experiment continued until 1945, when it foundered from lack of funding in peacetime.[148]

The project had two functions: it provided respite for children from bombed areas; and it was also a means by which children from 'bad' homes could be given a second chance to escape their home lives through their education. During the Blitz of 1940–41, and the V-2 bombing raids at the end of the war, the Country Schools took as many children as possible to safety.[149] In quieter times 'children whose home environment, for one reason or another, made it desirable to send them elsewhere' were admitted to the Country Schools. These included children who the local probation officer had begged to be admitted, along with children who had been abandoned by their mothers, and those from families with a history of domestic violence against the mother.[150] Aside from the probationers, these children had been processed not through the courts but rather through informal and formal networks of social workers, club leaders, neighbours and case work assessments.

Getting to Monmouthshire was no simple matter. Pressure on space meant it could be months before children could be admitted into the Country Schools. Parents had to agree not to remove their children from them without good reason, as well as to release the schools to provide their children with medical care if necessary. These conditions met, families had to obtain a medical examination certificate to ensure that the children had no infectious diseases, along with billeting certificates and travel warrants from the London County Council, as well as gathering together identity cards, ration books and the like.[151] Such conditions were necessary to ensure that the schools could provide for the children, as well as to minimise the potential disruption of parents collecting them only to return them days, weeks later. Yet they were not to be entered into lightly. Many children were naturally reluctant to leave their parents:[152] although they could come home for occasional, brief holidays, and likewise parents could arrange visits to the schools,[153] contact was normally limited to weekly letters.[154]

It was reported that most children settled down well into life in the countryside. Boys referred to the schools by probation officers were often found to 'calm down' quite rapidly, with the result that their improved behaviour led to early release from their probation terms.[155] Some found it harder. One small girl who had been left alone during air raids by her mother was terrified of being put to bed on her own; she gradually learned to trust adults and to sleep through the night by nodding off in the arms of the Matron. Other results were less dramatic, but nevertheless important, as those who had suffered from poor diet were able to build themselves up in the countryside on rations and fresh air.[156] There were other benefits, too: some children were able to make pen friends in the United States.[157] One boy was able to go to Bryanston, an experimental school in Dorset, through a scholarship provided by the Goldsmiths' Company, whilst another two boys were accepted by Dulwich Preparatory School.[158]

When the Oxford House Country Schools deliberately accommodated children with 'problems' they were directly engaging with this idea that an exigency of war could be used to remedy the perennial problem of children and young people misbehaving. For Winnicott the experience of being in a residential care setting was a therapeutic process in itself,[159] as it could provide the stability and warmth lacking in many of the children's lives.[160] Although there is no evidence to suggest that the Country Schools were informed by Winnicott's practice, this was nevertheless a vital element of their approach. Whilst Titmuss interpreted the development of hostels for difficult children as part of the evolution of more specialised and individualised services for needy children – and adults – from 1939,[161] this notion of the state acting through the court system, residential hostels and voluntary apparatus has a longer heritage. Hostels were already being used as a form of rehabilitation, as we saw earlier. But there was also very much a sense that the juvenile courts and their associates – including psychologists and psychiatrists, among others – helped in restoring the lacks of the family. For example, Anne Logan has shown how the ready inclusion of female magistrates in the juvenile courts in the inter-war period was connected with the idea of the court as a replacement 'family' which would offset the biological family's problems.[162]

What can be concluded from this study of the Oxford House Country Schools? On the one hand, they were one among many examples of the settlement movement experimenting with ways of trying to effect social change. The sources for this are frustratingly limited – we have no records of the children sent to the schools, so it is impossible, did the ethics allow it, to follow up their experiences some sixty years later. We are limited to the papers generated by those working at or with the Country Schools, and their perspectives on their work with the children. It is very much a narrative of social experimentation and control. What we do know from it is that evacuation threw into relief many of the problems that families experienced, as those problems 'moved out' of the family home and into the homes and lives of others. It also exposed many children and their parents to different expectations and ideas about parenting, for better and for worse. Whilst we understand more about the experiences of individuals in 'private' billets – so those living with families – there is still much more that we need to know about the children who lived in institutions, not least as psychologists and penal reformers used their work with such individuals to formulate attachment theory. This theory, developed by John Bowlby and D. W. Winnicott following their experience with evacuee children, concerns the ways in which infants form bonds of attachment with their primary carers, and which then shape the ways in which they interact with others as children and eventually as adults.[163] It still forms an essential part of current psychological thinking. This is a very different version of evacuation. At times, it is a view of evacuation which exposes some of the desperately unhappy families and children. But it also has some hope within it. Although we are still far from solving the problems faced by children and young people, those involved in working with children in hostels and Country Schools in the war believed that they were making progress towards solutions. In this case, two post-war projects had resonance with the experience of working with evacuated children: the Children's Country Holiday Fund and caring for the elderly.

The Children's Country Holiday Fund

As seen earlier, the Children's Country Holiday Fund (CCHF) began as a means of offering Victorian children a break from the urban environment, but its work continued throughout the twentieth century and beyond. Records of its activities at the settlements are limited, yet the documents suggest some strong consistencies over time. Although CCHF holidays lasted for an upper limit of two weeks, they had much in common with the experience of wartime evacuation, especially in terms of the tension that could exist between host and guest as well as the culture shock experienced by children in the countryside for the first time. This was as true of children in 1960s and 1980s as it had been during the war, as will be demonstrated in the following section.

Raising funds and resources remained a difficult task for the CCHF: demand often outstripped supply. Although the CCHF had a small core of paid staff at headquarters in 1981, it had to engage at least 2,000 helpers with the annual camps. These volunteers included host families, organising committees in London, camp leaders and supervisors, as well as volunteers who liaised with families and social services throughout each preceding winter. The CCHF derived its income from individuals' donations, from the contributions made by parents and carers, and fund-raising drives. In its publicity material the CCHF engaged with a complex discourse which on the one hand aimed to direct sympathy to the families whilst, on the other, being dismissive, if not condemnatory, of the parents' skills in managing their families. A 1981 flyer for the CCHF evoked an image of families suffering 'bad housing and over-crowding; parental neglect and desertion; parents mentally and physically ill; unsupported mothers or fathers coping alone; lack of space and play facilities – the list is endless'. Lest sympathy flow too readily for these families, the writer continued, 'Inadequate parents are usually incapable of budgeting properly, and will often buy unnecessary items, while failing completely to provide the family with the basic necessities of life . . . Many parents strive to do their best for the children despite great strain and difficulties; others seem almost to have given up trying and their children sadly lack affection and a sense of security.'[164] The CCHF presented itself as a body whose work could potentially correct these wayward parents, through volunteers' regular visits to families in the run-up to the annual holiday, co-operation between the CCHF and state welfare agencies, and, of course, the break itself with its exposure to 'good' families.[165]

The complexity of this relationship deepens when trying to ascertain something of the ways in which children responded to CCHF holidays. A further leaflet from 1981, 'Will there be a holiday for him this year?', reproduced a series of comments from children about their experiences in the countryside:

> Sir, I've just seen a sheep's head and it had a body joined on!
>
> There was no shops where we was staying, not even a little one. My mum wouldn't like that . . . They don't 'ave no buses, neither. Cor, what a place! The roads are so thin and even the flats are low. They 'aven't got a telly.
>
> I 'ad a bed all of me own. It's the first time I ever slept on me own. It was a bit scary at first, but then it was all right.
>
> I can ride a proper bike now. I was riding it round this big playing field all day. Sometimes Auntie let us take a picnic so we didn't have to go home for our dinners. It was great.
>
> Me and this boy I was staying with slept in the garden in a tent for five nights. One night it had rained and we didn't have to go into the house. We had all our food in the tent. I never been in a tent before.[166]

The comments were reproduced with misspellings and grammatical errors to suggest the vernacular speech of east London, and to convey the notion of the stereotypical 'Cockney' child bemused by the country-side and by the generosity of rural families. There is a sense of naivety and innocence suggested by the CCHF's selections; children whose experiences of life were likely to be seen as far from innocent by the CCHF's intended audience were thus restored as innocents abroad in the 'purer' rural environment. Further selections from people who had experienced the CCHF in the inter-war period were also included:

> Some sixty years ago my brother and I had a holiday on a farm near Edenbridge, and altho' it is so long ago I can still remember it – even the name and address where we stayed. I have pleasure in enclosing a cheque which I hope will help the good work you are doing for those in need. Sorry I cannot send more but when you are on a pension you don't have too much to spare.
>
> As a poor London boy (I lived in Bromley by Bow) I went to Cambridgeshire – I think – three times; my mother was widowed and had to slog for a living for us, my sister and I. They were the only country holidays I ever had as a schoolboy, and I've not forgotten them, and never will.
>
> I am in my eightieth year. Just seventy years ago, my young sister and I went for a couple of these holidays, never to be forgotten. The first one was to Sussex and our family were great. For the first time I saw cowslips growing wild. For the second holiday we went to Berkshire and again it was lovely. This time I was petrified by seeing frogs leaping around. We said grace at mealtimes and knelt to say our prayers at night – oh, it was wonderful![167]

The CCHF had no reason, in a piece of fund-raising literature, to delve into the experiences of children who had not enjoyed their holidays or to analyse the messages they were conveying to their audience. Some children did undoubtedly enjoy their stay in the country; for others the stay could be difficult or unpleasant. For others again it was somewhere in the middle. Parents may have welcomed the opportunity for their children to have a break; others may have resented the interference of CCHF volunteers or felt under pressure from their children to provide them with some sort of summer holiday. Although some of our understanding of the operation of the CCHF can be only speculative, it is necessary to deconstruct the complexity of the relationships that operated around and within the annual summer holiday. Rather than looking at the central operations of the CCHF,[168] this section will explore these issues through a case study of the Lady Margaret Hall Settlement branch of the CCHF from the late 1950s to the later 1960s.

In 1956, 83 children were sent away by the organising committee of the North Lambeth/Lady Margaret Hall Settlement CCHF. On the whole, the organiser remarked, the children had been well-clothed, although time had been spent on necessary mending; most were well-behaved, apart from one girl who was deemed unmanageable whilst another ruined a bed. Yet the organiser was more concerned about the ways in which parents behaved beforehand, causing difficulties for the voluntary organisers through cancelling or otherwise acting in ways that disrupted the undertaking. The organiser wrote, 'Had I to make this report in August, it would not be nearly as polite, for one feels then, is it worth it?'[169] This theme re-emerged in the 1960s, when Lady Margaret Hall Settlement was seriously considerng whether or not it should continue with the CCHF programme. The organiser felt that the programme did vital work in giving children a holiday and offering parents, especially single parents, a break from the rigours of child care. Yet there were problems with the children's behaviour, a few among the thirty to forty children sent away annually having to be returned home. Children could also find the exposure to new environments stressful, whilst other programmes, such as that of the Claimants' Union, allowed families to go away together.[170] The two reports, some ten years apart, highlight the ongoing tensions that arose between the parents and the voluntary organisers. Both parties saw the value of the holidays; but often neither appreciated the input of the other. It appears that the volunteer organisers felt put upon; the families often failed to match up to the organisers' expectations of them. The experience of the CCHF could be tense on all sides.

The files for the summer holidays of 1968 reveal much about the attitudes of the organisers and host families, as well as something of the family backgrounds of the children.[171] The average age of children sent away in that year was nine years, with the youngest child aged seven and the oldest twelve. In most cases, children were sent away in small groups of siblings, usually two or three of similar age. Just over half the children sent away were girls (54 per cent), whilst 26 per cent of all the children were black or came from a mixed background. The reasons why children were granted a holiday ranged from providing relief to single parents, which was the case for fifteen families, involving seventeen children, or families wherein at least one parent suffered from long-term or acute illness (seven families, accounting for thirteen children). In seven families, parents who were unemployed were able to send their children – a total of twelve – away on a summer holiday. A break from overcrowding was offered to six families (thirteen children in total), whilst two children from different families were taken away to give them an emotionally healthier environment for a short while. In some cases, families endured compound problems, such as the two single-parent families in which the parent suffered ill health, or the family in which long-term unemployment was accompanied by parental illness.

Each family was assigned a file which contained the notes of the CCHF organisers along with the reports of the host families. Through their reports the organisers painted the often sad lives of the children and their parents. Girls A and B were being brought up by their mother, a single parent struggling to make a living as well as cope with operations to rid her of cancer; the father of boy I had died, and he did not receive loving attention from his grieving mother. The mother of boys M and N had escaped from their abusive father, whilst boys P and Q were coping with the difficult aftermath of a father's nervous breakdown. Yet families who did not have such acute strains could still find it difficult to provide a treat for their children. Girl C's mother worked hard but was unable to get leave from work to take her daughter away, whilst the child of another single parent, boy A, had no financial or other support from his absent father. Girl N's mother had been abandoned by her father, and the pair lived in one very small room. The organiser noted, 'She has a very likeable character, easy to manage, and badly needs a holiday away from squalid surroundings.' Both acute and chronic situations needed to be addressed.

Growing up in a large family was another factor that impacted upon parents' ability to send their children on holiday. Girls D and E came from a family of nine, whilst for boys D and E and their sister, girl F, who came from a family of thirteen, getting away was impossible, as their father was unemployed and their mother was busy dealing with much younger children. Boys B and C came from a large family and their father was out of work. Although the organiser reported earlier problems – notably bedwetting and a period in a half-way home – which had since improved, it was noted that the 'boys are rough and ready but with unexpectedly good manners – and ready smiles. The family would prefer the boys to go together. They once went to Sussex and think it the best county!' These files provide us with a glimpse of the home lives of the children, if from the vantage point of the organiser. Apart from the recording of comments about how much the boys liked Sussex, we can know little of the children's hopes or fears or even of the processes of 'performing' for this important home visitor, of dressing up to impress or dressing down to inspire pity. Yet we have a sense of the visitor in the home, talking to the parents and the children, inspecting their environment and assiduously making notes on each case, from the specific needs of each family to comments on their ethnicity.

Although the visitors recorded the ethnicity of families who had black, mixed or non-British backgrounds, it does not appear to have been the case that such families were deemed to be necessarily more 'problematic' than white families by definition. The importance of this factor becomes clearer when examining the reports of the host families who received the children. Unlike the increasingly ethnically diverse communities of inner London, the host families were located in smaller, homogeneous rural environments. Although the host families had volunteered to take children in this instance, that did not mean that the relationship between London child and rural family was a smooth one. Such tensions have been explored in the case of evacuation in the early days of the Second World War, with middle- and upper-class families being repulsed by the manners of their 'alien' guests,[172] as well as with the host families of *Kindertransport* refugees from Germany,[173] and similar discourses appear to have operated in the context of the CCHF, despite the evident 'Britishness' of all the children. Girl C's host family were worried about what their neighbours would say about the presence of a little black girl in their village. The fears of the family subsided as girl C 'settled down perfectly naturally and was totally accepted by all, especially a little girl of $1^1/_2$ years, who followed her everywhere for the first few days'. Girl C

> was pleased by simple things like helping to make a cake, collecting snails, compiling a scrapbook of root cards [*sic*] and wild flowers and just playing in the garden. We look upon the two weeks as very happy

and rewarding and would have no hesitation in asking [Girl C] to stay with us next year.

There is in this account an undertone of surprise that a small black girl might be pleased by the same activities that small girls of any background might enjoy, but nevertheless the report was intended to be warm.

Boy W, on the other hand, did not have a particularly pleasant stay. His host's report began with the comment that 'considering the environment the boy came from his behaviour was quite good', suggesting that the hosts were expecting trouble from a small boy from a one-parent family, and, judging from the rest of their report, they found it. Boy W was repeatedly admonished for taking up and playing with toys that he found lying around, and the clothes his mother had packed were criticised by the hosts for being too small and full of holes. His hosts mended his clothes and provided him with new ones, but commented that:

> parents should at least be asked to send the child with sufficient items of clothing and those that are packed should at least be mended and have buttons on. Lack of money should not mean that the child need wear shirts and underpants which only need a needle and cotton. He was sent home in good order though.

Although Boy W's views on such reprimands and what must have been a sustained campaign to mend his clothes (and criticise his mother's parenting abilities) were not recorded, his response to his host family at the end of the stay suggests that his time had been unhappy:

> What disappointed me was that he did not say 'thank you' on leaving us at the station, only goodbye. I think, in fact he did say, he had enjoyed his stay perhaps he just forgot.

Whilst it is possible that boy W had indeed forgotten his manners, it appears more likely that he was the victim of his host's frustration. The host concluded her report with an angry comment about how the family had offered a place for a little girl:

> Why then did you send me a ten year old boy? Surely he could have stayed somewhere with other boys. It would have been a lot easier for me to handle a younger boy or girls of any age. As I have been used to girls and have all girls [sic] things in the house.

A degree of racism may be implicit in the host's expression of the view that the boy's mother was incapable of clothing him and that his behaviour was acceptable given the environment he had grown up in – it is not clear quite what the hostess implied through her statement.

Certainly the host, through over-justifying his or her actions, conveyed her thorough irritation at being given a young (black) boy to look after.

In many cases the host families had nothing to report other than the good behaviour of the children, which may mean simply that the children were well behaved in the eyes of the hosts, or that the hosts did not care to elaborate further on the forms. Others were less circumspect, as we have seen. Participating in CCHF holidays had the potential to expose children and their host families to happy memories and experiences; but it could also be unpleasant or even traumatic. That the majority of hosts wrote to praise the good conduct of the children in this case may suggest that, for the majority, such holidays were uneventful and pleasant. Although the intentions of all parties were ostensibly good, the process of going on holiday with the CCHF was by no means a simple one: loaded with the expectations and biases of the organiser and visitors, the experience of being visited at home for the assessment, the hopes and fears of the young children, and the welcome they received with their host families. By the 1960s the CCHF was no longer trying to rescue children from the urban environment *per se*, but from these surviving records we can see that they were attempting to reach out to particular groups of children and families in need – especially those single parents who had few other resources or forms of support, larger families and those with long-term illness or unemployment. Whether or not these children experienced happy home lives, all belonged to some of the neediest groups in post-war Britain, the children identified by *The Poor and the Poorest*[174] and the Child Poverty Action Group as being failed by the welfare state.[175] The CCHF did not have the means to lift the families out of poverty, but, despite the anxieties of the organisers, their hard work meant in many cases that such families were able to have a little respite for a short while.

Older people

From the 1950s onwards the settlements turned their attention to the question of family. On the one hand, this was a continuation of many pre-war projects, such as the provision of nurseries and clubs for young parents. Young parents were a particular area of concern as they moved into newly built council housing around settlements, such as in Poplar, near Fern Street Settlement,[176] or where families were moving through older housing estates, as near St Hilda's East in Shoreditch.[177] At the same time that many settlements were developing their provision for young parents they also turned their attention to the question of caring for the elderly.

Older people had always been at high risk of falling below the 'poverty line' once they were unable to work or if they did not have younger family members to support them.[178] The introduction of old age pensions in 1908 had gone some way to alleviating the problems of older people, yet it was evident in the Second World War that there were other issues that reduced older people's quality of life. During the war, the Friends' Relief Service was involved in removing older people from bombed areas, and developed a network of hostels to accommodate them.[179] The Friends did not see material impoverishment as the main problem facing older people, but rather loneliness. Whilst they did not recommend that older people be indiscriminately placed into residential care, the Friends advocated 'smaller, homelier places' to be provided for those who could no longer look after themselves.[180] Along with practical recommendations about the physical environment of the homes, the Friends were keen to advise on the importance of keeping the older people interested in the outside world. They suggested lending arrangements with local libraries, organising sales and bazaars, holding craft sessions and bringing volunteers in to help with indoor games and entertainments.[181]

The Royal Commission on Population of 1949 drew attention to the fact that Britain was experiencing a decline in the birth rate matched by an ageing population, and the consequences this would have for all aspects of public life.[182] Although the 1946 National Health Act and the 1948 National Assistance Act enabled local authorities to provide domiciliary services in addition to residential care, debate continued over how the care of the elderly should be divided between the state through local authorities, voluntary organisations and the family.[183] However, by the end of the 1960s the voluntary sector was heavily involved in the delivery of 'meals on wheels' (the preparation and administration often being the responsibility of the local authority), laundry services, lunch and recreation clubs, visiting schemes and counselling.[184] It was in this climate that the settlements greatly increased and expanded their provision for the elderly from the 1940s onwards, with particular growth from the later 1950s. For example, although Toynbee Hall already had its Veterans' Club for the elderly in operation from the late 1940s, the settlement took the decision to expand its services for older people in 1956 largely to provide friendship and company to the lonely. Toynbee Hall provided cheap meals over four days of the week, along with various types of entertainment, an annual holiday and other outings, access to chiropractice treatment and a warm day room. In 1957 it was also in the process of expanding its visiting programme in the local area. Volunteers and the central organiser were occupied in befriending and assisting those who were unable or unwilling to visit the day centre. The author of a 1957 report on the work with older people commented that:

the importance of visitation can be appreciated only when it is realised in what conditions of squalor and degradation some old people are living. In general these conditions arise from a combination of loneliness and declining faculties accentuated too often by poverty. The first condition to attack is loneliness.[185]

Settlements generally adopted the same model of working with older people. Fern Street established a luncheon club for older people in 1962, which was supplemented by crafts in the afternoon.[186] WUS offered Monday afternoon speakers and a Wednesday afternoon club, along with home visiting, meals and various outings,[187] likewise Mary Ward Settlement offered a handicraft centre for the elderly.[188] The Women's Fellowship at St Hilda's East ran a programme of lectures and musical performances for the elderly, as well as trips away from London.[189] From 1955 the settlement also organised the Daffodil Club, whose activities included handicrafts and singing. The club was able to muster a choir which in 1956–57 successfully competed in the Bethnal Green Festival of Arts, and even took part in Wilfred Pickles's *Have a Go* radio programme.[190] By 1962 St Hilda's had appointed a trained social worker, a Mrs Tuckman, to work closely with the older people. Tuckman's role was to keep in touch with them, especially if they were unable to get to the club, and to work alongside the Bethnal Green Old People's Welfare Committee to co-ordinate provision. Again, Tuckman was responsible for co-ordinating home visiting as a means of tackling loneliness and thereby hidden, but solvable, problems: 'Poverty, housing problems and emotional disturbances have in some cases been found and at least one couple has been literally put on its feet.'[191]

The settlements had a relatively consistent and extensive programme for the elderly which aimed to prevent loneliness as well as to circumvent problems caused by older people not knowing what they were entitled to or being too proud to claim it. They were typical of many other voluntary organisations – such as the Women's Voluntary Service – in providing the types of services and support which the state, through the local authority, was unable or unwilling to provide.

Therapeutic communities and support groups

The 1960s and 1970s saw increased interest in therapeutic communities of all kinds – the 'therapeutic community' as understood by psychologists and psychiatrists as treatment without medication and 'therapeutic community' as could be understood as signifying a support group. Some of these 'communities' involved ex-offenders, such as the bail hostel project attempted by NACRO and Lady Margaret Hall Settlement, the Blackfriars mentoring scheme, or the HM Prison, Grendon, outpost at Toynbee Hall, as discussed in Chapter 5.

One of the most controversial settlement health projects was launched in 1965 at Kingsley Hall Settlement: R. D. Laing's Philadelphia Association. The Philadelphia Association was founded in early 1965 by the psychologists David Cooper and Aaron Esterson and the psychiatrist R. D. Laing to provide a therapeutic community for people with mental health issues, especially those diagnosed with schizophrenia.[192] Laing was among the English pioneers of anti-psychiatry, a controversial school of thought which saw mainstream psychiatry as oppressive to the individual patient.[193]

Muriel Lester and the trustees of Kingsley Hall allowed the Philadelphia Association to establish a pioneering therapeutic community there. The space at the settlement was crucial to the development of this therapeutic approach: 'Kingsley Hall has been a melting-pot, a crucible in which many, if not all, of our initial assumptions about normal–abnormal, conformist–deviant, sane–crazy experience and behaviour have been dissolved.'[194] Although an earlier household community had been set up the previous year, the Kingsley Hall community was much larger, accommodating fourteen people at any one time. Between 1 June 1965 and 31 August 1969 113 people were accommodated at the Philadelphia Association project.[195]

The Philadelphia Association saw Kingsley Hall as a success. Only a very small number of people – eleven, or 9.7 per cent – went on to or were later hospitalised for their condition, and there were no suicides reported by 1969.[196] It was seen by some as an empowering experience for people whose lives might otherwise have been dictated by the routine of hospitals and the decisions of doctors;[197] but it was not without its detractors on both sides of the political spectrum as well as from feminists such as Elaine Showalter.[198] The experience of living at Kingsley Hall and her therapeutic journey was described by a former patient, Mary Barnes, in her memoirs,[199] later adapted into a play by David Edgar.[200] The experiment was popularly associated, in the words of one journalist, with 'adults reverting to babyhood' whilst in the Association's care.[201]

The Special Families Centre at Toynbee Hall was founded in 1974 in order to provide support for the families of people with a range of physical and mental disabilities, assistance that was not readily available elsewhere.[202] The centre evolved alongside an early Toy Library, started to help families on lower incomes have access to a range of educational toys, as well as other community projects in the area, such as the Spitalfields Project.[203] The Families Centre was originally funded by the King's Fund, but by the 1978–79 financial year had attracted joint funding from the London borough of Tower Hamlets and the local health authority. In practice, from 1978 funds came from the health authority rather than the borough council, and the amount set aside – £60,000 for two years in 1983 – did not meet the actual needs of the centre.[204] The centre offered a mixture of social and allied medical services – a wide range of clubs and support groups for service users of all ages as well as for their parents, social activities and the use of a training flat in nearby Evershed House to help users develop skills for independent living. The centre usually worked with families for a number of years as parents and children nego-tiated the challenges of growing up.[205] However, new forms of exclusion emerged in the course of the later 1970s and early 1980s, namely the need to provide support for Bengali families and mothers in particular.[206] Mothers or the main care providers of disabled children could find themselves doubly isolated if English was not their first language, and thus a research and information centre attached to the families centre had begun to provide English classes for those mothers. The organiser commented that although this duplicated other services in the area, 'the majority of families are more "comfortable" attending a service placed in the voluntary field than those of the statutory services'.[207] The Special Families Centre was under threat by the early 1980s, as its joint funding from the council and the health authority came to an end in 1984.[208] In that year it merged with the Stepney Children's Fund in order to form the Children's Department of Toynbee Hall.[209] By 1987, when the centre sought support from the European Poverty Programme, it had reconfigured itself as a service working with needy women and children from Bangladeshi backgrounds.[210] As a researcher pointed out in 1983, when the centre was founded in 1974 provision for families with disabled children in Tower Hamlets was limited, but by the 1980s stat-utory and voluntary provision had greatly increased.[211] The Special Families Centre no longer offered something original or distinctive to the community unless it was reconfigured. It was another example of a voluntary activity that came to an end to avoid unnecessarily duplication, and which evolved in response to new needs and fund-ing streams.

Conclusion

By the 1970s the remit of the university settlements with regard to health had changed dramatically. Where they had been major providers of health care, especially for women and young children, this was abandoned or transferred to the local authority or the National Health Service from 1945 onwards. Although 1948 can be seen as a watershed year, health care did not cease to be important at the settlements – rather it became entwined with the concept of 'well-being'. Well-being was not something necessarily provided by the NHS or the other social services, yet it drew on the pre-NHS experience of the settlements. Mothers' meetings were of vital importance to first-time mothers as well as to the more experienced, as a means of developing friendships, having something to do and to provide informal support. Although these tended to accompany activities such as infant welfare clinics, this spirit infused such post-war activities as centres for families with disabled children and the CCHF in its later incarnations. It was also about providing day centres for the elderly to have company and to retain an active role in society. Yet we should not see 1948 as a cut-off point: voluntary health services and interest groups continued to operate well into the 1950s and beyond, negotiating their remit as the National Health Service and local authority provision evolved, as well as in response to new streams of funding.

Notes

1 F. Engels, *The Condition of the Working Class in England*, trans. W. O. Henderson and W. H. Chaloner (Oxford: Blackwell, 1971).

2 J. A. R. Pimlott, *Toynbee Hall: Fifty Years of Social Reform* (London: Dent, 1935), p. 18.

3 H. Barnett, *Canon Barnett: His Life, Work and Friends*, 2 vols (London: John Murray, 1918) I, 177–9; S. Koven, 'Barnett, Dame Henrietta Octavia Weston (1851–1936)', in H. C. G. Matthew and B. Harrison (eds) *Oxford Dictionary of National Biography* (Oxford: Oxford University Press, 2004).

4 H. Cunningham, *Children and Childhood in Western Society since 1500* (London: Longman, 1995); H. Hendrick, *Child Welfare: England, 1872– 1989* (London: Routledge, 1994); R. Cooter (ed.) *In the Name of the Child: Health and Welfare, 1880–1940* (London: Routledge, 1992), *passim*.

5 A. Davin, 'Imperialism and motherhood', *History Workshop Journal* 5 (1978), pp. 10–11.

6 H. E. Meller, *Leisure and the Changing City, 1870–1914* (London: Routledge & Kegan Paul, 1976); J. Walvin, *Leisure and Society, 1830–1950* (London: Longman, 1978); P. Bailey, *Leisure and Class in Victorian*

England: Rational Recreation and the Contest for Control, 1830–1885 (London: Methuen, 1987).

7   See G. Darley, *Octavia Hill: A Life* (London: Constable, 1990), pp. 172–86; Barnett, *Canon Barnett* I, p. 178.

8   See especially Pimlott, *Toynbee Hall*, chapters 1 and 4 for an account of the development of adult education; chapter 10 more specifically for arts and musical provision.

9   Davin, 'Imperialism and motherhood', 11–12.

10   M. Sewell and E. G. Powell, 'Women's settlements in England', in W. Reason (ed.) *University and Social Settlements* (London: Methuen, 1898) p. 92.

11   *Ibid.*, p. 93.

12   G. Barrett, *Blackfriars Settlement: A Short History* (London: Blackfriars Settlement, 1985), p. 7.

13   *Burdett's Hospitals and Charities* (London: Faber & Gwyer, 1928), p. 39.

14   Newham Local Studies and Archives (hereafter NLSA), Canning Town Women's Settlement Executive Committee Minutes, 1891–94.

15   J. Sutherland, *Mrs Humphrey Ward, Eminent Victorian, Pre-eminent Edwardian* (Oxford: Clarendon Press, 1990), pp. 224–7; N. Scotland, *Squires in the Slums: Settlements and Mission Settlements in late Victorian Britain* (London: I. B. Tauris, 2007), p. 190.

16   Barrett, *Blackfriars Settlement*, p. 9.

17   Women's Library, 5WUS/1/J/1/b12–21 FL609, St Mary's Girls' Clubs, Workers' Sub-committee, 1925–27; Barrett, *Blackfriars Settlement*, 14–15.

18   British Association of Residential Settlements, *The British Association of Residential Settlements: Report, 1935–1938* (London: BARS, 1938), p. 14.

19   Sewell and Powell, 'Women's settlements in England', pp. 92–3.

20   NLSA, Mansfield House University Settlement, Mansfield House Hospital Letter Society, Minute Book. See also K. Bradley, 'Poverty and Philanthropy in East London, 1918–1959: The University Settlements and the Urban Working Classes' (PhD dissertation, University of London, 2006).

21   Pimlott, *Toynbee Hall*, p. 241.

22   *Ibid.*, pp. 241, 247.

23   S. Cordery, *British Friendly Societies, 1750–1914* (Basingstoke: Palgrave, 2003), p. 25.

24   W. J. Fishman, *East End, 1888: A Year in a London Borough among the Labouring Poor* (London: Duckworth, 1988), pp. 306–12.

25   M. Heller, 'The National Insurance Acts, 1911–1947, the Approved Societies and the Prudential Assurance Company', *Twentieth Century British History* (2007), doi: 10.1093/tcbh/hwm032, p. 2.

26   A. Hardy, *Health and Medicine in Britain since 1860* (Basingstoke: Palgrave, 2001), p. 45; L. V. Marks, '"They're magicians." Midwives, doctors and hospitals: women's experiences of childbirth in east London and Woolwich in the inter-war years', *Oral History* 23:1 (1995), p. 46.

27   L. V. Marks, *Metropolitan Maternity: Maternal and Infant Welfare Services in early Twentieth Century London* (Amsterdam: Rodopi, 1996), p. 169.

28   A. Briggs, 'Mallon, James Joseph (1874–1961)', in Matthew and Harrison, *Oxford Dictionary of National Biography.*

29   C. E. Grant, *Work and Clo' Fund* (London: Clara E. Grant, 1905), pp. 14–15.

30   *Ibid.*, p. 15.

31   C. E. Grant, *From 'Me' to 'We': Forty Years on Bow Common* (London: Fern Street Settlement, 1940), pp. 42–4.

32   *Ibid.*, pp. 44–5.

33   C. Steedman, 'Margaret Macmillan, 1860–1931', in Matthew and Harrison, *Oxford Dictionary of National Biography.*

34   C. Steedman, *Childhood, Culture and Class in Britain: Margaret McMillan, 1860–1931* (London: Virago, 1990), p. 51.

35   R. Tribe, 'Results of treatment at the Poplar School clinic', *School Hygiene* 2:5 (May 1911), p. 252.

36   *Ibid.*, p. 252.

37   C. E. Grant, *Farthing Bundles* (London: Fern Street Settlement, 1935), p. 83.

38   Tribe, 'Results of treatment at the Poplar School clinic', p. 258.

39   *Ibid.*, pp. 253–7.

40   *Ibid.*, p. 258.

41   Steedman, *Childhood, Culture and Class in Britain*, p. 52.

42   Steedman, 'Margaret Macmillan, 1860–1931'.

43   Grant, *Farthing Bundles*, p. 83.

44   See G. Sutherland, 'Education', in F. M. L. Thompson (ed.) *The Cambridge Social History of Britain, 1750–1950* III, *Social Agencies and Institutions* (Cambridge: Cambridge University Press, 1990), esp. pp. 143–6, 152.

45   V. Berridge, 'Health and medicine', in Thompson, *The Cambridge Social History of Britain, 1750–1950* III, p. 217.

46   Marks, *Metropolitan Maternity*, p. 170.

47   M. Gorsky and J. Mohan, 'London's voluntary hospitals in the inter-war period: growth, transformation, or crisis?' *Nonprofit and Voluntary Sector Quarterly* 30:2 (2001) pp. 263–5.

48   *Ibid.*, p. 265.

49   A. Briggs and A. Macartney, *Toynbee Hall: The First Hundred Years* (London: Routledge, 1984).

50   Canning Town Women's Settlement, 'A settlement hospital', in W. Reason (ed.) *University and Social Settlements* (London: Methuen, 1898), p. 160.

51   NLSA, CTWS Executive Committee, 5 December 1919.

52   Burdett's, *Burdett's Hospitals and Charities, being the Yearbook of Philanthropy and the Hospital Annual* (London: Faber & Gwyer, 1928). Queen Mary opened in 1861 as a dispensary, and as a hospital from 1890 (134), whilst St Mary's opened in 1892–93 (147).

53 D. Owen, *English Philanthropy, 1660–1960* (London: Oxford University Press, 1965), p. 528; also B. Abel-Smith, *The History of the Nursing Profession* (London: Heinemann, 1975).
54 S. Cherry, 'Before the National Health Service: financing the voluntary hospitals, 1900–1939', *Economic History Review* 50:2 (1997); M. Gorsky, J. Mohan and M. Powell, 'The financial health of voluntary hospitals in inter-war Britain', *Economic History Review* 55:3 (2002); Gorsky and Mohan, 'London's voluntary hospitals in the inter-war period: growth, transformation, or crisis?'
55 Gorsky *et al.*, 'The financial health of voluntary hospitals in inter-war Britain', p. 534.
56 See F. Prochaska, *Philanthropy and the Hospitals of London: The King's Fund, 1897–1990* (Oxford: Clarendon Press, 1992); K. Waddington, *Charity and the London Hospitals, 1850–1898* (Woodbridge: Boydell & Brewer, 2000); Cherry, 'Before the National Health Service', p. 315.
57 London Metropolitan Archives (hereafter LMA), A/KE/250/7, King's Hospital Fund for London, Invalid and Crippled Children's Society Hospital, formerly Canning Town Women's Settlement Hospital, 1898–1929, Letter, W. Hazell to King's Fund, 31 December 1915; Hazell to King's Fund, 29 December 1916; Letter, Hazell to King's Fund, 6 March 1922.
58 LMA, A/KE/250/7, Letter, W. Hazell (CTWS) to Maynard, King's Fund, 24 December 1918.
59 NLSA, CTWS Executive Committee, 18 September 1918.
60 *Ibid.*, 18 September 1918.
61 *Ibid.*, 24 November 1919.
62 *Ibid.*, 5 December 1919.
63 Burdett's, *Burdett's Hospitals and Charities*, p. 117; further references to the Invalid and Crippled Children's Society Hospital operating as a voluntary hospital can be found in British Hospitals Association, *The Hospitals Year-Book, 1947* (London: British Hospitals Association, 1947) pp. 47, 63, 126, and *The Hospitals Year-Book, 1948* (London: British Hospitals Association, 1948), p. 86. In 1948 it was subsumed into the North East London Metropolitan Regional Hospital Board for West Ham.
64 NLSA, South West Ham Health Society, Minutes, 1918–52 (hereafter NLSA, SWHHS Minutes), List of General Committee members, 1920.
65 NLSA, SWHHS Minutes, inserted newspaper clipping, no date.
66 Marks, *Metropolitan Maternity*, p. 159, p. 180.
67 NLSA, CTWS Executive Committee, 27 February, 27 March 1918.
68 NLSA, SWHHS Minutes, 24 April 1918.
69 *Ibid.*, 31 July 1918.
70 *Ibid.*, 23 October 1918.
71 *Ibid.*, 26 February 1918.
72 Grant, *From 'Me' to 'We'*, p. 45.

73   B. Harris, *The Origins of the British Welfare State: Society, State and Social Welfare in England and Wales, 1800–1945* (Basingstoke: Palgrave, 2004), 223.
74   NLSA, SWHHS Minutes, 20 March 1921.
75   *Ibid.*, 18 May 1921.
76   *Ibid.*, 18 May, 19 October 1921.
77   *Ibid.*, 4 July 1939.
78   *Ibid.*, 5 March 1947.
79   *Ibid.*, 11 February 1948; Newham Local Studies and Archives, South West Ham Children's Welfare Society, Trustee Minutes (hereafter NLSA, SWHCWS Minutes), 24 November 1948.
80   NLSA, SWHCWS Minutes, 29 April 1960 onwards, 4 November 1960.
81   B. Seebohm Rowntree, *The Human Needs of Labour* (London: Longmans Green, 1938).
82   C. Webster, 'Healthy or hungry thirties?' *History Workshop Journal* 13:1 (1982).
83   J. M. Winter, 'Infant mortality, maternal mortality and public health in Britain in the 1930s', *Journal of European Economic History* 8:2 (1979).
84   J. J. Mallon and E. Lascelles, *Poverty Today and Yesterday* (London: Student Christian Movement Press, 1930).
85   B. Leigh Hutchins and J. J. Mallon, *Women in Modern Industry, with a Chapter (Women's Wages in the Wage Consensus of 1906) contributed by J. J. Mallon* (London: Bell, 1915).
86   BRC, TOY/CEN/2/2/6, Letter, Mallon to Munro, 16 July 1936.
87   R. C. Garry and D. F. Smith (rev.), 'Cathcart, Edward Provan (1877–1954)', in Matthew and Harrison, *Oxford Dictionary of National Biography*; BRC, TOY/CEN/2/2/6, Letters.
88   *Report of the Committee on Scottish Health Services*, Cmnd 5204 (Edinburgh: HMSO, 1936).
89   BRC, TOY/CEN/2/2/6.
90   *Ibid.*
91   M. Spring Rice, *Working-class Wives: Their Health and Conditions* (London: Virago, 1981).
92   BRC, TOY/CEN/2/2/6.
93   *Ibid.*, Letter, Tennant to Mallon, 10 December 1936.
94   BRC, TOY/CEN/2/2/6.
95   Rowntree, *The Human Needs of Labour*, pp. 81–3.
96   BRC, TOY/CEN/2/2/6, Letter, Tennant to Mallon, 10 December 1936.
97   *Ibid.*, Letter, G. T. Kelly to Mallon, 25 November 1936.
98   BRC, TOY/CEN/2/2/6.
99   *Ibid.*, Letters, Mallon to E. T. Kelly, W. Clarke, C. Towers, Deaconess Truscott, H. W. Bryant and R. Parmley, 24 November 1936.
100 *Ibid.*, Letter, Peter Tennant to Jo Hodgkinson, 23 November 1936.
101 V. Markham, *May Tennant: A Portrait* (London: Falcon, 1949), pp. 13–18.
102 BRC, TOY/CEN/2/2/6, Letter, May Tennant to J. J. Mallon, 19 November 1936.

103 *Ibid.*, Letter, J. J. Mallon to Peter Tennant, 20 November 1936.

104 *Ibid.*, Letter, Eric Mawson to J. J. Mallon, 7 December 1936.

105 *Ibid.*, Letter, Jo Hodgkinson to Grace Drysdale, 21 January 1937.

106 *Ibid.*, Letter, Grace Drysdale to Jo Hodgkinson, 21 January 1937.

107 Although disrupted by the Second World War, this study was later published as Manchester University Settlement, *Ancoats: A Study of a Clearance Area: Report of a Survey Made in 1937–1938* (Manchester: Manchester University Settlement, 1945).

108 S. McLaurin, 'McGonigle, George Cuthbert Mura (1889–1939)', in Matthew and Harrison, *Oxford Dictionary of National Biography*. See also Webster, 'Healthy or hungry thirties?'; G. C. M. McGonigle, 'Poverty, nutrition and public health: an investigation into some of the results of moving a slum population to modern dwellings', *Proceedings of the Royal Society of Medicine* 26:6 (1933).

109 BRC, TOY/CEN/2/2/6, Waldorf Astor to J. J. Mallon, 29 April 1937, and attached papers.

110 *Ibid.*, Waldorf Astor to J. J. Mallon, 29 April 1937.

111 R. M. Titmuss, *Problems of Social Policy* (London: HMSO and Longmans Green, 1950), p. 101.

112 *Ibid.*, p. 115.

113 *Ibid.*, p. 111.

114 A. Calder, *The Myth of the Blitz* (London: Pimlico, 1992).

115 Titmuss, *Problems of Social Policy*, 122.

116 J. S. M. Rusby, 'Childhood Temporary Separation: Long-term Effects of Wartime Evacuation in World War II' (PhD dissertation, University of London, 2006), pp. 261, 171.

117 T. L. Crosby, *The Impact of Civilian Evacuation in the Second World War* (London: Croom Helm, 1986).

118 R. Glessner, 'Hosts of the *Kindertransport*: The Role of the Nation, the Organisation and the Individual' (MA dissertation, University of London, 2007).

119 P. Hayward, *Children into Exile: The Story of the Evacuation of School Children from Hellfire Corner in the Second World War* (Dover: Buckland, 1997); M. Parsons and P. Starns, *The Evacuation: The True Story* (Peterborough: DSM, 1999); R. Inglis, *The Children's War: Evacuation, 1939–1945* (London: Collins, 1989).

120 T. Enever, *Cockney Kid and Countrymen: The Second World War remembered by the Children of Woburn Sands and Aspley Guise* (Dunstable: Book Castle, 2001).

121 Evacuees' Reunion Association, *Sixtieth Anniversary of the East Kent Evacuation* (Liverpool: Brodie, 2000), p. 5.

122 See www.evacuees.org.uk (viewed 3 January 2008).

123 Calder, *The Myth of the Blitz*.

124 S. Isaacs (ed.) *The Cambridge Evacuation Survey: A Wartime Study in Social Welfare and Education* (London: Methuen, 1941).

125 *Ibid.*, p. 58.

126 *Ibid.*, p. 89.
127 R. Padley and M. Cole (eds) *Evacuation Survey: A Report to the Fabian Society* (London: Routledge, 1940).
128 Ministry of Health, *Report on Conditions in Reception Areas* (London: HMSO, 1941).
129 Ministry of Health, *Hostels for 'Difficult' Children: A Survey of Experience under the Evacuation Scheme* (London: HMSO, 1944).
130 Barnett House, *London Children in Wartime Oxford: A Study of the Social and Educational Results of Evacuation* (London: Oxford University Press, 1947).
131 Titmuss, *Problems of Social Policy*, pp. 378–87.
132 H. T. Lyons, 'Evacuation Problems: A Study of Difficult Children in Hostels' (MA dissertation, University of London, 1943).
133 Titmuss, *Problems of Social Policy*, p. 380.
134 *Ibid.*, p. 381.
135 Hendrick, *Child Welfare*.
136 *Ibid.*
137 D. W. Winnicott and C. Britton, 'Residential management as treatment for difficult children', and D. W. Winnicott, 'Children's hostels in war and peace', in C. Winnicott, R. Shepherd and M. Davis (eds) *D. W. Winnicott: Deprivation and Delinquency* (London: Tavistock, 1984).
138 Briggs and Macartney, *Toynbee Hall*, p. 126; 'Special war work', Toynbee Hall, *Annual Report, 1938–1946* (London: Toynbee Hall, 1946), pp. 12–13.
139 Kingsley Hall and Children's House, *Report, 1943–1944* (London: Kingsley Hall and Children's House, 1944), pp. 6–7.
140 Oxford House Country Schools, *Citizens in Readiness, being an Account of the Oxford House Country Schools* (London: Brakell, 1945), pp. 15, 56–9.
141 *Ibid.*, p. 5.
142 A. G. Clutton Brock, 'Homes, hostels, lodgings' 2, 'A. G. Clutton Brock, Principal Probation Officer for the Metropolitan Area', *Probation Journal* 3:2 (1938).
143 Oxford House, *The Oxford House in Bethnal Green, 1884–1948* (London: Brakell, 1948), p. 102.
144 *Ibid.*, p. 106.
145 Oxford House Country Schools, *Citizens in Readiness*, p. 5.
146 Oxford House, *The Oxford House in Bethnal Green, 1884–1948*, p. 106.
147 Oxford House Country Schools, *Citizens in Readiness*, p. 6.
148 *Ibid.*, pp. 7–9.
149 *Ibid.*, pp. 13, 39.
150 *Ibid.*, p. 13.
151 *Ibid.*, p. 13.
152 *Ibid.*, p. 14.
153 *Ibid.*, p. 16.
154 *Ibid.*, p. 15.
155 *Ibid.*, p. 43.

156 *Ibid.*, p. 23.

157 *Ibid.*, p. 45.

158 *Ibid.*, p. 60.

159 Winnicott and Britton, 'Residential management as treatment for difficult children', p. 57.

160 *Ibid.*, pp. 66–72.

161 Titmuss, *Problems of Social Policy*, pp. 382, 386.

162 A. Logan, '"A Suitable person for suitable cases": the gendering of juvenile courts in England, *c.* 1910–1939', *Twentieth Century British History* 16:2 (2005).

163 See J. Bowlby, *Attachment and Loss* (London: Hogarth Press, 1969); C. Winnicott, R. Shepherd and M. Davis (eds) *D. W. Winnicott: Deprivation and Delinquency* (London: Tavistock, 1984).

164 Children's Country Holidays Fund, *Children's Country Holidays Fund: What it's all About, How you can Help* (London: Children's Country Holidays Fund, 1981), p. 4.

165 *Ibid.*, pp. 6–11.

166 Children's Country Holidays Fund, *Will there be a Holiday for him this Year?* (London: Children's Country Holidays Fund, 1981), p. 5.

167 *Ibid.*, p. 11.

168 See London Metropolitan Archives, Children's Country Holidays Fund, 1884–1972, LMA/4040; also C. Jackson, 'The Children's Country Holidays Fund and the settlements', in J. M. Knapp (ed.) *The Universities and the Social Problem: An Account of the University Settlements in East London* (London: Rivington Percival, 1895).

169 Lambeth Archives Department (hereafter LAD), IV183/5/1F, Report on Children's Country Holiday Fund.

170 LAD, IV183/5/1, 'Children's Country Holiday Fund: Julia Stallibrass, work report', n.d.

171 LAD, IV183/5/1F, 'Children's Country Holiday Fund files for summer 1968'. References to individual cases have been anonymised.

172 Calder, *The Myth of the Blitz*, pp. 60–4.

173 Glessner, 'Hosts of the *Kindertransport*'.

174 B. Abel-Smith and P. Townsend, *The Poor and the Poorest: A New Analysis of the Ministry of Labour's 'Family Expenditure Surveys' of 1953–1954 and 1960* (London: Bell, 1965).

175 M. McCarthy, *Campaigning for the Poor: CPAG and the Politics of Welfare* (Beckenham: Croom Helm, 1986), p. 25.

176 R. Beer and C. A. Pickard, *Eighty Years on Bow Common* (London: Fern Street Settlement, 1987), p. 18.

177 St Hilda's East, *Annual Report, 1961–1962* (London: St Hilda's East, 1962), p. 6.

178 See P. Thane (ed.) *The Long History of Old Age* (London: Thames & Hudson, 2005).

179 Society of Friends, *Hostels for Old People* (London: Friends' Relief Service, 1945), p. 3.

180 *Ibid.*, p. 4.
181 *Ibid.*, p. 15.
182 *Report of the Royal Commission on Population*, Cmnd 7695 (London: HMSO, 1949), pp. 3–4.
183 R. Means and R. Smith, *From Poor Law to Community Care: The Development of Welfare Services for Elderly People, 1939–1971* (Bristol: Policy Press, 1998), pp. 219, 232.
184 *Ibid.*, p. 248.
185 BRC, DEP/3/3, Toynbee Hall Old People's Welfare Service, Report, 1957.
186 Beer and Pickard, *Eighty Years on Bow Common*, p. 18.
187 Women's University Settlement, *Annual Report, 1956–1957* (London: Women's University Settlement, 1957), p. 4.
188 Mary Ward Settlement, *Annual Report for the Year ended 31st August 1959* (London: Mary Ward Settlement, 1959), pp. 9–11.
189 St Hilda's East, *Annual Report, 1956–1957* (London: St Hilda's East, 1957), p. 7.
190 *Ibid.*, p. 7.
191 St Hilda's East, *Annual Report, 1961–1962*, p. 7.
192 P. Gordon and R. Mayo (eds) *Between Psychotherapy and Philosophy: Essays from the Philadelphia Association* (London: Whurr, 2004), p. xii.
193 Z. Kotowicz, *R. D. Laing and the Paths of Anti-psychiatry* (London: Routledge, 1997), p. 78.
194 Philadelphia Association, *Philadelphia Association Report* (London: Philadelphia Association, 1969), p. 7.
195 *Ibid.*, p. 7.
196 *Ibid.*, pp. 7, 10.
197 P. Gordon and R. Mayo, 'Introduction', p. xii, and R. Cooper, 'What we take for granted', in Gordon and Mayo, *Between Psychotherapy and Philosophy*, pp. 8, 14.
198 Kotowicz, *R. D. Laing and the Paths of Anti-psychiatry*, pp. 92–104.
199 M. Barnes and J. Berke, *Mary Barnes: Two Accounts of a Journey through Madness* (Harmondsworth: Penguin, 1973).
200 D. Edgar, *Mary Barnes* (London: Methuen, 1979).
201 V. Brittain, 'Is mad sane and sane mad? Myths of the family', *The Times*, Saturday 2 October 1971, p. 12.
202 BRC, TOY/DEP/10, Special Families Centre, Letter, Donald Chesworth to Fred Houghlin, Deputy Head of Special Education, Inner London Education Authority, 27 April 1983, attachment, 'Educational Ingredients of Special Families Centre, Sunley House'.
203 Briggs and Macartney, *Toynbee Hall*, pp. 172, 177.
204 BRC, TOY/DEP/10, Special Families Centre, Paper for Toynbee Council meeting, 21 May 1985, and Memorandum from Chesworth to John Profumo, 13 April 1984.
205 *Ibid.*, Letter and attachment, Chesworth to Houghlin, 27 April 1983.
206 *Ibid.*, Letter and attachment, Chesworth to Houghlin, 27 April 1983; Memo, Muriel Smith to Ruth Hindley, London Borough of Tower Hamlets

Directorate of Social Services, 7 September 1983, and Special Families Centre report of 21 September 1983.

207 *Ibid.*, Report of 21 September 1983.

208 *Ibid.*

209 TOY/DEP/9/4, Stepney Children's Fund, Leaflet, no date.

210 TOY/DEP/11/2, Family Centre, Report, 3 March 1987.

211 TOY/DEP/10/1, Special Families Centre, Rosalind Wyman, appraisal, May 1983.

4

Developing citizens, 1918–79

When the majority of settlements were established in the 1880s and 1890s, their mission was to alleviate intense social problems in the inner cities and larger towns. Those who went to live, volunteer and work at settlements in this period did so out of religious vocation. This could manifest itself as directly as a desire to fulfil Christian duties through serving the poor or, less directly, as part of a more general sense of Judaeo-Christian morality. In some cases it was also a means of working to serve political ends. Although settlements were by no means devoid of Conservative residents or supporters, the overwhelming majority were Liberal and later Labour supporters. This was especially true of Toynbee Hall in the inter-war period, where the warden, J. J. Mallon, was a Labour Party stalwart. Such motivations for social work continued well into the twentieth century.

The concept of citizenship

Citizenship and the role of the state are intrinsically linked both as concepts and as practice, along with the concepts of 'community' and being a 'good neighbour'. In 1867 working-class men received the vote in local elections, which allowed them to develop their political role in the community. Some working-class men also received the vote in the national parliamentary elections, and the reforms of 1867 and 1884 also opened up opportunities in local government for women of all backgrounds.[1] Yet, as Frank Smith noted in the early 1930s, the extension of these rights were not always openly welcomed, as some '[realised] that the Reform Act of 1867 had enfranchised a host of uneducated votes in this country'.[2] The extension of the franchise was accompanied by the apparent need to prepare and educate the new voters for their responsibilities. This became part of the remit of the university settlements when they were established from the 1880s onwards, along with their work to relieve poverty. Samuel Barnett was contemptuous of those working-class men who were able to participate in local government after 1884, believing them to act on emotions rather than reason generated by years of working in charities.[3] Barnett was involved in local government by virtue of being a clergyman, but he also held strong views on the role that his settlement had to play:

> Local government in East London needs the presence of a few people who will formulate its mission. To some degree this has been done by the residents of Toynbee Hall. Some of them as members of boards, all of them as neighbours, have shown something of what is not done and of what might be done. Whitechapel has been moved to get a library; political parties have been induced to adopt a social programme; the police have been encouraged to enforce order in back streets.[4]

Thus the settlements had three purposes: to provide help and assistance to those who needed it; to act as advocates for those individuals; and finally to ensure the self-realisation of those men and women involved with the settlement movement. But how did these men and women see their role and its functions?

There have been a number of discussions about the role citizenship played in the opinions of those working for or connected with the settlements. Julia Parker argued that prominent economists, theorists and policy makers, from T. H. Green and Canon Barnett to R. H. Tawney and William Beveridge, put the concept of economics – or more specifically work – in their perception of citizenship.[5] Parker argues that Beveridge's welfare state provided a framework for citizenship that was balanced on the duties, rights and responsibility of the citizen to work, as well as for the state to ensure that work was available.[6] But work was not the only issue in the formation of modern British citizenship. Tawney was keen to educate the British worker, partly for his or her own mental elevation but also so that the worker could participate fully in society.[7] Mutual aid and co-operation were examples of non-political citizenship practised by the working classes for the working classes.[8] Jonathan Rose has explored many of the reading groups and literary practices of the working classes in Britain, whereby the autodidact could meet other autodidacts to improve their knowledge and understanding of the world.[9] These were essential lifelines for those with an interest in furthering their education prior to the educational reforms that allowed greater numbers of Britons to access free education, either through schooling in childhood or later in life. Friendly societies provided a range of benefits to their members, from help with funeral costs to accessing medical care. As Garrard has shown, at the same time as these organisations provided their members

with benefits in times of crisis they also provided training in citizenship and civil society. These societies and other elements of working-
class civil society were a means by which people could claw back some
autonomy from their employers.[10]

T. H. Marshall's views on citizenship and social class were widely
seen, both at the time and since, as being highly influential in
mid-twentieth-century political thought. Education held a key role in
his argument. From the nineteenth century onwards, not only did the
individual have the right to be educated, it was also their duty to
educate themselves.[11] Marshall's view of citizenship was not based on
financial equality, but on an equality of *status*.[12] He wrote:

> Citizenship is a status bestowed upon those who are full members of
> a community. All those who possess the status are equal with respect
> to the rights and duties with which the status is endowed. There is
> no universal principle that determines what the rights and duties
> shall be, but societies in which citizenship is a developing institution
> create an image of an ideal citizenship against which achievement can
> be measured and towards which aspiration can be directed.[13]

Marshall attempted to reconcile the inequalities of advanced capitalist
societies and the concept of citizenship. Whilst citizens were equal
in terms of their ability to vote, and their rights and duties, there
would be disparities between the opportunities open to them. The
rights and duties of the citizen, therefore, were part of a contract bind-
ing the individual to participation in society. Marshall outlined the
mechanics of citizenship, whilst Beveridge and his blueprint for the
welfare state located the duties and responsibilities in 'work':[14] whilst
these rights and duties bind the individual to the nation, they do not
necessarily bind the individual to society and community. Central to
Beveridge's view of citizenship was that individuals should behave
altruistically towards their neighbours as well as to the state. In practice, citizenship could be about expanding the ways in which the
individual could engage with his or her society. Citizenship was
not just about the right to vote; it also concerned the individual's
right to make decisions in all areas of his or her life. Its danger – or
advantage – to the political system was that the acquisition of the
vote allowed the individual to demand representation and action on
issues of concern to them. The extension of the franchise to all men
and women had the potential to introduce a new range of concerns
into the political system.

In terms of social work in London, the period 1918 to 1979 was one
of immense change and readjustment. Until the 1950s many aspects
of the settlements' programmes – namely club work of various kinds,

education and legal advice – were relatively unchanged. The growth of the welfare state from the late 1940s necessitated many changes, as some types of work were taken over by the state. Other areas of work were expanded by the settlements, or explored for the first time. Certainly their work prior to the 1950s can be described as allowing the underprivileged to engage fully with all aspects of life. This was achievable through legislation and helping the working classes to be confident in accessing education, the arts, health and ultimately civic leadership. To deliver this, the settlements had to provide opportunities for their communities to explore the possibilities on offer:

> But even the remarkable expansion of Settlements throughout the civilised world is no adequate measure of the spread of Settlement ideas. We have seen how in England they have infiltrated all political parties and are embodied in social legislation which has given wider opportunities for the enjoyment of life . . . There is hardly any educated class and no community life [in the East End]. The London boroughs have signally failed to awaken the civic loyalty for the cultivation of which Toynbee Hall has so persistently striven.
>   To use the time-worn expression, Toynbee Hall and its fellow Settlements form oases in this desert. Their main function is to supply the intellectual life and the communal spirit in which the neighbourhood, taken as a whole, is so conspicuously deficient. Hardly less important is the investigation of social problems with a view to the formulation of appropriate measures for their remedy. Education, civic leadership, social research – in short, the very functions for which Settlements were founded in 1884.[15]

This view of citizenship was still based on the paradox that the ordinary working-class person had the right to participate in public life, but that he or she did not have the skill or ability to do so. The London County Council and the London boroughs had provided opportunities for Londoners to enter into local government at those levels, and had made major contributions to the educational and cultural life of the capital. The settlements in London and elsewhere did make important contributions to research into social issues, albeit amidst a burgeoning of such social research in the universities. The settlements certainly sold themselves as being experts in these areas, until the welfare state challenged their supposed hegemony. The settlement leaders of the 1950s were anxious about the role their charities should play in a world in which the state provided for basic needs, yet they soon found their role by targeting those needs that the state could not cater for, such as providing the lonely and the elderly with company. They also needed to reconsider the ways in which they went about their work, from developing partnerships with other settlements, charities and local government, and also to refresh the ways in which they organised volunteering. It did not follow, *pace* Prochaska,[16] that an increasingly secular nation and a welfare state had a deleterious impact upon volunteering. Rather, individuals continued to volunteer in their spare time and to make donations to the charities of their choice. If settlements 'lost' residential volunteers in the course of the 1960s and 1970s, that reflected the post-war expansion of higher education and rising levels of affluence. University students in the 1960s and 1970s challenged the model of collegiate living at Oxford and Cambridge, and elsewhere enjoyed greater freedom. The 'old' model of residential volunteering was not redundant – it competed with the other forms of engagement with public life open to university graduates. As seen in the first chapter, it also coincided with the increase in paid posts, often as part of specific, time-limited projects, from the 1940s. But what of the ways in which local people engaged with the settlements?

Going to the club

One of the most important ways in which local people engaged with the settlement movement was through the 'club'. The 'club' was one of the most popular means by which people accessed settlement services, from boys' and girls' clubs to mothers' meetings, clubs for the elderly and 'dry' clubs for men. The boys' or men's club was often the apogee of the settlement's work in the community, as it was the place in which 'good citizens' could and were made. Yet clubs were not solely about learning how to be a worthwhile member of society: it was a place in which friendships could be made and sustained, as well as a place for developing skills and status.

One area in which the settlement project to create 'good citizens' was most clearly articulated was youth work and the juvenile courts. As will be seen in Chapter 5, there were strong resonances between the two areas of work. Youth clubs – boys' clubs in particular – were seen as developing positive skills and confidence, and keeping boys out of trouble. Boys who came before the juvenile courts were seen as being deficient in the very qualities that boys' clubs could bestow upon them. It was not unusual for boys sentenced at the Inner London Juvenile Court to be required to attend a boys' club or other youth organisation as part of their probation terms. This view was best expressed by Basil Henriques in his memoir *Indiscretions of a Magistrate*:

To put the matter positively, very few children come before the court:

> Who have been brought up in a happy home;
>
> Who have united and loving parents with an income adequate to their needs;
>
> Who live in a district devoid of slums and with ample open spaces, in which they can give vent to their natural and thoroughly healthy high spirits;
>
> Who have been educated in a school which inculcates great self-discipline, and instils into them a sense of duty towards their neighbours and towards the State, team loyalty and true sportsmanship, humility and chivalry, self-control and a strong sense of 'I must because I ought';
>
> Who are not below average in intelligence;
>
> And who have felt, in their homes and in the school, such love and goodness, which have been taught them by example and not merely by precept, that they have got into the habit, on the one hand, of detesting meanness and vulgarity and beastliness, and, on the other, of seeking after beauty, loving-kindness, and truth.[17]

The physical nature of the boys' club activities was highly emphasised in the youth work literature of the time.[18] Boys were thought to need to release their energy through sporting activities. The release of energy was often valued over sporting prowess, as the priority of the club leaders was to channel adolescent male energy in this way, rather than allowing it to result in behaviour they found less acceptable.

This is a recurring theme in the literature about youth work in wartime, in peacetime, during economic depression and economic prosperity. Boys, far more than girls, were visible on the streets of east London and attracted attention and comment. Mallon wrote:

> The lot of the East End boy is not a happy one. He is mentally vigorous. He possesses a genius for adventurous play, but is denied opportunities. His district is not furnished with playing grounds; he is too poor to provide apparatus for games. He is cut off from the country and natural things. In these circumstances much of what is healthy and fine in him decays or is deflected into wrong channels. He takes to the streets. He makes evil friends and imitates bad models. He loses any ambition he may have cherished and finally may have only one: the ambition to possess money without working for it. At this stage the boy is in grave danger, and what may have been an inherently strong and healthy character is marred.[19]

Such comments were rarely made at the time about girls and young women, for whom the paramount issue in the minds of club leaders was whether or not they had appropriate home-making skills. A. E. Morgan, commissioned by the King George's Jubilee Trust in the 1930s to research young people's leisure, saw this attitude of the club leaders, partly shared by the girls themselves, as deriving from their high rates of participation in domestic service, and also a consequence of the influence of the women's religious groups that had done much to bring girls into the world of the club.[20] It offered opportunities for girls to gain skills in home making for later life. Club leaders saw domestic service as an important occupation, due in part to the privileged backgrounds of some of the leaders and settlers. Henrietta Barnett had been responsible for establishing the Metropolitan Association for the Befriending of Young Servants (MABYS), which provided guidance and placements to young female domestic servants.[21] Branches of MABYS could be found at most settlements, particularly women's settlements. The Princess Club in Bermondsey took this one step further, and before the First World War offered girls live-in training for domestic service.[22] Girls were generally seen as less of a problem, requiring training and the funnelling of their energies through creative pursuits such as singing or art, although some physical recreation was also encouraged.[23] Girls, it would seem, were assumed to spend their 'leisure' time in the home, or preparing for their own adult home; boys needed to be brought off the streets and into constructive leisure.

Girls' clubs were as likely as boys' clubs to be divided into sections by age, but in the case of boys' clubs there was thought to be a stronger need for this. Morgan suggests that, whilst mixing younger boys with older ones was frowned upon (possibly as the older boys might 'corrupt' the younger ones), leaders of girls' clubs saw the mixing of ages or the inclusion of a group of much younger children as useful for training girls in caring for babies and small children.[24] Successful boys' clubs had dedicated buildings, a variety of activities and a clear progression from the most junior clubs through to the men's club. Youth work grew out of the concern to find constructive outlets for the energies of urban working-class youth – boys more than girls, but not exclusively so. In the late nineteenth century there were a number of 'moral panics' about young urban working-class boys and their choice of entertainment. They began to be seen as delinquents who rejected the norms of so-called 'civilised' behaviour[25] and therefore posed a challenge to society as a whole. At the same time, Church reformers saw the need to fill young people's leisure time with constructive activities to prevent them from falling into criminality.[26] Youth work began, as Tony Jeffs has argued, with a distinct emphasis on welfare work. Between the late nineteenth century and the First World War it began to develop specialities of approach and to attempt to appeal to specific groups, tailoring its work to the needs of its client group.[27]

Following the Education Acts of the 1870s, there was a succession of legislation and official investigations into the needs of young people between the early 1900s and the 1950s. The concern about the nation's health that had been raised by the Boer War surfaced in the report of the Committee on Physical Deterioration in 1904, which recommended more physical training for young people. The 1908 Children Act gave welfare agencies greater powers to work with children in need.[28] From 1916 the Board of Education began to take a closer interest in leisure provision for young workers and encouraged local education authorities to start Juvenile Organisations Committees. This was included in the Education Act of 1921, but by 1936 only six local authorities had full-time workers on their Juvenile Organisations Committees.[29]

The need to address the so-called 'youth problem' continued through the 1930s. Unemployment, changing legal practices and the emergence of new media and leisure pursuits exacerbated existing concerns about youth. During the depression around 150,000 people aged fourteen to seventeen were unemployed,[30] although those who were employed also caused unease, as they had money to spend. The 1933 Children and Young Persons Act ensured that more matters relating to children were put through the courts, giving rise, however erroneously, to the perception of increased juvenile delinquency.[31] But the greatest concern in the early twentieth century was about young men entering 'dead end' jobs because they were unskilled. These jobs offered relatively high wages, at least for a young man with no responsibilities at the start of his working life. They offered little progression or opportunity to develop skills. Young men could find themselves out of a job when the next round of school leavers joined the labour force and they were old enough to command an adult wage yet with few skills to help them find another job.[32]

Young people caused concern when they were out of work. When they were in work the type of work they undertook, how they chose to spend their money and time also worried adults. Young wage earners from the 1930s onwards were prolific cinemagoers. In 1932 64 per cent of male and 65 per cent of female apprentices in the Manchester area went to the cinema three times a week.[33] The cinema was inexpensive, but it was a place where children and young people could avoid supervision by adults. In addition to concern about young men and women being unchaperoned in these places, educationalists and psychologists expressed fear about the impact on young minds of the realistic, exciting and absorbing images and fictions on offer. In the early twentieth century the Chicago school of sociology pioneered the 'hypodermic needle' model of mass communication. According to this model, cinema viewers passively accepted all that was presented to them as real and were incapable of forming their own reactions to or criticisms of the material. This model fell out of favour from the 1930s, but there was still great concern that children and young people could not differentiate between fiction and reality, and would emulate behaviour they had seen on the screen. Also many young wage earners were believed to spend their money on fashionable clothes and dances and nightclubs. The latter raised worries that impressionable adolescents would fall prey to drink or vice, the former that young people were concerned only with immediate gratification of their desires rather than saving their earnings wisely. In reality, as Selina Todd's work has shown, many young people were helping to support their families with their earnings.[34]

There were a number of responses to these concerns. As mentioned earlier, from 1935 the King George's Jubilee Trust surveyed adolescents' lives in every aspect, from their work through to their leisure pursuits, with the aim of improving services and conditions for young people. Much of the survey was carried out by A. E. Morgan (later warden of Toynbee Hall), whose findings were published in *The Needs of Youth*[35] and also in *Young Citizen*.[36] A 1936 report by the British Medical Association on the Health of the Adolescent looked at the provision in Czechoslovakia, Germany and Norway, and recommended the establishment of a National Fitness Council to promote sporting activity among British youth, but this was not implemented due to the war. There was a raft of wartime memoranda on youth provision, from Memorandum 1486, *In the Service of Youth*, in November 1939 through to 1577, *The Registration of Youth*, in December 1941.[37] The Education Act of 1944 raised the school leaving age to fifteen and introduced tripartite schooling. The Youth Service was also set up to cater for the leisure needs of young people who were no longer attending school. The state was gradually playing an ever greater role in the lives of young people, partly as a result of public pressure to cope with the 'youth problem' and partly because of the growing recognition that the state had the responsibility to ensure that its younger citizens had a 'good' start in life. A good start could be given through health and education; but providing young people with opportunities for constructive leisure was also important.

The issues of developing citizenship and community spirit among young people and attempting to prevent future juvenile delinquency continued after the Second World War. Osgerby argues that films like *Brighton Rock* and *The Blue Lamp* suggested that war was a major contributing factor in juvenile crime, and that the media emphasised younger, working-class criminals – and particularly their taste for American clothes – to create the sense that British culture had been degraded, stimulating juvenile delinquency,[38] despite the lack of evidence to corroborate this link between juvenile crime and the cinema or evidence that juvenile crime was especially high. Although youth work had been embraced by the state as well as by the settlements and other organisations, 'moral panics' about the behaviour of young people from the 1950s onwards ensured that, politically, youth work retained its importance. In theory, if not necessarily in practice, youth work through the club or Scout or Guide company was intended to curb the apparently criminal tendencies of youth as well as their sexual behaviour.

Why was constructive leisure time so important to social reformers? In one respect the answer is simple. The processes of urbanisation and industrialisation had changed the social landscape, drawing people together in larger cities, and encouraging a culture of consumption. For A. E. Morgan these processes had resulted in a world of automated, repetitive work for many, coupled with the passive leisure provided by sport spectatorship and the cinema.[39] Like Josephine Macalister Brew, a prominent writer on the training of youth workers,[40] and Pearl Jephcott, an authority on girls' clubs,[41] Morgan was convinced of the need to provide children and young people with the citizenship skills they needed for future life.

The need to find positive role models for young urban boys and to get them off the streets was strongly argued from the nineteenth century to the 1950s and beyond. Nor were girls immune to attempts to take them away from apparently wandering aimlessly around their district, as Morgan commented on the early formation of girls' clubs.[42] It is unlikely, however, that young people joined youth organisations in order to avoid becoming a delinquent – they went because the clubs or organisations provided something for them. Successful clubs – those with strong, creative leadership, good facilities and a range of interesting activities – allowed young people the opportunity to do the things that interested them in their spare time, often making them feel part of a wider community.[43] This was a mutual need – the young people wished to be entertained or instructed, whilst adults were happy that they were not getting up to mischief. The boys' and girls' clubs at Mansfield House and CTWS provided structured activities, and it was likely that members of the child's extended family and neighbours attended the club. The clubs could appeal to the 'delinquent' and non-delinquent young person alike. Whilst juvenile court magistrates often saw youth clubs as building moral fibre and strengthening character, clubs could offer 'delinquent' teenagers a safe refuge from problems at home, 'bad' company, and the friendship of other young people and of the club leaders.

Work with children and young people was common to most settlements. In 1951 the British Association of Residential Settlements sent a survey to forty-two settlements. Of these, all had activities for children of school age or under, and thirty-four had youth clubs or other provision for teenagers.[44] Youth organisations were popular across the nation. In the United Kingdom there were approximately 815,800 fourteen- to eighteen-year-old members of youth organisations in the last years before the war, some of whom may have joined more than one organisation or moved between them. In 1937 there were 3.5 million adolescents aged between fourteen and eighteen in the UK population, of whom around a quarter could be said to be a member of at least one youth organisation.[45] Even taking into account the uneven spread of youth clubs and organisations across the country, this was a significant proportion of young people. Some children and young people were simply uninterested in joining; for others there may have been obstacles such as having to travel a long distance to get to a club. These figures demonstrate that children and young people had, then as now, a desire to be active and involved in things and escape boredom. Young people are keen to belong to groups, gangs and wider communities as part of learning how they fit into the world around them. Clubs and youth organisations therefore played an essential role in assisting children and young people to grow up.

Canning Town Women's Settlement

Although the university settlers and youth workers tended to suggest that boys were more in need of clubs than girls, girls were no more content to stay at home helping their mothers or participating in more individual, home-based forms of leisure. Girls were desperate to get out and have their own clubs and groups. The girls of Bethnal Green pestered the staff of Oxford House for their own club for many years but did not succeed until the Second World War, and then only with the enlightened support of Guy and Molly Clutton-Brock.[46] At CTWS the girls of West Ham and Plaistow were more fortunate in having access to the extensive club network established by the women settlers from the early 1890s. Where women were in control, the girls had access to a wider range of activities, and the girls could and did derive far more from their club than when male settlers were determining the agenda. Of all the youth organisations in Morgan's survey of youth in 1938, the Girl Guides had the largest membership of fourteen- to eighteen-year-olds, even exceeding that of the Scout Association.[47] Young women and girls looked forward to opportunities to meet, to learn new skills and to try out a range of activities, from crafts to public speaking, dancing and camping. Girls as much as boys needed an outlet for their energies and skills, and the clubs provided it in a safe, organised environment.

Girls' club activities at CTWS can be dated back to February 1892, around a month after the settlement opened.[48] By 1918 the girls' clubs were going strong, despite the war. In the summer of 1918 the girls were competing in the East London Federation of Clubs competitions, performing a display as part of the National Organisation of Girls' Clubs event at the People's Palace in Mile End, as a result of which one team were successful in going through to the 'Great Display' at the Old Vic the following May.[49] In 1919 the Senior Club offered girls the opportunity to explore dramatics, first aid, cookery, singing, needlework and drill, whilst the Junior Girls were offered dramatics and singing.[50] By the 1930s the girls were also offered a housekeeping class.[51] Beauty and keep-fit lessons were later included.[52] At first sight, this appears to be a relatively limited range, concentrating, as with the Girls' Dinner Club, on opportunities for girls to express themselves through the arts or to train in the domestic sciences. The emphasis on domestic training was in part a result of the belief that girls and women needed to acquire these skills in order to protect and improve the health of the nation. There is evidence that young women wanted to be trained in domestic skills to prepare them for married life and running their own home.[53]

The girls who attended the clubs at Canning Town were strongly encouraged to take pride in their achievements and to succeed at whatever they turned their hand to. To take one example, in 1921 the Senior Girls' Club took an array of prizes at the East London Federation of Girls' Clubs, with the Shield for General Excellence at the top of the list.[54] The girls were also supported in their efforts to take responsibility, with the Seniors offering to run the Old Canning Town Club, whilst one girl was keen to take the Sunday afternoon Bible class.[55] By 1930 the older club girls were running the Junior Club.[56] Like their male counterparts at the Fairbairn, as will be seen, the girls were able to assert their authority and gain skills in the management of their club and related activities.

The girls also long had the opportunity to contribute paintings and art works to the annual Lees Hall art and crafts exhibitions, although in 1934 there was an attempt to extend this exhibition by introducing loans from art galleries. The settlement succeeded in obtaining loans from the Victoria and Albert Museum and the Tate Gallery.[57] The exhibition which resulted included work from local people alongside the loaned items, and 'several thousands of people had been admitted, including many children'.[58] The coronation of 1937 gave CTWS a further opportunity to encourage a sense of personal pride and self-worth. One girl from the club represented West Ham at the ceremony, and a further two girls signed the National Council of Girls' Clubs' Queen's Book. This was also the year that a former CTWS club girl became the first female mayor of West Ham – Daisy Parsons. Parsons worked as a domestic servant before joining the East London Federation of Suffragettes (ELFS) and was a member of the only deputation of working-class women to H. H. Asquith, then Prime Minister, in 1914. Back in east London, she was heavily involved in the ELFS's women's health work. Her career as a suffragette, and her subsequent work as a Labour councillor in West Ham, was heartily supported by her husband.[59] Parsons returned to CTWS in 1937 to address the settlement on her work during the year as mayor.[60]

The Canning Town Women's Settlement girls' clubs were part of a larger network of clubs at the settlement, but they were some of the most prominent activities there. There appear to have been cases where, as at Mansfield House, girls would move in later years to become involved with the Co-operative Women's Guild, the Townswomen's Guild, the various Mothers' Meetings and similar adult women's activities, or turn to the settlement during periods of unemployment, such as immediately after the First World War. The clubs did not offer an explicitly feminist programme, but they offered working-class girls the opportunity to excel in their chosen field of activity and to take pride in their achievements. The girls also benefited from contact with a range of role models, from local women like Daisy Parsons to nationally well-known figures such as Margaret Bondfield, the first female Cabinet Minister, who addressed a mass meeting for the club girls in December 1924.[61] In this respect the girls' programme at CTWS was far superior to anything else provided for youth across the settlements in this study. There was no sense of the residents or youth workers being unwilling to support girls whose futures may not have extended much further than local factories, marriage and child rearing; on the contrary, the CTWS staff appeared to have had a wholesale commitment to supporting women whatever their future might hold. Whether those women were mothers in need of assistance through the infant welfare clinic, women doctors or nurses, or young girls at a loose end, the settlement made the effort to enrich their lives.

The Fairbairn Club at Mansfield House

The address books of the Mansfield House men's and boys' clubs for the years 1906–10 are one of the few surviving records to demonstrate actual use of settlement clubs by local people.[62] Analysis of the records reveals that brothers often joined at the same time, and it was not uncommon for younger brothers to join their older brothers at the club once they reached the appropriate age. Older boys progressed to the men's club on reaching the age of twenty-one. There were also geographical clusters of boys' addresses, suggesting that groups of boys from the same street or cohort in school joined the club together. These children and young people joined the club at the direction of their parents, perhaps just to get them out of the house; they also joined in order to have a place to go locally that was affordable and offered the activities they wanted. This was very much a 'local' club, and the neighbourhood and workplace networks of Canning Town flourished in the club environment. This phenomenon was remarked upon by the settlement management in 1918:

> They [the club members] have made an atmosphere, and in Fairbairn House the beginnings of gambling are soon checked, bullying is discouraged, a foul word is seldom heard, clear eyes look into clear eyes, and boys can grow up to be strong, healthy, clean-minded, helpful men. One can watch the progress. The newcomer is brought in by a pal; he is welcomed to the Club, and put in the friendly care of an older member; he is shown the glories of the place, the gym., the boxing room, the tennis court, the library.[63]

In this account, boys were recruited to the clubs by their friends, and thus the process of becoming a member of Fairbairn House began, through accepting the explicit rules of the club and the more implicit ones relating to the expected behaviour of the members. As was the case in the men's club, the boys were also able to set their club rules, as well as to police the membership. These patterns of behaviour were also entrenched and normalised through the practice of boys graduating to the men's club, and close interaction between the two. This mode of teaching by example, or peer-based training, had become common in club leadership manuals by the inter-war period. Drawing upon the reputation of the high priest of Victorian self-improvement, Samuel Smiles, James Butterworth described the process as follows:

> The peculiar thing about it all is that no one has preached at him [Sam Smiler, composite club inductee]. In a most natural way Smiler has fallen under the powerful spell of the club spirit. In the silent suggestiveness

of all around him he has seen for himself the worthwhileness of a completely new way of life.

Amid the bewilderment of the first years in employment he will feel that the club is the one place in the world of which he is sure. Ideals which he might otherwise throw to the wind become dear to him when he is conscious that other fellows feel as he does. However vaguely, he knows that he is not alone but part of an understanding fellowship. What this means to those acutely conscious of loneliness amongst crowds cannot be estimated. It is when everything is going wrong at work, at home, or within himself, that he draws inspiration from the unspoken comradeship of the club.[64]

Whilst this was a noble ideal, it did not always exist in practice. Relations between the club members could be tense and unpleasant at times.

Fairbairn House had a standing committee, drawn from its membership, whose role was to oversee the daily management of the clubs. The chairman was a member of the Mansfield House staff. The duties included disciplining club members. There was a range of offences for which members could be disciplined, one of the most common being failure to attend regularly. Such members were called before the standing committee and asked to account for themselves. Two boys were expelled from the club for not turning up to play football and leaving the team short of players,[65] whilst another young man was called to explain his absence through holidays and a bout of diphtheria. This young man offered to pay the subscriptions he owed from September, but the committee decided he should be fined 1s and made to pay his subscriptions for January.[66] Rejoining the club was not a simple matter. Five members were called before the committee in August 1945 to make an application to rejoin. The committee felt that the boys had not been sufficiently active in club activities when they first joined, and made it a condition that they should be more active in future. They were also fined 1s and made to pay their subscriptions for the month.[67] A further young man found himself before the committee for missing swimming, despite having alerted a member of Mansfield House staff in good time.[68] Commitments to sporting teams aside, these were strict terms of membership requiring considerable commitment from the young men to attend each week.

Regular attendance did not equate with best behaviour. The club sports ground was a popular place for under-age smokers to indulge their habit, with little successful interference from adults or standing committee members.[69] A fourteen-year-old boy challenged the standing committee when he was caught smoking in the club by arguing that his father allowed him to smoke; the committee pointed out that, regardless of his father and his wishes, smoking under the age of sixteen was illegal and not permitted in the club.[70] During an apparent shortage of billiard cue chalk in October 1945 others provoked the ire of the committee by chalking their cues up on the ceiling.[71] Another boy caused trouble by loitering with girls at the entrance to Fairbairn House – and objecting to a reprimand issued by a standing committee member.[72] He was duly brought before the committee, to be told by the chairman that 'the members of the standing [committee] held responsibility and authority and due deference was to be paid to any proper action taken by them to ensure the smooth running of the club'.[73] The billiard room was evidently a hotbed of trouble, for it was from the window of that room that one young man decided to throw fireworks out on to the busy Barking Road below. This resulted in the police visiting the club and one of the committee members setting up an investigation to track down the offender. The committee originally resolved to have the firework thrower 'suitably spoken to' at the police station[74] but recanted when they realised that it would result in him being charged and summoned to appear at the juvenile court. They opted for ticking him off themselves instead.[75]

There is no doubt that membership of the standing committee was a responsibility to be taken on only by those who were dedicated to the club and prepared to police their friends and neighbours. The boys' attitude to occasional non-attendance was perhaps more draconian than that of adult club leaders. Certainly, adult club leaders had to make friends with the boys and gain their respect,[76] especially when they came from a very different background. Although it was the responsibility of the adult club leader to ensure that membership subscriptions were regularly paid,[77] being too firm risked losing members. The relationship between club member and club leader was in no way the same as that between club member and club member: age, experience and background meant that, no matter how successful the club leader in engaging the young people, he or she was always and by definition an outsider.

Clubs, fellowship and the Second World War

Although relations could be strained from time to time, the boys' club often occupied a special place in the affections of its members. This was most clearly seen during the Second World War, when young men regularly wrote home to their club leaders with news of what was happening in their lives and to catch up with events at home. Basil Henriques received many letters from his former club boys, in both the First and Second World Wars, and published selections as *Fratres: Club Boys in Uniform* in 1951.[78] Likewise, William 'Bill' Harris of Fairbairn House painstakingly pasted letters from old club boys into a scrapbook, and kept up correspondence with all who wrote to him.[79] Oxford House had an 'Unseen Club', a database of over 500 former club members stationed around the world who kept in touch with settlement and club activities through a monthly newsletter as well as writing to the settlement with their news.[80]

A common feature of many of the letters was the feeling that the experience of being in a boys' club in their youth had helped to prepare them for the trials of war:

> It's surprising how, in time of danger, various thoughts flash through your mind, and the thought of letting down the Club and your people at home, and setting an example to your men, gives you courage and strength to see the job through.[81]
>
> Whenever I feel down and fed up, I just look back to the spirit of the Club I left behind me, and something inside me starts ticking.[82]
>
> I have been telling the fellows here so much about Fairbairn that they have nicknamed me 'Fairbairn'.[83]
>
> I still have my badge and I am never without it. Even now, as I write, I have it here in front of me, and it seems to say, 'Don't worry, I am here, I am Fratres.'[84]
>
> I think you deserve a lot of gratitude from me and will do my best to return a lot by giving Jerry a rough time.[85]
>
> The spirit of the Club has made each of us, I am sure, give that little extra bit over the next man. All those little extra bits add up to something, and the final amount is but part of the Club's total effort.[86]
>
> Above the noise of exploding shells, crashing bombs, and the whizzing of bullets, I hear the rumble of Commercial Road traffic calling me back to my brothers and sisters in Berner Street.[87]
>
> Sorry to hear that the Lambourne Camp has been bashed about. I will have to get my shovel out after the war and build it up like we did the shelter. I will close now and jump into the old hammock, crash my head down and start to dream of all the good times, past and future, which there will be when we are all home.[88]

'Club spirit' gave the young men something to believe in, and helped them to see their hardships as part of a bigger picture of sacrifice and preparation. Club fellowship could also be a reality in times of need, as one ex-Bernhard Baron boy posted in the Middle East found out after hearing that his wife had been killed by 'enemy action'. A fellow club member joined his unit the same week:

> It is more than 'just some help' to know how you all feel about it back in the Club. Never before have I needed the Club so much as I need it

now. The bond of brotherhood has proved itself a thousandfold. J.C. has been posted to this camp. I have spent every available minute with him. Believe me, I needed someone like him at this particular time. It was a blessing from above.[89]

The crises also gave members the opportunity to reflect upon what the clubs had offered them as boys and young men:

It was only after I had left school that I began to think and understand the physical, mental and moral aspects of life. Millions of youths, because of lack of opportunities, have retrogressed. The Club definitely transformed my life to such an extent that words cannot express my gratitude.
   Over the impressionable ages of boyhood and youth, the Club convoyed me safely through the temptations that breed on the street corners of slums, where youth is like a high-speed ship without a rudder.[90]

The former youth club members believed that the experience of the clubs had changed their lives. Some saw the experience as putting them on the right path, or as providing opportunities they might not otherwise have experienced. But, for many, clubs provided opportunities to make new friends and to further develop their sense of identity and self. The club badge was a powerful metonymy of this sense of brotherhood. It could be a little something to look at and reflect upon when a long way away from home and in mortal danger. It appeared to signify something moral and good in a time of peril, as the testimony of this former member and shows:

I do not know whether you remember me. Some seventeen years ago I handed back my Club badge. I did not consider that I had the right to ask for it back again until November 1941. I then wrote to you from Ceylon and asked for it. A few weeks later I went into action at Malaya and was subsequently taken prisoner when Singapore fell. Three days ago I was liberated by the American Air Force, and I now make the same request to you that I made four years ago. Will you accept me as a member of the Oxford St George Club once again?[91]

Writing back to the club also gave the young men a sense of stability in a world which was both boring and dangerous. Bill Harris wrote regularly to ex-Fairbairners in the services, sending them socks and a copy of the local newspaper, the *Stratford Express*. The club boys wrote back to him with their thanks and to give him news of their lives:

Am glad to get the weekly copy of *Stratford Express* with the local news and note with pleasure that the athletics section is still doing its best to function. You will be interested to know that I was recommended for appointment to a commission as a physical fitness officer – to promote, encourage and stimulate sport and recreational games in the RAF. My social service with F[airbairn] H[ouse] was a good recommendation, also but unfortunately – or fortunately – my 'lazy' eye failed to reach the standard required for a non-flying commission.[92]

Others appeared to remain engaged with the club and its doings as a means of passing the time:

> I am having a lovely time down here it is just like being on my holidays down camp. The worst of it is through that I am with a class of about fifty Scotchmen and every time I play football with them it ends up in a free fight. I would be very much obliged if you could send me down the *Stratford Express* every week so that I could keep in touch with the club news. I hope all the boys enjoy their holidays down camp August week for I know they was looking forward to it.[93]

It was not only ex-club members who looked back fondly upon their early experience in the clubs who were attracted to the club model. Prisoners of war in Oflag 79 decided to work towards setting up and supporting boys' clubs, producing a booklet which was sent to and reproduced by the National Association of Boys' Clubs. They also raised £13,000 between themselves for this club project. They believed that the best way to 'build a better Society where freedom could be real and creative' was through a boys' club, 'promoting the fitness and character of boys especially those handicapped by environment'.[94] Like the old 'boys' who wrote back to their club leaders, the prisoners of war shared a common interest in developing 'moral fibre' among boys and young men. To these men, stationed around the world or waiting in prison camps, training young men through clubs was a very real, very positive way of ameliorating the world of the future.

However, the club was not always a force for good in the local community. It was possible for club leader and other roles of responsibility to be exploited by child abusers. Seth Koven has pointed to the ways in which some of the Victorian settlers, notably C. R. Ashbee, used work with boys' clubs as a means of exploring their sexuality and gaining access to 'rough lads'.[95] Although such abusive or exploitative relationships were rare, they were none the less destructive. Mansfield House never truly recovered from its warden, Ian Horobin, being charged with the indecent assault of boys under the age of sixteen in 1962.[96] At Horobin's trial it emerged that he had indecently assaulted a number of young boys during his wardenship of the settlement. Horobin's activities had gone unreported until September 1961, when a young man with whom he had committed some of the offences began talking about them around the settlement whilst Horobin was on holiday. On his return Horobin was confronted by the deputy warden and secretary of the settlement, and immediately resigned. For those who had known Horobin as warden, their admiration of his work at the settlement and as an MP, and his courage as a prisoner of war of the Japanese in the Second World War, was thrown into horrific relief by the facts that emerged. Sentencing Horobin to four years in prison, Justice Mocatta pointed to his previously exemplary reputation but added that 'a man in your position owes a duty to others to set an example, and however unfortunate your own make-up may be it cannot be allowed to be said that these Courts are prepared to allow this sort of conduct with boys to be carried on by people of education, position and responsibility'.[97] Following his release, Horobin left Britain to live in Tangier, where he died in 1976.[98]

Although the Horobins of clubland were rare – or at least undetected – they constituted the underbelly of the club movement. For all that Henriques and others emphasised the need to act as sympathetic role models for their young charges, they essentially left space for others to abuse and exploit that relationship and trust. Horobin claimed to have had many of what he called 'sweethearts' over the forty years he was at Mansfield House,[99] but we know little of his actual impact upon those boys and young men, apart from the recollections of Terence Stamp, a former Mansfield House club boy. In his memoir, *Stamp Album*, Stamp recalled his enjoyment of life at Fairbairn House, from the anticipation of waiting for the doors to open to enjoy the comfortable surroundings of the clubhouse to the joys of discovering the theatre.[100] However, shortly before Stamp stopped going to the settlement, he was sexually assaulted by Horobin.[101] For Stamp, as doubtless for other boys, the club was a place to go to learn how to box or to spend time with your friends or to make new ones. Horobin was a character to be feared on account of his ferocious temper, as well as a figure of fun to the boys who made jokes about his sexuality.[102] In some cases, as Stamp discovered, his attentions could be unwanted and abusive.

Post-war experiments: generation and location

The post-war period was a challenging one for settlement youth clubs. Whilst membership of youth organisations remained high, supported by the growth of the National Youth Service and the Albemarle report of 1960, the National Association of Boys' Clubs came under pressure to encourage its members to reform. The NABC was loath to mix its clubs, whilst the clubs affiliated to the National Association of Girls and Mixed Clubs saw a growth in numbers. It was accused

of being hidebound by tradition in insisting on retaining such homosocial space for its members, and the views of the NABC leaders
likewise came to be seen as hideously outdated by the 1960s. Marcus
Collins has explored this issue in the context of the changing relationship
between the sexes in the 1950s and 1960s, pointing out the increasingly outmoded nature of the homosocial boys' club in the ever more
mixed mid to late twentieth century.[103] Yet it is apparent that boys'
clubs retained an important place in youth leisure into the 1970s and
beyond, especially where they had a reputation for sporting prowess.
For example, the Port of London Authority Boxing Championships
of 1977 attracted amateur contenders from such settlement clubs as
Fairbairn House and clubs of a similar vintage such as the Repton and
Arbour clubs.[104] The question is perhaps not why did some boys' clubs
insist on resisting the tide of change, but rather what was attractive
about boys' clubs to young men? Certainly some boys wished to access
sports facilities, and boys' clubs remained a convenient and affordable
means of doing so. Clubs continued at settlements throughout the 1960s
and 1970s, although many became mixed 'youth clubs' offering social
fare such as discos and outings. It was also true that many clubs became
a focal point for particular youth subcultures, associated with particular groups and sectional interests, as will be seen in the following
discussion of the Hoxton Café.

The issue was also generational and local. For example, the Bernhard
Baron Settlement clubs were always strongly associated with Basil
Henriques and his wife, Rose Loewe. When Henriques retired from
the settlement in 1947[105] it became harder for the clubs to continue
as per the model he had established. But Bernhard Baron was able
to establish itself as a hub for Jewish youth by the 1960s. The
Association of Jewish Youth was operational at the settlement by
1966, when it occupied itself with forging links between other East
End Jewish clubs – notably the Brady Clubs – and those outside
London.[106] However, by the early 1970s, Bernhard Baron Settlement
was experiencing intense problems. It was required to function as a
Jewish charity, but this was increasingly difficult as the Jewish
community gradually moved out of the East End into the suburbs
of north and east London.[107] The trustees were unwilling to keep the
settlement running beyond 1973 if they could not offer it to the
community as a whole, rather than to one particular group.[108]

There was also concern about white working-class youth, especially
in areas like Hoxton. Hoxton was seen as a deprived and underprivileged neighbourhood on the fringes of the East End that had a
reputation for high levels of crime.[109] Various philanthropic activities

had established themselves in the area at various times, such as Hoxton Hall, run by the Bedford Institute,[110] and the women's settlement set up by Hannah Morten.[111] It attracted settlement attention again in the early 1960s, when Toynbee Hall and other parties became involved in the Hoxton Café project, an experiment in meeting the needs of working-class youth.[112] It and its sister project, the Hoxton Club project, were an attempt to combat the problems of isolation that young people in the Hoxton area were believed to experience. As an experiment in detached youth work it was to function as a café rather than as a traditional 'club', to attract those young people who would not normally be welcome at such venues.[113] It was also to be a bold experiment in youth work, through deliberately employing youth workers with unorthodox approaches to work with some of the most challenging young people.[114] The project carefully selected its trustees to include individuals with a keen interest in the local area, such as borough councillors, schoolteachers, local clergy and a youth leader in an attempt to engage the community with the project.[115] The Hoxton Café project also had high-calibre supporters: Eileen Younghusband served as its president, whilst Lady Cynthia Colville, royal courtier and local juvenile court magistrate, served as a trustee.[116]

Despite this, the café failed to become a beacon of light in Hoxton as intended. It swiftly came to be seen as a 'den of thieves', a hang-out for young delinquents rather than a place for their reform and renewal.[117] It targeted the neediest young people, and not those 'natural' club leaders who might otherwise have provided the café with a less anarchic profile. The project was treated with suspicion by young people, who were unsure what to make of it. Brother Joseph, an Anglican monk attached to the project, reported that some of the youngsters thought he was a detective attached to the local police, whilst others could not cope with his being a monk. The situation changed when one boy recognised Brother Joseph from his work with inmates at Wormwood Scrubs prison, and thus he gained the trust of the young people.[118] Brother Joseph and his colleagues had their work cut out for them: the young people who attended the café acted out in various ways, often as a result of coming to the café whilst high on drugs.[119] Many of the clients found themselves in borstal or prison, and much of the café's efforts went into trying to convince these young people that there were meaningful alternatives to crime.[120] One young man reportedly told youth workers that:

> Hoxton's like a prison, you can't escape from it. There seems to be no way out, you always come back to what you know, your friends. The

only way out I've found is in the West End, but that's no good, really, it isn't like Hoxton. Mind you, I like the idea of an easy life and I've got some good friends in the West End (naming several celebrities) but in the end I always go back to Hoxton. But what can you do there? It's always the same old grind and you generally end up 'doing a job' (committing a crime) just because there's nothing else to do, and then you come up against the 'Fuzz' (police) and there you are in trouble again.[121]

The project floundered in 1968 when the youth workers challenged its aims and a general review of the project began.[122] The Hoxton Café would not reopen, although it was hailed by the Youth Service in the 1970s as one of the longest-running coffee bar outreach and community development experiments.[123] After some reflection, Dr H. M. Holden, a consultant psychiatrist at the Tavistock Clinic, and the project consultant, concluded that the major mistake of the project had been to assume that ordinary Hoxtonians wanted to be like the middle classes; there had not been enough consultation with and listening to the local community and what they wanted. Holden felt that the project workers gained far more from the project than the local community. He felt that the Hoxton Café project had singularly failed to ask its clientele what it was they wanted from these social workers. Holden concluded, 'We should perhaps ask them not only what it is they want for themselves – but also what they might be able to contribute to our future happiness – what we can learn from them.'[124]

Settlement work evolved from trying to provide leadership to a community which appeared – to the settlements at least – to lack it to providing a form of support to the community through clubs. Clubs were both a vehicle for transmitting ideas about citizenship and a means by which the community could access leisure and support services. Like many other areas of settlement life, clubs worked well when they were directly relevant to the community. They offered space to meet friends, to learn new skills and activities, and, for some, stability. Clubs and similar projects had the potential to be exploitative; and it was essential that they avoided the temptation to impose values upon a particular community, as was the case with the Hoxton Café project. Settlement activities of all varieties had to engage with and negotiate these dynamics. Although they tried hard to empower local people, they often spoke for them rather than allowing them a true voice.

Notes

1 P. Hollis, *Ladies Elect: Women in English Local Government, 1865–1914* (Oxford: Clarendon Press, 1987), esp. pp. 1–68.

2　F. Smith, 'The nation's schools', in H. Laski, W. Ivor Jennings and W. Robson (eds) *A Century of Municipal Progress, 1835–1935* (London: Allen & Unwin, 1935), p. 231.

3　S. A. Barnett, 'Charity versus outdoor poor relief', *Nineteenth Century*, November 1899, pp. 818, 826.

4　S. A. Barnett, 'University settlements', *Nineteenth Century*, December 1895, p. 1023.

5　J. Parker, *Citizenship, Work and Welfare: Searching for the Good Society* (Basingstoke: Macmillan, 1998), p. 13.

6　*Ibid.*, pp. 145–6.

7　*Ibid.*, pp. 130–9.

8　*Ibid.*, p. 13.

9　J. Rose, *The Intellectual Life of the British Working Classes* (New Haven CT: Yale University Press, 2001).

10　J. Garrard, *Democratisation in Britain: Elites, Civil Society and Reform since 1800* (Basingstoke: Palgrave, 2002), pp. 2, 283, 6.

11　T. H. Marshall, 'Citizenship and social class', in T. Bottomore and T. H. Marshall (eds) *Citizenship and Social Class* (London: Pluto, 1992), p. 16.

12　*Ibid.*, p. 53.

13　*Ibid.*, p. 18.

14　Parker, *Citizenship, Work and Welfare*, p. 146.

15　J. A. R. Pimlott, *Toynbee Hall* (London: Dent, 1935), p. 225.

16　F. Prochaska, *Christianity and Social Service in Modern Britain: The Disinherited Spirit* (Oxford: Oxford University Press, 2006).

17　B. L. Q. Henriques, *The Indiscretions of a Magistrate: Thoughts on the Work of the Juvenile Court* (London: Non-fiction Book Club, 1950), pp. 177–8.

18　M. Collins, *Modern Love: An Intimate History of Men and Women in Twentieth Century Britain* (London: Atlantic, 2003), p. 62.

19　BRC, TOY/SPE/1, *Toynbee Hall, 1884–1925: Fortieth Annual Report, 1926*, p. 16.

20　A. E. Morgan, *The Young Citizen* (Harmondsworth: Penguin, 1943), pp. 118–19.

21　S. Koven, 'Barnett, Dame Henrietta Octavia Weston (1851–1936)', in H. C. G Matthew and B. Harrison (eds) *Oxford Dictionary of National Biography* (Oxford: Oxford University Press, 2004).

22　K. Bradley, *Bringing People Together: Bede House Association, Bermondsey and Rotherhithe, 1938–2003* (London: Bede House Association, 2004), p. 18.

23　P. Jephcott, *Clubs for Girls: Notes for New Helpers at Clubs* (London: Faber & Faber, 1943), pp. 32–3.

24　Morgan, *The Young Citizen*, pp. 120–1.

25　C. Griffin, *Representations of Youth: The Study of Youth and Adolescence in Britain and America* (London: Polity Press, 1993).

26　T. Jeffs, 'Changing their ways: youth work and "underclass" theory', in R. McDonald (ed.) *Youth, the Underclass and Social Exclusion* (London: Routledge, 1997), p. 155.

27 *Ibid.*, p. 156.
28 *Ibid.*, p. 157.
29 J. Macalister Brew, *In the Service of Youth: A Practical Manual of Work among Adolescents* (London: Faber & Faber, 1943), p. 21.
30 B. Osgerby, *Youth in Britain since 1945* (Oxford: Blackwell, 1998), pp. 7–8.
31 *Ibid.*, p. 10.
32 See esp. A. Greenwood, 'Blind-alley labour', *Economic Journal*, 22 (1912).
33 D. Fowler, *The First Teenagers: The Lifestyle of Young Wage-earners in Inter-war Britain* (London: Woburn Press, 1995), p. 116.
34 S. Todd, 'Poverty and aspiration: young women's entry to employment in inter-war England', *Twentieth Century British History* 15:2 (2004).
35 A. E. Morgan, *The Needs of Youth: A Report made to the King George's Jubilee Trust Fund* (London: Oxford University Press, 1939).
36 Morgan, *The Young Citizen*.
37 Brew, *In the Service of Youth*, pp. 22–5.
38 Osgerby, *Youth in Britain since 1945*, pp. 11–12.
39 Morgan, *The Young Citizen*, pp. 83–4.
40 Brew, *In the Service of Youth*.
41 Jephcott, *Clubs for Girls*; Pearl Jephcott, *Rising Twenty: Notes on Some Ordinary Girls* (London: Faber & Faber, 1943).
42 Morgan, *The Young Citizen*, p. 119.
43 Jephcott, *Clubs for Girls*, p. 28.
44 British Association of Residential Settlements, *Residential Settlements: A Survey* (London: British Association of Residential Settlements, 1951), pp. 11–12.
45 Morgan, *The Young Citizen*, p. 7.
46 Oxford House, *The Oxford House in Bethnal Green, 1884–1948* (London: Brakell, 1948), p. 102.
47 Morgan, *The Young Citizen*, pp. 100–36.
48 Newham Local Studies and Archives, London, Canning Town Women's Settlement (henceforth NLSA, CTWS), Committee Minutes, 2 March 1892.
49 NLSA, CTWS Executive Committee, 15 May 1918.
50 *Ibid.*, 17 October 1919.
51 *Ibid.*, 22 October 1930.
52 *Ibid.*, 23 February 1938.
53 Jephcott, *Clubs for Girls*, p. 53.
54 NLSA, CTWS Executive Committee, 27 May 1921. The General Excellence shield was awarded to the club with the greatest number of successes across the competitions.
55 *Ibid.*, 27 January 1922.
56 *Ibid.*, 22 October 1930.
57 *Ibid.*, 25 October 1934, 23 January 1935.
58 *Ibid.*, 26 June 1935.
59 T. Wales, 'Parsons [*née* Millo], Marguerite Lena [Daisy] (1890–1957)', in Matthew and Harrison, *Oxford Dictionary of National Biography*.

60 NLSA, CTWS Executive Committee, 27 October 1937.

61 *Ibid.*, 24 October, 19 December 1924.

62 Aston-Mansfield Collection, Men's and boys' club address books, 1906–10.

63 'The need for boys' clubs', *Mansfield House Magazine*, March, April 1918.

64 J. Butterworth, *Clubland* (London: Epworth Press, 1932), pp. 52–3.

65 NLSA, 27/2, Fairbairn House Standing Committee, October 1943–July 1945, Minutes, 24 January 1944.

66 NLSA, 27/1, Fairbairn House Standing Committee, 1945–46, Minutes, 7 January 1946.

67 *Ibid.*, 13 August 1945.

68 *Ibid.*, 17 September 1945.

69 *Ibid.*, 6 October 1945.

70 NLSA, 27/2, Fairbairn House Standing Committee, October 1943–July 1945, Minutes, 22 November 1943.

71 NLSA, 27/1, Fairbairn House Standing Committee, 1945–46, Minutes, 6 October 1945.

72 NLSA, 27/2, Fairbairn House Standing Committee, October 1943–July 1945, Minutes, 6 December 1943.

73 *Ibid.*, October 1943–July 1945, Minutes, 13 December 1943.

74 NLSA, 27/1, Fairbairn House Standing Committee, 1945–46, Minutes, 22 October 1945.

75 *Ibid.*, 1945–46, Minutes, 29 October 1945.

76 B. L. Q. Henriques, *Club Leadership* (London: Humphrey Milford, 1933), p. 59.

77 *Ibid.*, p. 27.

78 B. L. Q. Henriques, *Fratres: Club Boys in Uniform* (London: Secker & Warburg, 1951).

79 NLSA, 34/1, Wartime correspondence.

80 Oxford House, *The Oxford House in Bethnal Green, 1884–1948*, p. 100.

81 Henriques, *Fratres*, p. 107.

82 *Ibid.*

83 NLSA, 2/83, Warden's Letter, p. 2.

84 Henriques, *Fratres*, p. 107.

85 NLSA, 2/83, Warden's Letter, p. 4.

86 Henriques, *Fratres*, p. 107.

87 *Ibid.*

88 NLSA, 2/83, Warden's Letter, p. 4.

89 Henriques, *Fratres*, p. 114.

90 *Ibid.*, p. 117.

91 *Ibid.*, p. 110.

92 NLSA, 34/1, Wartime correspondence, Letter, Ray Perry to William Harris, 6 January 1940.

93 *Ibid.*, Letter, R. H. Rust to William Harris, 9 May 1941.

94 NLSA, 2/81, *Citizens of Circumstance*, insert.

95   Koven, 'From rough lads to hooligans: boy life, national culture and social reform', in A. Parker *et al.* (eds) *Nationalisms and Sexualities* (London: Routledge, 1991), *passim*.

96   'Sir Ian Horobin on indecency charges', *The Times*, Wednesday 16 May 1962, p. 9.

97   'Sir Ian Horobin sentenced to four years' imprisonment', *The Times*, Wednesday 18 July 1962, p. 9.

98   'Sir Ian Horobin', *The Times*, Thursday 8 July 1976, p. 18.

99   'Sir Ian Horobin sentenced to four years' imprisonment'.

100 T. Stamp, *Stamp Album* (London: Bloomsbury, 1987), pp. 81–5.

101 *Ibid.*, pp. 126–7.

102 *Ibid.*, p. 126.

103 Collins, *Modern Love.*

104 Port of London Authority Amateur Boxing Club, *Port of London Boxing Championships, 1977* (London: Port of London Authority Amateur Boxing Club, 1977).

105 S. McCabe, 'Henriques, Sir Basil Lucas Quixano (1890–1961)', in Matthew and Harrison, *Oxford Dictionary of National Biography.*

106 British Library of Political and Economic Science, London School of Economics (hereafter BLPES), Peter David Shore Papers, 19/10, *You* 9 (June–July 1966), p. 1.

107 *Ibid.*, 19/79, Letter to Peter Shore from Simon Benedictus, 28 September 1972.

108 *Ibid.*, 19/79, Memorandum, Bernard Baron settlement, 3 November 1972.

109 H. M. Holden, *The Hoxton Café Project: Report on Seven Years' Work* (Leicester: Youth Service Information Centre, 1972), p. 4.

110 E. St John Catchpool, *Candles in the Darkness* (London: Bannisdale, 1966), p. 16.

111 M. Vicinus, *Independent Women: Work and Community for Single Women, 1850–1920* (London: Virago, 1985), p. 222.

112 Holden, *The Hoxton Café Project*, p. 55.

113 *Ibid.*, p. 5.

114 *Ibid.*, pp. 19–20.

115 *Ibid.*, p. 9.

116 Hoxton Café, *The Hoxton Café Project, 1966: Report No. 3* (London: Hoxton Café, 1966), p. 2.

117 Holden, *The Hoxton Café Project*, p. 23.

118 Hoxton Café, *The Hoxton Café Project, 1966: Report No. 3*, p. 8.

119 *Ibid.*, pp. 9–14.

120 Hoxton Café, *Hoxton Café Project, 1967: Report No. 4* (London: Hoxton Café, 1967), pp. 9–10.

121 Holden, *The Hoxton Café Project*, p. 41.

122 *Ibid.*, p. 5.

123 *Ibid.*, p. 3.

124 *Ibid.*, p. 61.

5

The settlements, the citizen and the law

There was one distinct arena in which the settlements acted as a buffer between the state and the individual citizen: the law. There were two ways in which this manifested itself: first, through work to prevent juvenile delinquency and to help adult former prisoners re-engage with society; the second was through the provision of free legal advice and advocacy.

The restoration of citizenship

As seen previously, the 'boy labour' question was an issue that pre-occupied the settlements into the mid-twentieth century. The settlements tried to tackle the problem in two ways. The first, the boys' club, was a means of providing constructive leisure pursuits as well as training in citizenship and leadership, as seen in the previous chapter. But the settlements were also involved in the juvenile courts. Settlements such as Toynbee Hall and Bernhard Baron Settlement housed juvenile courts or offices for probation workers, and several East End settlement wardens – Basil Henriques of Bernhard Baron, J. J. Mallon of Toynbee Hall and Miriam Moses of the Brady Clubs – served as magistrates.[1]

Yet this agenda underwent considerable evolution after 1945 as the settlements' emphasis shifted from the young offender to the adult ex-offender. It was partly the result of those older settlement staffs such as Henriques and Mallon retiring, and also a response to a vacuum in the care available for those leaving prison, a result of both the extension of the welfare state and changes in the funding and the remit of the probation service. The probation service had become part of the state by the 1960s, at which point it gained responsibility for the after-care of prisoners and, by the 1970s, it was also given the responsibility for reintegrating these ex-offenders back into society through community service. Likewise, the state took more responsibility for children and young people through the 1948 and 1969 Children and Young Persons Acts, which also corresponded with expansions and

reorganisations of the social services, especially following the 1968
Seebohm report. These shifts did not push the voluntary sector out
of working with children and young people: it encouraged charities
like the settlements to work with under-considered groups as former
prisoners. Whereas their pre-1945 work had concentrated on the
prevention and reduction of juvenile delinquency, their later work
aimed to rehabilitate adult ex-offenders. This included such projects
as befriending schemes, running probation hostels, counselling prisoners' families and helping ex-prisoners to set up small businesses.
This work also refreshed ideas about the application of residential
living as a means of working with needy groups.

This section will begin by looking more closely at the evolutions of
attitudes to the 'problem' of childhood. Settlements were by no means
unique in attempting to tackle the 'boy labour problem' but were
part of a much broader discourse about childhood, parenting and
citizenship. As Harry Hendrick has shown, clubs were seen as a means
of directing the spare time and energies of young workers from the
mid-nineteenth century onwards, when they were set up by churches
and public school missions, and later by the settlement movement.[2]
This interest was fuelled in turn by increasing fears that feckless
working-class parents were allowing their children to run wild, thereby
generating gangs of hooligans terrorising towns and cities.[3] By the 1880s
fears about social degeneration stemming from childhood causes
were conflated with poverty, creating the notion that children needed
to be 'saved' from their environment.[4] Correlations were made between
need, abuse and criminality as campaigners and commentators began
to look closely and critically at the working-class family as an agent
of social 'degeneration'.[5] Thus child abuse became a social 'evil' and
a matter of concern to the nation as a whole.[6] Child abuse was the
main focus of the National Society for the Prevention of Cruelty to
Children (NSPCC), which campaigned in the 1880s for the 'Children's
Charter' of 1889, which gave the state power to intervene in matters
of child abuse. The NSPCC continued to call for extensions of the power
of the state, alongside investigating and prosecuting cases.[7] There were
various pieces of legislation passed in the course of the 1890s and early
1900s, much of which was codified in the 1908 Children Act.[8]

However, one innovation of the 1908 Act was the introduction of
the juvenile court. The first juvenile court was established by the Chicago
Women's Club and the Hull House Settlement in 1899. This court, the
Cook County Juvenile Court, was a highly influential experiment in
adapting legal procedures in order to take the impact of poverty and
bad parenting into account when dealing with the crimes of children

and young people.[9] The basic principle of the court was that children broke the law when their family or society had failed them, and if the family could not correct itself, then the state should intervene. This meant rehabilitating the child and his or her family to prevent problems in the future, rather than necessarily punishing the child. This approach had resonance for British welfare campaigners, especially the NSPCC and the Howard League for Penal Reform, who worked hard to instigate a similar scheme in the United Kingdom. The first British juvenile court was set up in Birmingham in 1905. Yet the court was part of a longer process of separating the treatment of children from that of adults under English and Welsh law, as seen by the series of Youthful Offenders Acts passed in 1854, 1857, 1861 and 1867.[10]

There have been a number of studies of the history of juvenile delinquency and its relation to youth welfare. Andrew Davies's work has explored a range of themes, from the leisure pursuits of young people and various aspects of 'gang' culture and 'hooliganism'.[11] Some of his most interesting work has focused on girl gang members in the late nineteenth-century Manchester area, which found that, although gangs were dominated by young men, young women were keen participants. Young women were condemned for their gang activities in the press, yet often received milder treatment in the courts than their male counterparts.[12] From a different perspective, Louise Jackson has looked at the ways in which women officers of the Metropolitan Police force were assigned to 'specialist' work with needy and vulnerable women, girls and younger children.[13] Harry Hendrick's work encompasses both studies of the 'boy labour' problem and the development of child welfare in the course of the nineteenth and twentieth centuries.[14] George K. Behlmer has also focused on the child welfare aspects of juvenile justice through a Foucauldian analysis of the court as a means of exercising social control over working-class families.[15] Victor Bailey explored the connections between delinquency and citizenship by focusing on juvenile justice as an important element of British social policy formation in the period 1914 to 1948. Bailey traces the evolution of policy, the interplay of reformers and policy makers and the complexity of the development of the Children and Young Persons Act of 1933.[16] Abigail Wills looked at the working-out of citizenship and ideas about healthful masculinity in reform schools in the 1950s and 1960s, finding that the reform of male juvenile delinquents was inextricably linked with a discourse on the creation of 'manly' young citizens, healthy in body as well as in mind.[17] There are parallels between the work of Davies and Pamela Cox. Cox explores the ways in which 'delinquent' girls were treated by the legal system, the state and voluntary organisations, concluding that gender had important role in shaping the ways in which girls and boys were treated. Girls committed fewer crimes than boys, but there was no substantive difference in the categories of crimes committed. But girls' crimes were heavily connected with fear of their being led astray, and this influenced the ways in which they were dealt with. Cox also found that young women were often referred to charitable bodies or state care homes instead of being taken to court, especially those with venereal disease or who were pregnant.[18] Anne Logan has explored the connections between the establishment of the juvenile courts from 1908 and the encouragement of female magistrates in those courts.[19] Logan foregrounds the importance of gender not only in the ways in which children and young people were treated, but in how this influenced the recruitment of magistrates and the development of the court in the inter-war period.[20] Before the Sex Discrimination (Removal) Act of 1919 the lay and stipendiary magistracy was open only to males. Women's rights and juvenile justice campaigners actively worked for the introduction of women magistrates as 'specialist' magistrates in the juvenile courts, as they were believed to be especially able to deal with children's cases, regardless of whether or not they were themselves married or had children.[21] Women magistrates formed part of a discourse in which the juvenile court was seen to function as a surrogate or replicated parent, and came to be accepted as fulfilling a 'motherly' role alongside the male magistrates' patriarchal role.[22]

Although the research outlined above covers the question of juvenile delinquency from a range of perspectives, there are still areas that require fuller exploration. First, we know more about the ways in which girls and young women were treated by the courts than we do about boys and young men, largely thanks to the work of Pamela Cox. What of those young men and boys? Whilst Logan's work has pointed to the particular role of female magistrates, knowledge about the sentencing patterns and rationales of magistrates of both genders remains limited.[23] Likewise, although Davies's work explores the role of gangs, his focus is upon the late nineteenth century through to the inter-war period. Did this change from the Second World War, and, if so, how? How did teams of magistrates – which had to consist of both genders – deal with offences? What were the prevalent trends in youth offending, as far as we can know from the cases that were brought to court? How did all these factors intersect with the work of the settlements and others in the voluntary sector? The first part of this chapter will explore these issues through a quantitative analysis of the Inner London Juvenile Court, which was based at Toynbee Hall from 1929 to 1954.

Toynbee Hall and the juvenile courts

By the inter-war period, boys' club work at a settlement had become an important precursor to a career in penal reform or research into juvenile delinquency, as Victor Bailey noted. Alexander Paterson, borstal reformer and member of the Prison Commission, began his career as a club leader at the Oxford and Bermondsey Settlement and wrote the influential *Across the Bridges* about his time in south London;[24] Charles E. B. Russell, inspector of industrial and reformatory schools, was a youth worker in Manchester; Sir Cyril Burt, the influential child psychologist, worked as a young man at the Liverpool University Settlement.[25]

Toynbee Hall began working with prisons in the early 1920s, as an offshoot of its extensive adult education programme. Residents from the settlement ran classes and gave lectures on a variety of topics to both adult and juvenile inmates at Wormwood Scrubs and young men at Feltham Borstal Institution in 1921.[26] Four years later, in 1925, Egerton St John Catchpool, then sub-warden at Toynbee, was inspired by a visit to Chicago, with the encouragement of his friend, Alexander Paterson, to work on a programme of classes at Pentonville prison.[27] Catchpool had visited the Hull House Settlement in Chicago the previous year, and had avidly followed the Leopold and Loeb trial. Leopold and Loeb were two brilliant teenage University of Chicago graduates convicted of murdering a relative, apparently for fun. The trial gripped the US media, prompting questions about the nature of evil and its causes. Although the two were far from being 'normal' juvenile delinquents, Catchpool was determined on his return to London to undertake preventative work with young people.[28] With Paterson, a friend from his days at the Oxford and Bermondsey Club, Catchpool organised a voluntary prison visiting scheme, classes for small groups of prisoners, a library and a series of guest lectures and concerts.[29] Catchpool went further. He visited prisoners in their cells, brought in books for them to read, talked to them about sport and tried to give them moral support as they neared release. Catchpool came to believe that 'most of them, whether consciously or unconsciously, were antisocial partly because society had denied them the benefits of a happy childhood'.[30] He felt that at least a partial remedy lay in getting young people into youth organisations, as well as using outdoor activities in the countryside to boost their confidence.[31] He continued to explore these ideas through his work with hostels for young working men and later with the Youth Hostels Association from 1929.[32]

Catchpool's interests resonated with other areas of the settlement's work. In 1925 Toynbee Hall took over the John Benn Hostel, which had previously formed part of the Dr Barnardo's complex on Stepney Causeway. It took its name from John Benn, who had been the MP for St George's in the East and Wapping, as well as a major figure on the early London County Council.[33] Benn had also been a champion of schemes to provide lodging houses for young men in the 1890s.[34] The hostel was funded by Ernest Benn Ltd, the Benn family publishing house, and the Carnegie Foundation, and it operated as a home for working boys aged fourteen to eighteen[35] into the 1940s, despite closing down on the outbreak of the Second World War like many other voluntary or Ministry of Labour hostels.[36] The hostel became home to over 100 boys, some of whom were referred there as part of care and probation orders, others by voluntary and state agencies, whilst others again came by word of mouth.[37] It was successful enough to attract the attention of Sir William Clarke Hall. Clarke Hall was a major, if controversial, figure in juvenile court reform in the early twentieth century. He studied at Oxford, before becoming a prosecutor for the NSPCC as well as the son-in-law of its founder, the Reverend Benjamin Waugh. He entered the magistracy in 1913, and became the president of the Old Street and Islington Juvenile Courts. His policy was never to send a child to an institution that he did not know of or had not visited, and he also made great efforts to keep up correspondence with the children who came through the courts, a massive endeavour.[38] Clarke Hall recruited Basil Henriques to the juvenile court magistracy,[39] and, among his many other commitments, was a member of the board of the John Benn Hostel.[40] Clarke Hall became increasingly interested in the possibility of holding a juvenile court at a settlement. At his request the Inner London Juvenile Court took up residence at Toynbee Hall in 1929, where it would remain until 1953.[41]

The Inner London Juvenile Court

The Inner London Juvenile Court originally formed part of the Metropolitan Police court system, and grew out of the Old Street Magistrates' Court. In accordance with the 1908 Children's Act, the juvenile court split away from the main or adult proceedings of the Old Street court. The 1908 Children Act made various recommendations for the running of juvenile courts, notably that they should not be held at the same time as sittings of 'adult' courts, and that they should ideally be held elsewhere. Part of the rationale for the court moving to Toynbee Hall in 1929 was to make it less intimidating to young people, a key point made in the 1908 Act but which was not always applied.[42] Juvenile courts were often held in rooms normally used by the adult courts, which had often been designed to intimidate, or on the same day that the police courts were sitting, potentially bringing children and young people into contact with adult criminals. Removing the courts to other locations was one way of circumventing these issues. In the case of Toynbee Hall, it was also to place the court closer to welfare services that families could call upon or be directed to as part of routine court and probation business. The court was housed in various rooms around the settlement until the opening of the 'New Block' in 1938. The New Block was built as part of the settlement's fiftieth anniversary celebrations, and included purpose-built classrooms, a rooftop playground and a music room which doubled up as the court.[43] As per the requirements of the 1933 Children and Young Persons Act, the court dispensed with the more formal furnishings favoured by adult courts, and used normal tables and chairs laid out in close proximity – so that children would not have to raise their voices to be heard by the magistrates and court personnel.

5 Interior view of the Inner London Juvenile Court: the magistrates' bench

6 Interior view of the Inner London Juvenile Court: the defendant's
seating area

The court sat one day a week throughout the year, with three magistrates in attendance. Three main types of event were handled – summonses, charges and remands. Summonses introduced cases to the courts, often being brought by the Metropolitan Police, but also by individuals, family members, the London County Council and private companies. It was quite common for summonses to be brought by individuals or groups who were not the Metropolitan Police, but it did not follow that such cases were 'civil'. It was common for employers to bring employees who had stolen or attempted to defraud them to court, whilst the LCC brought children to the court in order to instigate care proceedings. At the charge hearing, children and young people were able to enter a plea. Children and young people could be remanded in custody at any stage. Some were bailed on their own recognisance or by their parents and other family members, but many were sent to remand homes. Remand was used as a period in which to gather information on the child and his or her family, and in some cases to refer the individual involved for medical and psychological tests. In some care and protection cases it appears to have been used as a means of keeping children away from potentially harmful home environments for as long as possible.

Juvenile court records, where they survive, are exempt from the Freedom of Information Act 2000, which was in operation at the time of writing. The papers generated by these courts on the cases they held are closed, but juvenile court registers – listing the business of the courts – are in the public domain. From these documents it is possible to glean information about the ways in which the court functioned. Here a sample of the months of January, February and March in the years 1930, 1935, 1940, 1945 and 1950 were examined. Cases are referred to in the aggregate, or anonymised as appropriate. The registers provide insight into the average ages of children and young people brought to the courts, the severity of the offences they were accused of committing, and the relation of offences to age and gender. Ethnicity and religious affiliation are not effectively recorded in the registers. Some surnames are suggestive of a Jewish, Irish or Asian background, but are no firm indicator of the children's ethnicity and/or religion.[44] On occasion, the committing of children to particular homes or approved schools – such as the Roman Catholic St Vincent's in Dartford, or Montefiore House in Stamford Hill – may suggest the professed religion of the defendant and their family, but is still far from suitable index. But the records do provide a clear picture of the sentencing decisions of the magistrates, and the strategies used by the courts, the community and the probation officers to police children's behaviour in this period. The court registers themselves are not an indication of the extent of juvenile crime in the East End in the period, but they do help us to understand the kinds of crimes that children and young people were arrested for and the ways in which such detected crimes were handled. The snapshot approach also enables us to see the ways in which 'new' crimes were invented, the formation of new crazes, and the attitudes of the magistrates to these offences.

Temptations

Larceny (unlawful taking) and breaking and entering were by far the most common offences that boys – and occasionally girls – were charged with. Boys were keen thieves at all ages, branching out into other forms of crime only as they entered their later teenage years. Their thefts tended to be opportunistic and petty. They were also creative, quickly picking up new ideas for getting hold of desirable items. Automatic vending machines proved an enormous temptation to boys of all ages. One gang in 1930 set themselves the task of stealing 2s 11d from a machine, along with eleven 'Oh Boy!' nuggets.[45] Cigarettes were also popular for theft from these machines, although one ingenious young man used a brass disc in order to trick the machine.[46] Another group of boys in 1935 were keen to remove the chocolate from a vending machine in Old Street Underground station.[47] Stealing from these machines was still a popular activity in 1940, 1945 and 1950, but an activity that gained ground was theft from gas and electricity meters. In both cases, potentially large sums of money in small denominations were kept in these devices, often away from immediate adult surveillance. Many East End homes paid for their utilities in this manner, so meters were readily accessible. Such thefts seemed 'victimless', as one stole from an inanimate object or a public space rather than taking an object from a person's body or private domestic space. But it was also true that children and young people stole from meters for less nefarious reasons. Betty, a young woman befriended by Edith Ramsay, stole 2s 6d from a meter in the house where her mother lodged in order to be able to pay a visit to her beloved elder brother, who then lived with his wife and new baby on the outskirts of London. Betty was caught, prosecuted and sentenced to probation with a residential requirement to live at a Jewish girls' hostel.[48]

Yet boys were by no means beyond more 'traditional' forms of stealing, with several cases of shoplifting or theft from market stalls coming to the court throughout the period. But their methods altered to accommodate the opportunities around them. Motor vehicles in particular provided new means of acquiring goods that could be used by the defendants, passed on to friends and family, or sold. By the 1930s Sainsbury's the grocers had developed an innovative scheme of using lorries to deliver goods to homes in urban and suburban areas.[49] Such grocery vans, with the back doors left open whilst the driver completed the delivery, were tempting in several cases where 'jump-up jobs' were committed. One boy liberated a turkey from such a van in the week before Christmas,[50] whilst another helped himself to jars of spice.[51] Commercial and private vehicles were equally at risk. Theft from inside cars was common and opportunistic. One group of boys helped themselves to a driver's carefully assembled picnic hamper.[52] In one case, two boys stole a pair of spectacles from a car. It emerged from the minute of adjudication that one of the boys had stolen the glasses in order to correct his poor sight. Whilst the court sent him to an ophthalmological hospital in Swanley, Kent, to receive treatment, he still gained a criminal record.[53] And older means of transport still provided ample opportunities. One boy was a serial taker of ponies and carts across the East and West Ends, operating under at least two names over several months, and stealing around £50 worth of property.[54] On rare occasions children were brought before the court on counts of automobile theft. There were a small number of cases in which cars were stolen, but which were often prosecuted as larceny cases with accompanying road traffic offences.

Table 5.1 Types of theft as percentage of sample

Offence	1930	1935	1940	1945	1950
Stealing from commercial property	40.2	32.6	32.48	28.9	10.77
Breaking and entering commercial property	5.9	17.9	9.5	10	16.15
Stealing from private dwelling houses	2.9	7.1	6.37	15.5	6.92
Breaking and entering private dwelling houses	2.9	0	0.6	2.7	0

In both cases of larceny and cases of breaking and entering, the majority of cases involved theft from commercial rather than domestic property. Yet not all breaking and entering charges resulted in full prosecution, as a number were downgraded to stealing cases. Receiving stolen goods and being in possession of stolen goods or goods believed to be stolen accounted for a very small proportion of cases. As with stealing from vending machines or gas meters, the young stole desirable items from shops and warehouses, in what might be perceived to be 'victimless' crimes – taking from those who already had more than enough.

Whilst breaking and entering or stealing from dwelling houses remained a minority pursuit in the period, the number of appearances appears to have risen dramatically by the end of the Second World War. Only a small number of cases of breaking and entering homes were recorded in the sample period (three in 1935, one in 1940 and four in 1945), whilst stealing from homes grew from 2.9 per cent in 1930 to 7.1 per cent in 1935, dropping slightly to 6.37 in 1940 to a high of 15.5 per cent in 1945 before falling again to 6.92 per cent in 1950. There was also a small but nevertheless perceptible increase in stealing in other places, such as street robbery and theft from air raid shelters. These accounted for two and three cases seen in the 1940 and 1945 samples respectively, although these were not present in the 1950 sample. The war marked a subtle change in the nature of theft. The apparent decline in thefts from commercial properties was accompanied by a small rise in thefts from dwelling homes, and a change in the types of items taken. Whereas pre-war breaking and entering had resulted in the theft of such items as a silver watch and chain,[55] chocolate,[56] razors,[57] jewels[58] and several cases of relieving young men of bicycles left in yards or passages, wartime theft took on a different nature. In 1945 a gang of boys stole £20 from a house – a considerable amount for the time.[59] The theft of cash from homes was not unusual in the period, with three separate cases involving this crime.[60] Another boy stole eighteen racing pigeons from a back yard,[61] valuable in themselves but priceless to the owner whose pets they were. Savings stamps were also stolen from homes, whilst items of identification – identity cards, driving licences and the like – were also desirable items for thieves, along with wallets and handbags.[62] In one case a girl stole a handbag from a woman seeking refuge in the Bethnal Green Tube shelter.[63] Given that many people took to carrying all their documentation and valuable items with them during air raids, we can only imagine the victim's distress at potentially having lost everything – but also the increased value of papers and coupons in an economy in which rationing books and paperwork were paramount and where there was a lively black market in such items.

   This evolution from taking items that were convenient yet valuable to taking items that were valuable yet personal is a fine one. Whilst there were many consistencies in approach and method, the frequency with which more personal items were stolen within this overall trend is striking. With the limited nature of the sources, this leads to further questions. Did playing on bombed sites inadvertently encourage looting, or less identification of personal items with individuals? If families were regularly losing their precious items, did that lessen the value of other people's precious items, and increase the importance of gaining coupons and other useful items through illicit means? In terms of patterns of reporting and arrest, the change could be attributed to the police not having the same volume of young people to deal with as they did before the war as a result of the waves of evacuation; it could have been a result of greater vigilance of property through the efforts of firewatchers, bombed site rescue and safety efforts, as well as people keeping an eye on activity around the bombed-out homes of friends and neighbours. Given the shame attached to stealing from neighbours in popular memory,[64] it is possible that some people were more likely to report seeing personal items on the black market out of distaste for stealing from the dead and wounded, or because of the inconvenience it would cause another. It is also surely the case that the importance and value of these items led to people reporting their loss or theft to the police rather than writing them off or pursuing the matter informally. Nonetheless, the picture of boys and young men generally and typically engaging in the various types of theft remains consistent with the earlier court records. It is also consistent with the findings of numerous studies on the nature of crime in the East End. Dick Hobbs pointed to the market culture of the East End in which stealing from commercial bodies and selling the goods via the black market was common if not 'normal' behaviour.[65] Oral history work undertaken by Hood and Joyce found that respondents recalled that stealing from 'your own' – your neighbours or people of a similar economic background – was considered shameful, although they also noted that, given this taboo, it was less likely that their respondents would admit to such behaviour in their past.[66]

Clearly boys and some girls were willing to explore the boundaries of respectability in this area. It is difficult with the constraints of access to legal records and rigorous ethical practice as well as the willingness of oral history participants to talk comfortably about such issues to push this topic further at the present time. Although it is possible to propose that the experience of the war loosened concepts of morality and respectability – as well as presenting greater opportunities to transgress boundaries – these findings in relation to the Inner London Juvenile Court must remain speculative for now.

Care and control

The other main area in which prosecutions were brought 'against' children and young people concerned the civil remit of the court. These were divided into two types – 'beyond control' and 'in need of care and protection'. Unlike entries for other offences on the court registers, these entries usually provided the minimum information required. Boys of all ages were brought to the court by mothers who appeared to be reaching the limits of their patience with bad behaviour, whilst older girls were typically brought to the court for being out of control. This often meant in practice that they were spending time with boys. As with reports of 'bad' behaviour of young female evacuees,[67] spending time with boys was a wonderfully vague complaint, which could extend from a girl incurring the displeasure of her parents and guardians by chatting with boys to those girls who were engaging in pre-marital or promiscuous sex. But it is apparent from some of the notes on those girls brought to court on 'beyond control' charges that they were referred for medical examinations. Occasionally the minutes note that the medical examination was in respect of a pregnancy, but on the whole there is little information from which to build up a picture of girls' 'misbehaviour' as handled by the Inner London Juvenile Court. Although there were some notable exceptions. One young woman had warrants out for her arrest after escaping from an approved school. She was remanded to Holloway prison for adult women prisoners, where she managed to gain recognition for being an 'unruly' inmate – such behaviour being noted in the registers for the information of the magistrates.[68]

'In need of care and protection' encompassed a wide range of problems. The children of alcoholics were often brought to court under this category,[69] as were children found fending for themselves on the streets.[70] There were many cases in which the parents were simply described as 'not exercis[ing] proper guardianship', a loose term which could include alcoholism or drug abuse, lack of supervision and discipline, or general failure to secure the child's needs.[71] In many cases the parents or guardians were too involved in the lives of their children – several were brought to court having been found living in circumstances liable to encourage seduction or prostitution or for the similar charge of being exposed to moral danger. In 1930 two large families with very young children were prosecuted under this section of the 1908 Children Act.[72] Ten years later the children of one household were removed by the courts following an offence under the Punishment of Incest Act 1908 against a female member of the household.[73] The Children and Young Persons Act of 1933 also introduced the category of Schedule One offences against the young. In 1940 a fourteen-year-old girl was sent to the East London Maternity Hospital as part of an interim order following a Schedule One offence against her – in other words, another person had sexually or otherwise assaulted her, resulting in her pregnancy.[74] One boy was committed to a home after being found living in a house used by a prostitute for prostitution: a last resort, it would seem, after being left destitute when his mother was placed in custody.[75] Children brought to the court as 'in need of care and protection' were unlikely in most cases to go home once the case had been brought. Cases were usually remanded over a period of weeks whilst evidence was generated, buying time for the case to be built, but also to keep children away from allegedly abusive parents, guardians or home environments. The number of 'in need of care and protection' cases rose during the Second World War, mirroring the NSPCC's campaigns about mothers who left their children alone during air raids and the abuse of evacuee children.[76]

Adjudications

The overwhelming majority of cases were dealt with in the following way: from after being summoned and then charged, young people were typically remanded or bailed for at least a week. Before 1939 the standard amount for which defendants were bailed was 40s. This was a not inconsiderable sum, and in the majority of cases the defendant's parents or guardians were responsible for their good behaviour. Being bound over to keep the peace was often accompanied by a probation order, typically for a year, but less often for two years. Yet this was occasionally a rather heavy-handed sentence for relatively minor crimes. A boy who stole a bottle of milk from a doorway was bound over for 20s and given a probation order for twelve months[77] – whilst a boy who had been part of a gang which broke into a property with intent to commit a felony received the same sentence for what was a more serious crime.[78]

Probation orders were the most common outcome that young people could expect. Probation orders for twelve-month periods were the most popular, accounting for 22 per cent of all cases sampled, whilst probation orders of all durations were the outcome of a third of all cases. Probation orders came with various conditions. Young people could be required to live away from the parental home, or to avoid bad company; others were required to attend a youth club or a uniformed organisation. There was often a requirement of 'good behaviour', to avoid coming into further contact with the law. Although probation officers appeared to have heavy work loads, they were nevertheless involved in the lives of their charges. Films such as *Children on Trial* (1942) picture the probation officer as walking confidently around the slums to find Fred, her charge, and going to his home to assess its overcrowded, squalid conditions.[79] The speed with which probation officers brought young people to court for breach of the condition of their orders suggests that visits at least on a weekly basis were common.

However, the likelihood of a probation order forming the main part of a sentence was dependent upon the offence prosecuted. In cases involving larceny – stealing and breaking and entering (the latter often being downgraded to the former) – probation orders of twelve or twenty-four months were common. In 1930 36.59 per cent of cases involving theft from commercial properties were concluded with twelve-month probation orders, whilst 24.39 per cent were given twenty-four-month orders. Five years later, breaking and entering commanded a rate of 51 per cent of defendants being given twelve-month sentences whilst only 3 per cent were committed to institutions. Stealing from commercial properties likewise had a rate of 21.6 per cent for twelve-month orders, with a 5 per cent committal rate – although those who stole from dwelling houses in that year could well expect to be committed, as the committal rate was 15 per cent, compared with 30 per cent being put on probation for twelve months. The same patterns held true in 1940 (29.41 per cent received twelve-month probation orders) and 1945 (15.38 per cent for twelve-month orders for stealing from commercial properties, 46.43 per cent for stealing from homes). With the exception of 1930, in all other years around 30 per cent of all larceny defendants were dismissed under the Probation of Offenders Act or discharged under the Summary Jurisdiction Act. Dismissal under the Probation of Offenders Act 1907 usually meant that the case against the defendant was dismissed on the grounds of the trivial nature of the offence, the defendant's normally good character or extenuating circumstances. Likewise, there were similar provisions under the Summary Jurisdiction Act.[80]

Children and young people who were brought to the court on such 'civil' charges as being beyond control or in need of care and protection were the most likely to be committed of all groups. Over 50 per cent of the 'beyond control' cases in 1930 were given probation orders of twenty-four months, with 18.75 per cent of defendants being committed to institutions. 76.9 per cent of the 'care and protection' cases resulted in committals in 1930, a trend which continued throughout the intervening years. Whilst it was quite common for most cases to stretch over a number of weeks, with defendants being bailed or remanded, the 'care and protection' cases took this to a further level. It was common for cases to be repeatedly put back as evidence was gathered, the children living in homes or with court-appointed persons. In many cases, children were committed to a home until they were sixteen or seventeen years old and theoretically able to fend for themselves, but in a handful of cases older children and their parents were given supervision orders, administered in a similar way to probation orders. However, the Second World War disrupted these patterns. The number of such cases rose during the war, arguably in parallel with the disruption of family life. In 1940 44 per cent of care cases were committed to institutions, whilst an additional 16.67 per cent of the cases were referred to maternity hospitals as a condition of their committal. In these cases the circumstances in which the girls – all under fourteen – fell pregnant are largely unclear, although in one case the girl appears to have been the victim of an offence under Section 1 of the 1933 Children and Young Persons Act. Committal rates had decreased to 10.34 per cent by 1945, although 65.52 per cent of cases were on interim orders pending completion – suggesting that the war was perhaps slowing up the rate at which cases were closed, but not that practice in removing children from homes had changed.

Young offenders and the Inner London Juvenile Court

These findings demonstrate that the majority of crimes committed by youths and prosecuted by the courts were, on the whole, relatively minor, involving petty theft from commercial properties. The court statistics lend weight to the concept of the 'slide into criminality', as outlined by Jerry White in *Campbell Bunk*, the process by which young people were slowly drawn into semi-criminal behaviour through friends, acquaintances and family members. Rather than setting out to be 'bad', many young people committed crimes that were opportunistic.[81] Likewise, the overwhelming concentration of girls on the 'care' side of the equation complements many of Pamela Cox's findings on girls and young women and the ways in which they were treated by the judicial system.[82] The picture we may derive from this is one of mischievous boys 'pinching' goodies from shops and automatic vending machines, with a few very bad girls who ran riot, refusing to listen to their parents and keeping bad company. Yet this overview can only be a limited one, given the crimes that are likely to have gone undetected. That it was common for gangs of boys to indulge in criminal behaviour together would support the findings of the Carr-Saunders, Mannheim and Rhodes survey of the Inner London Juvenile Court in the late 1930s. One of the findings of this report was that juvenile crime in east London – but not elsewhere – was linked with high 'gang' membership, as well as limited access to leisure and club activities, and low rates of employment among fathers.[83] It would appear that the efforts of the settlements to provide opportunities for constructive leisure in the East End failed to reach all young people, or rather those who most needed it. Some problems – such as abusive parents – could not be solved by club attendance alone. However, the magistrates in the court in this period were keen to keep children or young persons within their community for as long as possible. The financial implications of being bound over, especially if the money was found by a family member, placed the onus of policing that agreement upon the family, if only so that the money should not be lost. Probation likewise kept young persons in their own community in many cases, but brought the young persons and their family into a close relationship with the probation officer. The probation officer attended to the holistic needs of the child and his or her family, and acted promptly when things went wrong. Although the magistrates at the court were keen to point out the problems that a bad environment could cause for a young person – Basil Henriques was especially vocal on the subject[84] – they nonetheless kept the majority of young people in their home environments and local communities. The onus on the courts was to provide a means by which the 'bad' influences could be checked.

The not so young offender

As seen earlier in this chapter, the settlements saw themselves as having an important role to play in preventing young people from falling into crime and rehabilitating those who did. Adults appeared in this discourse as 'bad' or absent parents who were either unable or unwilling to provide their children with support and discipline, or as the corrupters of the young – as abusers, pimps, gang leaders and the like. The spectre of the adult offender – the child who grew up to be beyond the reforming capacity of settlement clubs and juvenile courts – was less often seen in such discussions. Little consideration was given to these 'failures' by the settlements, although their obvious existence prompts a series of questions. Why did these individuals fail to respond to the prescriptions of Henriques and others? Was it really the case that such 'failures' were caused by young people not having access to clubs and suitable role models? Did crime in young adulthood and beyond have different causes? Or, alternatively, was it the case that some problems could not be solved by boxing, bagatelle and a probation officer?

Aside from studies and reports prepared for practitioners, the history of the probation service and after-care for prisoners has remained understudied. The origins of the probation service lay in the late eighteenth century, when a Philanthropic Society was set up in 1788 to provide training for homeless children.[85] In 1876 Frederic Rainer worked with the Church of England Temperance Society (CETS) to establish the London Police Court Mission, in an attempt to reduce crime through tackling the problem of drunkenness.[86] The London Police Court Mission grew throughout the late nineteenth century, and by 1907 there were 124 male and nineteen female missionaries.[87] Following the Probation Act of 1907, those missionaries became formally attached to the courts as probation officers. They worked with both adult and juvenile courts, having great responsibility, as we have seen in the case of the Inner London Juvenile Court, for working on the rehabilitation of young offenders. These 'probation officers' were under the control of the Home Office as well as the CETS or other voluntary body, such as the Church Army, the Salvation Army or the NSPCC. This system of dual control continued until 1936, when the probation service came fully under the control of the Home Office.[88]

Yet probation officers did not just work with those who had been given probation orders by the courts. By the 1960s their work load included: producing reports on the offenders' family or other circumstances for the courts; dealing with applications for marriage by young people under the age of eighteen whose parents did not consent to it; acting as a guardian *ad litem* in adoption cases; and assisting with divorce cases.[89] During the 1960s policy makers became increasingly interested in community-based approaches to dealing with offenders of all ages. The 1964 Longford report recommended that young people should be treated within the community, but that the juvenile court should be retained; similar recommendations were made by *Children in Trouble*, a 1968 White Paper.[90] The Criminal Justice Act of 1967 introduced greater emphasis on dealing with offenders on parole,[91] whilst the Seebohm report of 1968 recommended that probation officers should work with those over the age of seventeen, whilst local authorities would have responsibility for younger offenders.[92] There were also powerful trends towards introducing 'community service' for adult ex-offenders, which drew partly on new thinking about the causes of criminality and partly on reducing pressure on the prison system. The Wootton report, upon which much of the Criminal Justice Act of 1972 was based, recommended the use of a period of community service under the supervision of a probation order as part of a sentence. Thus 'community service' was punitive, acting as means of punishing offenders without incarcerating them. But it also drew upon ideas of rehabilitating offenders and provided a means for them to give something back to the society they had offended against.[93] By the 1970s the Home Office had clearly defined the role of probation officers as working with offenders over the age of seventeen in the community.[94] Historians of probation have generally focused on denoting the changes in policy and its welfare mix in the course of the twentieth century,[95] but not necessarily on the complex ways in which this operated on the ground.

The impetus for settlements to work with older offenders in the 1960s drew on similar impulses to Catchpool's work in the early 1920s, but this time the emphasis was on supporting former prisoners to reintegrate successfully back into society and thereby reducing recidivism rates. In 1965 Michael Sorenson, a senior prison welfare officer at Pentonville prison, was seconded to Blackfriars Settlement by his employers, the National Association of Discharged Prisoners' Aid Societies (NADPAS).[96] As with probation, prisoners' aid associations, the forerunners of NADPAS, can be traced back to the eighteenth century. In 1862 a central organising committee was established to co-ordinate activities, which was then refounded in 1918 as the Central Discharged Prisoners' Aid Society, and again as NADPAS in 1936. By the late 1950s the responsibility for the after-care of prisoners following their release lay with the various Discharged Prisoners' Aid Societies (DPAS) and NADPAS. Such schemes in London were critically overstretched, with a few NADPAS officials, a DPAS at the Royal London Hospital in Whitechapel, a Jewish and a Catholic DPAS, and a couple of other small schemes left to cover the capital.[97] NADPAS began to appoint welfare officers to prisons from 1953, and these welfare officers were concerned with preparing prisoners for life outside prison as their release date drew closer.[98] From 1959 Sorenson and colleagues began to draw upon the expertise and collaborate with external organisations such as Alcoholics Anonymous, as well as developing teams of Hungarian and Caribbean volunteers to work with prisoners from those backgrounds. An opportunity to work closely with the settlement movement came when the warden of Women's University (shortly to be renamed Blackfriars) Settlement expressed an interest in establishing an after-care scheme for newly released prisoners.[99]

The Blackfriars after-care scheme began in earnest in 1960 with financial backing from the Nuffield Foundation. By late the following year the settlement employed a full-time organiser for the scheme, Alan Markham, whose job was to manage the befriending project and the Top Floor scheme.[100] The Top Floor scheme provided short-stay accommodation for six men, whose daily routines were overseen by a housekeeper, who was 'expected generally to take a motherly interest in them' as well as having support from the Blackfriars residents.[101] As with the Grendon Prison scheme outlined later in this chapter, the Top Floor scheme was an adaptation of the settlement residence principle, allowing the men to live among supportive people as they adjusted to life outside prison.

The scheme ran in tandem with a befriending initiative. The befriending initiative involved prison welfare officers from Pentonville, Wandsworth and Holloway referring prisoners nearing release to the befriending service, which then paired up applicants with volunteer befrienders. This began some time before the prisoner's release date, in order for a stable relationship between the befriender and be-friendee to be established.[102] A large number of the volunteers were men in professional or administrative jobs who were looking for some additional voluntary work experience to add to their *curriculum vitae*[103] or to prepare them for entry to social work training courses.[104] Others again were employed as social workers, or had previously worked as such beforehand.[105] Volunteering for the scheme was not an endeavour to be entered into lightly. Prospective volunteers were sent a leaflet, 'The role of the voluntary associate', and were expected to attend a series of preparation courses before references were taken up. Suitable candidates were invited to interview with a panel of psychiatrists and psychiatric social workers, and those who were successful would then be required to sign the Official Secrets Act before entering into their first befriending contract.[106] Although there were good reasons for the training and application to process to be highly rigorous, it meant that it took a long time to build up a pool of suitable volunteers who could be called upon to work with prisoners.

In 1963 the Advisory Council on the Treatment of Offenders recommended that all after-care duties should be passed on to the probation service. Probation officers already carried a heavy work load: there was scope for voluntary organisations to assist them. Blackfriars subsequently led a bid to the Inner London Probation and After-care Service (ILPAS) which aimed to support ILPAS in this endeavour. The proposed Blackfriars scheme aimed to extend the befriending scheme to cover more of the geographical area covered by ILPAS, and included Toynbee Hall, Bishop Creighton and Christian Teamwork as partners, although Christian Teamwork left the partnership in 1966.[107] Sorenson replaced Markham in 1965 when this project commenced.[108] Sorenson inherited a list of 130 volunteers from Blackfriars, but he found that only about twenty were willing to continue their work; his tar-gets for 1966 were to recruit 100 volunteers to work from Blackfriars and a further fifty at both Toynbee Hall and Bishop Creighton. A promotion drive in early 1966 recruited a further thirty-five volunteers, who were promptly allocated to prisoners.[109] Recruitment was to be an uphill struggle for the project – not only were the pre-service demands rigorous but successful volunteers would remain in contact with prisoners for extended periods of time, taking them out of the general pool of volunteers.[110] Other problems emerged in the course of the scheme's first year – Wandsworth Welfare Department was unable to provide probation officers to support the scheme, and the volunteers at Toynbee Hall and Blackfriars were not integrating well within the general life of the settlement.[111] Sorenson and others continued the

Blackfriars scheme until 1971, when they handed the project over to NACRO.[112] Toynbee Hall withdrew its interest in the project, although it retained connections through the Business Advisory Bureau and developed its own work with the Grendon Prison outpost.

Walter Birmingham, warden of Toynbee Hall from 1964 onwards, was a keen supporter of empowering advice projects. His wife, Maisie Birmingham, wrote a novel called *You Can Help Me*, a murder mystery with a young Citizens' Advice Bureau worker as its central character,[113] which, murder aside, aimed to evoke the atmosphere of the settlement in the 1960s as a place of intended empowerment. One of the advice initiatives developed at the settlement alongside the Blackfriars scheme was the Business Advisory Bureau (BAB) from 1965 onwards. The premise of the scheme was simple. Ex-prisoners often had problems in finding paid employment after release, and so established their own businesses as a means of supporting themselves legitimately. Problems arose, however, with managing the books, taxes and cash flow, or with appropriate business planning; hence the need for BAB.[114] BAB, however, was a short-lived project. In 1967 the BAB organiser, Neville Shulman, applied for separate charitable status in order that the bureau could apply to the Home Office for assistance,[115] but financial support was not forthcoming from this source and the service was kept running on a shoestring through Shulman's offices in Wigmore Street.[116]

As the settlement's involvement with the bureau came to a close, another opportunity presented itself. John Profumo arrived at Toynbee Hall to volunteer in the fund-raising department at the end of 1963, following his scandalous exit from the House of Commons. Despite his public humiliation, Profumo retained his connections and standing among the political elite. Profumo was able to draw upon his contacts to support events and appeals, and on occasion he was offered an opportunity of further public service. In 1968 James Callaghan, then Home Secretary, invited Profumo to join the board of HM prison Grendon Underwood in Buckinghamshire.[117] Grendon was no ordinary prison. It was set up in 1962 to deal with 'abnormal and unusual types of criminals' by operating a therapeutic community or social learning model. It aimed to investigate and treat mental disorders, to explore mental morbidity among offenders, and to concentrate upon the question of dealing with psychopaths.[118] Following Profumo's acceptance of the board place, the prison psychiatric social worker approached Toynbee Hall to explore the possibility of establishing an outpost at the settlement.

The social workers attached to HMP Grendon had begun experimenting with 'outposts' in April 1967, when a weekly meeting of ex-prisoners was held at the Circle Trust in Camberwell, south London. The Circle Trust mainly catered for those former prisoners who had been institutionalised for a long period of time, and problems arose between the 'old lags' and the 'nutters', which was how the Circle Trust regulars referred to themselves and the ex-Grendoners. As a result, Margaret Miller Smith, then the psychiatric social worker at Grendon, suggested that ex-prisoners from Grendon and the psychiatric wings of Wormwood Scrubs and Holloway prisons should have their own dedicated meeting space.[119] Dr W. J. Gray, the medical superintendent and governor of Grendon, lent his support to her request to the Home Office,[120] emphasising that much of the therapeutic work the younger men needed, especially in terms of building relationships with females, simply could not be undertaken whilst they were in prison.[121] Yet when the proposal was passed around the Home Office and its branches for review the plan was not avidly seized upon. The assistant principal probation officer for Inner London reported no special difficulties with ex-Grendon prisoners, which led R. H. Beeson, a senior figure in the Probation Branch, to be sceptical of the plan.[122] As will be seen shortly, Miller Smith's project went ahead regardless with voluntary-sector support whilst she sought official recognition from the Home Office. However, even at this early stage of the project, the Home Office was unable and unwilling to support the project.[123]

The weekly 'outpost' meeting moved to Toynbee Hall in 1968,[124] and Miller Smith began to attempt to integrate the project within the life of the settlement. The outpost discussion group met in the Old People's Welfare Service day room on two weekday evenings. They repaid the favour by redecorating the room,[125] whilst in November the following year an exhibition of ex-prisoners' art was held at Toynbee.[126] Miller Smith was keen to expand the support services offered by the outpost. An opportunity to do so offered itself through the Toynbee Housing Association. The Toynbee Housing Association was founded around 1965 to provide social housing in London and the south-east. One of its earlier projects was Evershed House, a street away from the settlement. Evershed House was originally built by the Greater London Council, but the Toynbee Housing Association acquired the block and allowed it to be used for specific social housing experiments by the settlement.[127] One flat was used to enable experienced social workers, medics and others to engage with settlement living, whilst another was used as a training flat by the Special Families Centre.[128] Thus the Grendon flat was not in a typical residential setting, nor, as Miller Smith pointed out, in a typical residential area, located as it was in the 'vivid and anonymous environs of Petticoat Lane'. The flat was able to establish itself without protest from neighbours and the ex-prisoners were not a conspicuous presence in the community.[129]

The Grendon flat was not funded by the state: rather the men paid £3 10s a week for their rent and bills, whilst the Gulbenkian Foundation underwrote the rent on those occasions when the men were unable to pay or if the flat was not fully occupied. The organiser, Margaret Miller Smith, commented that, for many of the men, their immediate priorities were establishing themselves in their new lives, but some of the longer-staying residents were happy to get involved with the Special Families Centre club which met in another part of Evershed House.[130] The Evershed House flat remained in use until around 1973, when the Home Office proposed to take over the running of the flat from the Gulbenkian Foundation.[131] It is not clear why the Evershed House flat or indeed the Grendon outpost closed in the course of 1973–74: it appears to have been a combination of rising rents and the cessation of funds from the Gulbenkian along with the refusal of the Treasury to allow the Home Office to support it financially.[132] What this project highlighted was the potential for the voluntary sector to work in innovative ways, but how the work was ultimately vulnerable through being dependent upon short-lived funding streams. The St Leonard's Housing Association, founded in 1963, moved to Toynbee Hall in 1967, providing affordable housing to former prisoners and their families.[133] St Leonard's was a separate charity which rented accommodation at the settlement until 1974, when it too moved on. Although the outpost and the Blackfriars scheme could not be sustained at Toynbee Hall, the two activities were part of a period in which the settlement refocused its attention on the need to rehabilitate adult offenders back into society and to support them as they negotiated their way through critical times.

The final manifestation of work with adult ex-offenders was the bail/after-care hostel run by NACRO and Lady Margaret Hall Settlement (LMHS) from 1972. LMHS approached NACRO to investigate the possibility of the settlement adapting its residential accommodation in order to provide a bail hostel for eight women, staff and social work support, along with after-care support for a further seven people going through training or further education. The centre would 'ensure that accused persons, by not being unnecessarily remanded in custody, may be able to take advantage of the opportunities the community has to offer in the remaking of their lives'.[134] The project was a means of fulfilling the Community Service by Offenders Act, which came into force on 1 January 1973.[135] This in turn drew upon the recommendations of the Wootton report of 1970, which advised that community service was particularly suitable for what the Inner London Probation and After-care Service described as 'the isolated and withdrawn individual, the under-achieving and purposeless, those who act out and the socially disadvantaged'.[136]

The LMHS/NACRO bail and after-care hostel received its funding, and welcomed its first tenants – women on bail in one part of the building, and young offenders in another. But the project collapsed in 1975 through a combination of legal problems, local resistance and the loss of rents. Despite the value attached to the hostel by the Inner London Education Authority and Lambeth Social Services, the debts run up by the project were sufficient to cripple the settlement as a whole. On 1 April 1975 the settlement owed £3,059, with a further £8,125 in liabilities, including a disputed account with NACRO for £1,889. With the threat of the Inland Revenue and the London Electricity Board suing the settlement for debts in the region of £2,500, the trustees voted to put the settlement into liquidation.[137] The settlement rallied in the course of 1975, but the financial problems with NACRO led to the termination of the project.[138]

None of the settlements was able to develop sustainable projects with ex-offenders. In all cases the settlements were responding to changes in the law relating to ex-offenders, and they exploited related funding opportunities. However, the funding streams were precarious: project funding could be granted by bodies such as the Gulbenkian Foundation or the Nuffield Foundation, with a view to the state taking on the work once it had been established. Although the projects could be innovative and successful, the state did not commit to taking on the responsibility for funding the work in the longer term. The Blackfriars scheme aimed to provide voluntary-sector support to the Inner London Probation Service, by pairing up volunteers with prisoners. The Grendon Prison outpost had similar impulses, whilst the LMHS bail hostel aimed to integrate offenders into the community through undertaking voluntary social work. The projects were based on the premise that engagement with the community could reintegrate ex-offenders back into society. Some aspects of this were more immediately practical, as in the case of the Business Advisory Bureau, or somewhat more esoteric, such as painting the walls of a day centre for older people. The projects all considered the need for the community – defined as the settlement – to reach out to those at risk of exclusion, and to re-engage them with the community. These were the same principles applied in the inter-war period to young people and their use of clubs – the discourse of citizenship, of participation, of renewal through collective effort.

Legal advice and advocacy: 'From a charity to a social service'?[139]

In their sociological studies of the legal profession in the late 1960s Brian Abel-Smith and Robert Stevens made an important observation about the Legal Aid and Advice Act of 1949. Whilst the Labour governments had initiated nationalisation programmes in health, education, the social services and social security, legal advice remained in and controlled by the 'private' sector. There were valid reasons for this: it was felt that the law should remain independent of the government, and furthermore the legal system had sufficient influence in the House of Lords to protect its needs and interests.[140] Yet access to legal advice, both before and after the advent of the welfare state, was an important right for British citizens. As will be seen, being able to access legal advice and support was a powerful means of alleviating some of the acute pressures of poverty – as well as a means of checking the abuses or mistakes of the welfare state.

Access to good, affordable legal advice and aid was extremely limited throughout the twentieth century, with the exception of the period immediately after the 1949 Legal Aid Act. The Act extended legal aid to 80 per cent of the population in 1950,[141] but by the end of the decade, inflation and the narrow limits of the scheme meant that only the very poorest could access civil legal aid by 1959.[142] However, all British citizens were and are required to follow the requirements of the various British legal systems. Despite the fact that their compliance was required, it was difficult for the majority of people to access a means of interpreting the law or guidance on how it applied to them. On the jurisprudential and ethical levels, this was a gross inequality that effectively meant that Britons were not equal under the law, and technically, that Britain's claim to be a democracy was somewhat premature. But for the ordinary working person this was not a philosophical matter: it had very real repercussions for those seeking to leave an unhappy marriage, obtain redress from an errant landlord, get assistance with hire-purchase problems, resolve an employment dispute or write a will.

As with probation, the history of civil legal aid and advice is largely under-researched, although there are a plethora of guides for lawyers, magistrates, Citizens' Advice Bureau staff, social workers and the general public reflecting the changes of legal provision in the course of the post-war period. As Richard I. Morgan points out, the historical development of legal aid is often treated as a preamble covering what went before in many studies and guides to the law.[143] Yet there are some exceptions. As mentioned at the beginning of this section, Abel-Smith and Stevens's books on the English and Welsh legal systems of the 1960s were rigorous accounts of the historical development of legal aid and advice both as a manifestation in themselves and as part of the welfare state.[144] Robert Egerton's 1940s works on legal aid for the poor contained limited, if useful, guides to the evolution of the system of Poor Procedures and the Poor Man's Lawyer before the 1949 Act.[145] A further useful account is Alan Paterson's 1971 study of civil legal aid as a form of social service, with a particular emphasis on the role of the state in the Second World War and the evolution of legal aid from 1949.[146] Finally, Morgan has traced the pressures for and against the reform of access to legal advice from 1914 to 1949, and is one of the best sources for understanding the interaction between the highly conservative attitudes of the majority of the legal profession and the radical fringes involved with legal aid for the poor.[147] Accounts of the development of the Poor Man's Lawyer are likewise limited: Diana Leat's 1975 article erroneously attributes the foundation of the movement to Toynbee Hall, whilst she locates the phenomenon within the heritage of the Charity Organisation Society and the Barnettian view of settlements.[148] Other historical accounts include Paterson[149] and a 1940 survey of the Poor Man's Lawyer scheme undertaken by Cambridge House.[150] Accounts of the Citizens' Advice Bureau are equally thin on the ground, although Jean Richard's 1989 study of the CAB is a useful guide to its development during the Second World War and beyond.[151] The under-researching of legal aid means that its impact is often overlooked, despite its important role. Whereas the other works in the field have looked at the institutional development of legal aid, this chapter will look at a legal advice centre in action, and how its business was shaped by larger structures: especially how the changes in the administration of an expanding welfare state caused increased problems for the most vulnerable.

From the thirteenth century to the early twentieth, poorer Britons had highly limited access to civil law through the *in forma pauperis* procedure. Regulations passed in 1883 stipulated that claimants should be worth less than £25 and that applications were to be supported by a barrister and a solicitor's affidavit verifying their means. But as this required both the barrister and the solicitor to act for free, the procedure was rarely carried out.[152] As Paterson notes, widened access to divorce in the course of the late nineteenth and early twentieth centuries had a decisive impact upon the Poor Persons' procedures: they needed to be opened up to greater numbers of people in order that couples should be able to access their legal right to divorce.[153] In 1914 the role of Prescribed Officer was introduced into the High Court to administer the

Poor Persons' Department, in turn overseen by the Lord Chancellor's Office. Prescribed officers were responsible for assessing the viability of cases and the means of the litigant before passing them on to an approved lawyer.[154] As Morgan outlines, this was still an imperfect system in the eyes of the legal profession, especially after a boom in matrimonial cases and a shortage of solicitors during the First World War.[155] There were several committees commissioned in the 1920s and 1930s to investigate the potential reform of the civil legal aid system: the two Lawrence reports of 1919 and the Finlay Committee report of 1928. The Lawrence reports recommended the retention of the voluntary principle of the Poor Persons' scheme, but that this might be shared more equally among the profession:[156] lawyers were likely to find them-selves out of pocket after taking on a Poor Persons' case, and as divorce cases had to be heard in London solicitors in the capital took on most of this work.[157] The Finlay report was concerned with the extension of the Poor Persons' procedure to the county court. The county court predominantly heard debt cases, and therefore was the other main civil court where working-class people could find themselves.[158] However, despite an increased work load caused by a further reform of the divorce laws – the 1937 Matrimonial Causes Act – little alteration was made to access to civil legal aid and advice before the Second World War. A major development was the Services Divorce Scheme. This was set up in 1942 by the War Office and the Law Society in order to keep up morale among the Forces by making it easier for them to access legal advice on matrimonial matters: a Poor Persons' Civilian Depar-tment was also established.[159] Both these initiatives were dismantled with the end of the war,[160] although the Rushcliffe Committee was appointed in 1944 to explore the possibility of a new, post-war scheme to improve access to legal advice for the poor.[161] The Haldane Society, a group of socialist lawyers which included many involved in the Poor Man's Lawyer scheme, pressed for improvements in the accessibility of legal aid, calling in 1942 for legal aid to be run by the government.[162] Following much negotiation and deliberation, the findings of the Rushcliffe Committee finally formed the basis of the 1949 Legal Aid and Advice Act.

It would be incorrect to see the development of civil legal aid to 1949 as a Whiggish narrative of unbridled progress. As Morgan ably demonstrates, the legal profession mounted stiff opposition to reforms which would lead to their members losing income and professional status, yet they favoured the retention of a voluntary element as a means for young solicitors and barristers to gain further experience.[163] And there were other bodies which provided the poor with legal advice or support with legal matters. In their 1947 *Guide to Legal Aid for the Poor* Ernst Cohn and Robert Egerton recommended that individuals having problems with paying their rent, nuisance neighbours or sanitation problems should consult the Family Welfare Association (the COS as freshly rebranded) or their local Council of Social Service.[164] Matrimonial issues could also be referred to probation officers,[165] as seen earlier in this chapter. Likewise, Cohn and Egerton recommended approaching a hospital almoner for initial help in pursuing accident compensation claims, and the British Legion as a first point of call for claims regarding war wound pensions and payments.[166] The trade unions were an important and powerful resource for dealing with employment issues, often using their ability to provide such legal advice as a means of drawing in new members.[167] In the inter-war period, political parties also ran free legal advice centres.[168] Newspapers' legal advice 'problem pages' provided a major service, especially after the Second World War. The John Hilton Bureau of the *News of the World* was established in the late 1940s,[169] and within twenty years the bureau and others at the *Mirror* and the *People* were handling 300,000 enquiries a year.[170] From the mid-1960s onwards such campaigning charities as the Child Poverty Action Group, the National Council for Civil Liberties and Shelter provided advice and referrals to solicitors.[171] As mentioned earlier, the Citizens' Advice Bureau (CAB) was established by the National Council of Social Service as part of its war preparations in 1938.[172] The CAB was intended to provide rapid and accessible advice to those who had all manner of problems resulting from the impact of the war, and continued to operate after the end of the war: 430 CABs were in operation in 1948.[173]

Alternative providers of legal advice had one uniting feature: all straddled a line between legal advice as clarification of one's rights and legal advice as litigation or the pursuit of a case through the courts. This was an important aspect of the dynamic of legal advice from the 1950s onwards, as will be seen from the following discussion of the ways in which the CAB and the settlements co-operated. The CAB could not provide legal advice unless they had the support of an honorary legal adviser. One solution to this presented itself at those settlements which had a Poor Man's Lawyer (PML) scheme in existence. Cambridge House and the Mary Ward Centre combined their PML and the CAB to form Free Legal Advice Centres, which were open in the daytime as well as evenings to hear both legal and CAB enquiries.[174] A similar centre was opened at Oxford House in 1943.[175]

The first Poor Man's Lawyer scheme was set up at Mansfield House in 1891 by Frank Tillyard, who was then a young lawyer in residence.[176] The Poor Man's Lawyer had a simple premise: settlement residents with legal training gave advice free at evening clinics. It was immensely popular, and was replicated at a number of settlements, including Toynbee Hall, Cambridge House and Mary Ward in London, as well as at the Manchester University Settlement.[177] It could either draw upon the expertise of residents and former residents or provide a means for lawyers to give their time *pro bono*. It provided valuable training for lawyers at the start of their career, as well as a vital resource for the community. The Poor Man's Lawyer and other free legal advice schemes were popular, although their presence was generally limited to London and the major cities. By 1940 there were around 125 free legal advice centres in England, fifty-five of them in London.[178] Demand was high. Figures for 1938 demonstrate that the Poor Man's Lawyers Associations in Birmingham saw 4,328 cases whilst Manchester saw 4,238; Cambridge House Settlement in London saw over 3,000,[179] whilst Toynbee Hall saw about 1,600.[180]

The view of those involved in free legal advice schemes and the Haldane Society by 1940 was that citizens needed to be informed of their rights and the legal and advice professions should act as a buffer between the state and the individual; or at least as a translator:

> It may be that the modern State-aided system of education has made poor persons more sensitive in the matter of their legal rights, or more readily disposed to assert them, than they were then . . . These facilities in the form of the Poor Persons Procedure and the Poor Man's Lawyer, are now so much a part of the social welfare system of this country, that they are, in the present condition of society, indispensable. Indeed, so much of the ordinary work that voluntary social workers used to do has been shouldered, or taken over, by the State, that it is frequently said that the Poor Man's Lawyer is the most valuable part of social welfare work to-day.[181]

It was a view expressed in popular legal publications, such as Derek Hene's guides to legal aid published in the *Daily Express* Legal Guides in the 1950s:

> The laws of a nation exist for the benefit of the people, the same laws for all, men or women, old or young, rich or poor. Therefore everyone is entitled to justice, and none should lack the help of a lawyer just because he cannot afford to pay for the lawyer's services.[182]

Hene's rhetoric of legal advice as an integral part of the rights of the citizen had echoes in his advice to those navigating the early welfare state:

> The citizens are the State. The machinery of the modern State is an intricate mechanism, involving much administrative organisation. It is YOUR

money which keeps this machinery working, and it is kept working so that you and your fellow citizens can live at a reasonable standard and in adequate comfort and security.[183]

Remember, all the Services, Benefits, Grants and other amenities which are discussed in this book are yours by RIGHT. They are not charities – you have paid for them by taxes, rates, contributions, and in many other ways. You are ENTITLED to them, but more often than not you may have to prove your entitlement.[184]

In this discourse, civil legal aid and advice formed the means by which the ordinary person could defend and claim his or her rights in the welfare state. As will be seen later in this chapter, by the late 1960s advice workers and lawyers were acutely aware that the welfare state tended to assume a certain level of confidence and literacy among the public. Not all were able to understand byzantine benefit claim forms or complete them correctly. Others were intimidated in dealings with functionaries to correct mistakes. In the 1940s and 1950s the CAB, providers of free legal advice and such media lawyers as Hene had an important role to play in enabling people to take advantage of the rights and benefits open to them. Some people were not aware of the new resources available; others were still wary of taking up anything which had connotations of the Poor Law.

The free legal advice movement had a long track record of campaigning to improve legal access for those on lower incomes. They were concerned that good legal advice should be readily accessible to all who needed it: representatives of Poor Man's Lawyer programmes advised on the Finlay Committee on Legal Aid for the Poor of 1929 as well as the Poor Prisoners' Defence Act of 1930. Although it was one of the smaller legal advice centres, the Toynbee Hall Poor Man's Lawyer scheme and their associates were connected with a number of inter-war legal innovations. On the criminal law side, R. H. Turton, a former Toynbee Hall resident, was among those MPs who enabled the passing of the Poor Prisoners' Defence Act of 1930.[185] This Act was a significant revision of the 1903 Poor Prisoners' Defence Act, which introduced provision for magistrates to arrange for the legal fees of defendants to be paid from local funds on the proviso that they disclosed their defence at an early stage in the legal proceedings. The 1930 Act removed this proviso and gave magistrates extended powers to grant aid to those on low incomes.[186] Turton was also involved with the development of the Summary Jurisdiction (Appeals) Act of 1933, which enabled people on low incomes to have legal aid to appeal to Quarter Sessions against decisions taken in magistrates' courts.[187]

One of the most significant pieces of work in civil law was the passing of the 1937 Hire Purchase Act, which was drafted by a Toynbee Hall solicitor and Haldane Society member E. S. Watkins.[188] The Act regulated the terms under which hire-purchase agreements could be made, and specifically aimed to prevent retailers and others from changing the terms of those agreements with little notice or negotiation with the purchaser. Many people on lower incomes subsequently had immense difficulties in meeting the new payment schemes or, when required, in repaying the full amount. The Act had its origins in the early 1930s, when there was growing awareness of an increase in cases coming to Poor Man's Lawyers sessions regarding problems with hire-purchase. At Toynbee Hall, Mallon and Watkins undertook research into the impact of coupon trading, which they later presented to the Board of Trade committee, whilst in 1932 the British Association of Residential Settlements (BARS) held a conference on the problems of hire-purchase.[189] Ellen Wilkinson, the Labour MP for Jarrow, was alerted to the problem of hire-purchase by a Middlesbrough solicitor who described to her some of the problems faced by poorer families, who used the scheme as a means of buying goods and clothes without fully understanding or being given an explanation of the contracts they were entering into.[190] Mallon and Wilkinson knew each other from the former's work on the establishment of the trades boards before the First World War, and the pair joined forces to pursue the hire-purchase matter through a new Act. Watkins drafted the Bill, and Wilkinson steered it through Parliament with the support of both sides of each House.[191]

The Toynbee Hall Poor Man's Lawyer was joined by a Citizens' Advice Bureau at the start of the war, although, with the intense pressure on space at the settlement after the war, the CAB moved on. By the end of the 1950s the Poor Man's Lawyer had rebranded itself as the Toynbee Hall Legal Advice Centre, but otherwise its aims and general work remained the same. Cases dealt with by the centre in the later 1950s and 1960s were assiduously recorded by the honorary organiser, James Dow, providing important data for understanding the evolution of the service from the 1950s to the 1970s. Dow retired from several years' service to the Centre in 1963 in order to take up duties as a juvenile court magistrate, around the same time that a branch of the CAB returned to Toynbee Hall.[192] The CAB had employed a mixture of salaried and voluntary workers from its creation in 1939: the local authority paid for the full-time case worker, with additional funds provided by philanthropists and the Ministry of Health.[193]

The two most common causes for enquiry at the legal advice centre from Dow's statistics of the late 1950s and early 1960s through to 1979 remained constant: at any one time, around 50 per cent of enquiries concerned either personal/family matters or housing. These were the main issues identified in the 1940 survey of settlement legal advice centres[194] and, further back again, the principal concerns of the Poor Man's Lawyers of the 1890s. Personal and family matters generally involved such work as helping people to prepare a will, although there could also be matters of contention between parties to deal with. Housing issues often involved repairs, tenancy agreements and the like, although overlap between the two areas was common. Other issues dealt with included employment matters, common assault and nuisance, with a small number of criminal cases. The organiser noted in 1963 that, following the reopening of the CAB, new cases coming to the legal advice centre increased as a result of referrals.[195] This trend continued in the course of the 1960s. The CAB – which was open in the daytime and had longer opening hours than the legal advice centre – naturally had a larger case load (around 6,000–7,000 cases annually)[196] than the legal advice centre. As it attracted more enquiries, the number of cases being referred to the legal advice centre increased. Yet this was not in proportion to the general increase in cases taken on by the legal advice centre, as 47 per cent of its cases by 1967 came from the Toynbee CAB.[197] The other significant change which occurred was the development of a greater catchment area. Until 1962, 69 per cent cases heard by the legal advice centre came from Whitechapel – the immediate neighbourhood – but by 1967 this had declined to 49 per cent. Enquirers from other areas of east London remained consistent, with a slight rise in enquirers from Hackney and Islington, in north-east London, whilst cases from 'other areas' rose from 11 per cent to 20 per cent.[198] Although the centre had always attracted people from outside the local area, as those who had left the area returned to use a service they knew or others were alerted to it by word of mouth, this was a significant change. Both the CAB and the centre found themselves under increasing pressure to meet a growing demand for legal advice and support, as other CABs in east London referred their clients to the legal centre for detailed advice.

Demand continued to grow. Changes in legislation – reforms of the divorce, housing and employment laws – successively increased the number of people seeking advice from the CAB and the legal advice centre.[199] This increase involved greater specialisation both in the types of and medium of delivery of advice. A business advisory bureau had been set up to help former prisoners at Toynbee in 1965; a similar but more extensive scheme for the whole community – the Money Advice Centre – was started by the settlement and Barclay's

Bank in 1974.[200] But there was also an increase from 1965 onward in the number of people seeking assistance with what were described as matters of 'civil and national information' or 'social security'. These cases often involved individuals' failure to complete social security forms correctly, with the result that they received the wrong benefit or support or were chased to repay money. Other cases involved those who were frightened or unable to assert themselves with Social Security clerks in order to prevent demands or proceedings that had been entered into in error.[201] Both centres noted a particular need to provide advice to members of the Bengali community in Sylheti or Bengali, which was in part solved by the establishment of the Immigrants' Advice Bureau (IAB).[202] The IAB – which is discussed at greater length elsewhere in this book – was set up to concentrate upon the needs of immigrants. This partly involved the provision of advice in a language the enquirer felt comfortable with, but it also became clear that the IAB clients had a different hierarchy of needs from the standard CAB or legal advice centre clients. Although difficulties with housing were also regularly encountered by these clients (23.7 of cases in 1969), they also were more likely to come to the IAB seeking assistance with social security queries (16.8 per cent), communications and travel (11.8 per cent) and employment issues (11.1 per cent), with family and personal matters the least frequent category of enquiry in the later 1960s (8.7 per cent).[203] However, in the early 1970s there was a significant increase in housing and family cases, which corresponded with the maturation of the Bengali community and the establishment and entrenchment of family units. Family and personal cases accounted for 11 per cent of cases in 1971,[204] whilst there was a rise in immigration cases dealt with by 1973.[205] Both the CAB and the legal advice centre at Toynbee Hall and elsewhere found that the elderly, the mentally ill[206] and the precariously employed, such as seamen,[207] had the greatest difficulty in negotiating the welfare state – and were also the most severely hit by national events such as the three-day week and the industrial disputes of the late 1970s.[208] The mentally ill often needed a great deal of support in completing the paperwork necessary for disability and housing benefits; older people could be too 'proud' to claim benefits or poor eyesight could make form filling tricky; many workers on lower incomes found themselves out of pocket – or a job – through misunderstandings arising over contracts during the three-day week.

Part of the increase in cases was undoubtedly due to the changing availability of funds for people on lower incomes to pursue cases, but the increase in non-family matters and cases relating to the social services would suggest that in many cases the welfare state failed to provide support to its neediest members. Those who had the greatest need of benefits were often the least able to complete forms without the help of a CAB or social worker; others felt intimidated at the prospect of challenging a clerical or computing – as was increasingly the case by the 1970s – error which threatened their livelihood. The CAB, the legal advice centre, the IAB and others were reactions to an increasingly complex world which bewildered those whose literacy skills or competence in articulating themselves fell below the expectations of the social security services. The problems that the poor took to lawyers in the early twentieth century did not disappear: rather the introduction of mechanisms to protect the needy only complicated their lives.

Conclusion

Through their work first with young offenders and then with adult ex-offenders the settlements were attempting to address the social causes of crime, from the petty disappointments or frustrations of children acting out to the adult ex-offender who fell back into crime through lack of moral support or difficulty in finding employment. Their aim was to bring these individuals back into society. This was not always easy, and the settlements were not always successful. By the late 1960s the settlements and their work in rehabilitating adult ex-offenders in the community was at the cutting edge of government thinking. However, financing these projects proved difficult. Blackfriars passed its befriending scheme on to NACRO, a specialist body in the field, whilst Lady Margaret Hall Settlement came close to collapse following its association with NACRO. Toynbee Hall's work with Grendon prison failed to secure Home Office funding to continue its outpost flat. But these attempts to aid individuals negotiate society successfully should not be seen as the exclusive preserve of the 'criminal'. Legal advice and advocacy work was another important, if not essential, way in which the settlements were able to help the needy to overcome the problems that prevented them from playing a full part in society. This was especially true of those who found it difficult to negotiate their way around the welfare state. If the settlements' work with the juvenile court to 1954 was the enabling of a state service with voluntary organisation input and expertise, then their work with ex-offenders and those seeking legal advice was an attempt to help those individuals negotiate an increasingly complicated state and wider society. By the 1960s the settlements were again acting as a buffer between the state and the individual.

Notes

1   A. Briggs, 'Mallon, James Joseph (1874–1961)', S. McCabe, 'Henriques, Sir Basil Lucas Quixano (1890–1961)', and S. Kadish, 'Moses, Miriam (1884–1965)', in H. C. G. Matthew and B. Harrison (eds) *Oxford Dictionary of National Biography* (Oxford: Oxford University Press, 2004).

2   H. Hendrick, *Images of Youth: Age, Class and the Male Youth Problem, 1880–1920* (Oxford: Clarendon Press, 1990), pp. 167, 170, 173.

3   G. Behlmer, *Friends of the Family: The English Home and its Guardians* (Stanford CA: Stanford University Press, 1998), pp. 235, 239.

4   H. Hendrick, *Child Welfare: England, 1872–1989* (London: Routledge, 1994), pp. 50–4.

5   *Ibid.*, pp. 33–5.

6   L. Murdoch, *Imagined Orphans: Poor Families, Child Welfare, and Contested Citizenship in London* (New Brunswick NJ: Rutgers University Press, 2006), p. 7; M. Flegel, 'Changing faces: the NSPCC and the use of photography in the construction of cruelty to children', *Victorian Periodicals Review* 39:1 (2006), 1–2.

7   See extended discussion in Flegel, 'Changing faces'.

8   Hendrick, *Child Welfare*, p. 122.

9   G. H. McNamee, 'The origins of the Cook County Juvenile Court', in G. H. McNamee (ed.) *A Noble Social Experiment? The First 100 Years of the Cook County Juvenile Court, 1899–1999* (Chicago: Chicago Bar Association with the Children's Court Centennial Committee, 1999), pp. 16–17; E. J. Clapp, 'The Chicago Juvenile Court Movement in the 1890s' (Leicester: University of Leicester: 1995), reproduced at www.le.ac.uk/hi/teaching/papers/clapp1.html (viewed 14 May 2004), see p. 1.

10   Hendrick, *Child Welfare*, p. 27.

11   A. Davies, *Leisure, Gender and Poverty: Working-class Culture in Manchester and Salford, 1900–1939* (Buckingham: Open University Press, 1992); 'The police and the people: gambling in Salford, 1900–1939', *Historical Journal* 34:1 (1991); 'These viragoes are no less cruel than the lads': young women, gangs and violence in late Victorian Manchester and Salford', *British Journal of Criminology* 39:1 (1999).

12   Davies, ' "These viragoes are no less cruel than the lads" '.

13   L. A. Jackson, 'Care or control? The Metropolitan Women Police and child welfare, 1919–1969', *Historical Journal* 46:3 (2003).

14   Hendrick, *Images of Youth*.

15   Behlmer, *Friends of the Family*.

16   V. Bailey, *Delinquency and Citizenship: Reclaiming the Young Offender, 1914–1948* (Oxford: Clarendon Press, 1987).

17   A. Wills, 'Delinquency, masculinity and citizenship in England, 1950–1970', *Past and Present*, 187 (2005).

18   P. Cox, *Gender, Justice and Welfare: Bad Girls in Britain, 1900–1950* (Basingstoke: Palgrave, 2003).

19 A. Logan, '"A suitable person for suitable cases": the gendering of juvenile courts in England, *c.* 1910–1939', *Twentieth Century British History* 16:2 (2005).

20 *Ibid.*, p. 131.

21 *Ibid.*, pp. 132–3.

22 *Ibid.*, p. 139.

23 P. Rock, 'Rules, boundaries and the courts: some problems in the neo-Durkheimian sociology of deviance', *British Journal of Sociology* 49:4 (1998), p. 594.

24 A. Paterson, *Across the Bridges, or, Life by the South London Riverside* (London: Arnold, 1911).

25 Bailey, *Delinquency and Citizenship*, pp. 2, 10–12, 15.

26 BRC, TOY/SPE/1, *Annual Report, 1921–1922*, pp. 19–20.

27 *Ibid.*, *Report, 1962–1963*, p. 9.

28 E. St John Catchpool, *Candles in the Darkness* (London: Bannisdale, 1966), pp. 129–30.

29 *Ibid.*, p. 131.

30 *Ibid.*, p. 132.

31 *Ibid.*, p. 132.

32 *Ibid.*, pp. 133–8.

33 M. Brodie, 'Benn, Sir John Williams, First Baronet (1850–1922)', in Matthew and Harrison, *Oxford Dictionary of National Biography*.

34 A. G. Gardiner, *John Benn and the Progressive Movement* (London: Dent, 1925), p. 119.

35 Pimlott, *Toynbee Hall*, pp. 216–17.

36 'Editorial', *Probation Journal* 8:3 (1939), p. 115.

37 BRC, TOY/SPE/1, *Toynbee Hall, 1884–1925: Fortieth Annual Report, 1926*, p. 6.

38 NSPCC Archives, NSPCC London (hereafter NSPCC), 209/8, 'Sir William Clarke Hall', *The Child's Guardian* 62, November 1932.

39 B. L. Q. Henriques, *The Indiscretions of a Warden* (London: Methuen, 1937), p. 233; L. L. Loewe, *Basil Henriques: A Portrait, based on his Diaries, Letters and Speeches and collated by his Widow, Rose Henriques* (London: Routledge & Kegan Paul, 1976), p. 72.

40 NSPCC, 'Sir William Clarke Hall', p. 10.

41 Pimlott, *Toynbee Hall*, p. 245. See also K. Bradley, 'Juvenile delinquency, the juvenile courts and the settlement movement, 1908–1950: Basil Henriques and Toynbee Hall', *Twentieth Century British History* (2007), doi: 10.1093/tcbh/hwm038.

42 Bailey, *Delinquency and Citizenship*, p. 22.

43 A. Briggs and A. Macartney, *Toynbee Hall: The First Hundred Years* (London: Routledge, 1984), p. 120.

44 See C. Bressey, 'Invisible presence: the whitening of the black community in the historical imagination of British archives', *Archivaria* 61 (2006), pp. 47–61.

45 London Metropolitan Archives (hereafter LMA), PS/IJ/O/019, Charges, 11 March 1930.
46 LMA, PS/IJ/O/019, Charges, 25 February 1930.
47 LMA, PS/IJ/O/027 and PS/IJ/O/028, Charges, 5 February 1935.
48 B. Sokoloff, *Edith and Stepney. The Life of Edith Ramsay: Sixty Years of Education, Politics and Social Change* (London: Stepney Books, 1987), pp. 51–2.
49 www.j-sainsbury.co.uk/index.asp?pageid=188&caseid=inter-war#inter-war (viewed 16 January 2008).
50 LMA, PS/IJ/O/027, Remands, 11 January 1935.
51 LMA, PS/IJ/O/019, Charges, 11 February 1930.
52 LMA, PS/IJ/O/027 and PS/IJ/O/028, Charges, 15 January 1935.
53 LMA, PS/IJ/O/027 and PS/IJ/O/028, Remands, 15 January 1935.
54 LMA, PS/IJ/O/027 and PS/IJ/O/028, Remands, 1 January 1935, 12 February 1935, 26 February 1935.
55 LMA PS/IJ/O/027 and PS/IJ/O/028, Remands, 15 January 1935.
56 *Ibid.*, Summonses, 12 March 1935.
57 *Ibid.*, Remands, 8 January 1935.
58 LMA, PS/IJ/O/028, Charges, 26 February 1935.
59 LMA, PS/IJ/O/058, Charges, 5 February 1945.
60 *Ibid.*, Charges, 8 January 1945; Remands, 15 January 1945; Charges, 22 January 1945.
61 *Ibid.*, Charges, 26 February 1945.
62 *Ibid.*, Remands, 1 January 1945, 15 January 1945; Charges, 19 February 1945.
63 *Ibid.*, Remands, 22 January 1945.
64 R. Hood and E. Joyce, 'Three generations: oral testimonies on crime and social change in London's East End', *British Journal of Criminology* 39:1 (1999): 136–60, p. 142.
65 D. Hobbs, *Doing the Business: Entrepreneurship, the Working Class and Detectives in the East End of London* (Oxford: Oxford University Press, 1989).
66 Hood and Joyce, 'Three generations', p. 142.
67 See Winnicott and Britton, 'Residential management as treatment for difficult children'; Winnicott, 'Children's hostels in war and peace', in C. Winnicott, R. Shepherd and M. Davis (eds) *D. W. Winnicott: Deprivation and Delinquency* (London: Tavistock, 1984), p. 56, and S. Isaacs (ed.) *The Cambridge Evacuation Survey: A Wartime Study in Social Welfare and Education* (London: Methuen, 1941), pp. 88–9.
68 LMA, PS/IJ/O/027 and PS/IJ/O/028, Special hearing, 12 January 1935.
69 LMA, PS/IJ/O/019, Charges, 21 January 1930.
70 *Ibid.*, Remands, 18 March, 25 March 1930; PS/IJ/O/027 and PS/IJ/O/028, Remands, 29 January 1935.
71 PS/IJ/O/027 and PS/IJ/O/028, Remands, 8 April 1930.
72 *Ibid.*, Charges, 4 February 1930.

73 PS/IJ/O/045, Cases, 13 February 1940.

74 *Ibid.*, Cases, 5 March 1940.

75 PS/IJ/O/027 and PS/IJ/O/028, Remands, 14 January, 11 February 1930.

76 NSPCC, 'Children and air raids', *Child's Guardian*, winter 1940, pp. 4, 6; 'Child evacuees and the Society', *Child's Guardian*, spring 1941, p. 3.

77 PS/IJ/O/027 and PS/IJ/O/028, Remands, 5 February 1935.

78 *Ibid.*, Remands, 29 January 1935.

79 J. Lee, *Children on Trial* (United Kingdom, Home Office: Crown Film Unit, 1946).

80 L. A. Atherley Jones and H. H. L. Bellot, *The Law of Children and Young Persons (in relation to Penal Offences), including the Children Act 1908* (London: Butterworth, 1909), p. 44.

81 J. White, *The Worst Street in North London: Campbell Bunk, Islington, between the Wars* (London: Routledge & Kegan Paul, 1986); R. Samuel, *East End Underworld: Chapters in the Life of Arthur Harding* (London: Routledge, 1981).

82 Cox, *Gender, Justice and Welfare*, pp. 3–10.

83 A. M. Carr-Saunders, H. Mannheim and E. C. Rhodes, *Young Offenders: An Enquiry into Juvenile Delinquency* (Cambridge: Cambridge University Press, 1942), pp. 75, 81, 92, 110.

84 See Henriques, *The Indiscretions of a Magistrate*, *passim*.

85 See Rainer Society, www.raineronline.org/gen/m1_i3_ourhistory.aspx (viewed 16 January 2008).

86 F. V. Jarvis, *Advise, Assist and Befriend: A History of the Probation and After-care Service* (London: National Association of Probation Officers, 1972), pp. 2–3.

87 *Ibid.*, p. 5.

88 P. Whitehead and R. Statham, *The History of Probation: Politics, Power and Cultural Change, 1876–2005* (Crayford: Shaw, 2006), p. 28.

89 P. Parsloe, *The Work of the Probation and After-care Officer* (London: Routledge & Kegan Paul, 1967), p. 6.

90 Whitehead and Statham, *The History of Probation*, pp. 45–6.

91 D. Bochel, *Probation and After-care: Its Development in England and Wales* (Edinburgh: Scottish Academic Press, 1976), p. 225.

92 *Ibid.*, p. 235.

93 Whitehead and Statham, *The History of Probation*, p. 47.

94 Bochel, *Probation and After-care*, p. 240.

95 *Ibid.*; Jarvis, *Advise, Assist and Befriend*; M. Vanstone, *Supervising Offenders in the Community: A History of Probation Theory and Practice* (Aldershot: Ashgate, 2004); Whitehead and Statham, *The History of Probation*.

96 Women's Library, 5/WUS/142/[1], Michael Sorenson, 'The Blackfriars Scheme: a Personal Report by Michael Sorenson' (London: Blackfriars Settlement, 1968), p. 1.

97 *Ibid.*, p. 4.

98   NACRO, 'Nacro: Frequently Asked Questions', www.nacro.org.uk/mediacentre/FAQ.htm (viewed 3 January 2008).

99   WL 5/WUS/142/[1], Sorenson, 'The Blackfriars Scheme', p. 1.

100   *Ibid.*, p. 1.

101   *Ibid.*, p. 5.

102   *Ibid.*, p. 3.

103   *Ibid.*, p. 21.

104   *Ibid.*, p. 22.

105   *Ibid.*, p. 21.

106   *Ibid.*, p. 3.

107   *Ibid.*, p. 5.

108   TOY/SPE/1, *Annual Report, 1967*, p. 38.

109   *Ibid.*, p. 38.

110   *Ibid.*, p. 39.

111   Sorenson, 'The Blackfriars Scheme', p. 6.

112   *Ibid.*

113   M. Birmingham, *You Can Help Me* (London: Collins, 1974).

114   BRC, TOY/SPE/1, *Annual Report, 1966*, p. 28.

115   *Ibid.*, *1967*, p. 36.

116   *Ibid.*, *1968*, p. 39.

117   '*Times* Obituary: John Profumo', *The Times*, www.timesonline.co.uk/tol/news/uk/article739657.ece (viewed 12 December 2007).

118   E. Cullen, *Grendon and Future Therapeutic Communities in Prison* (London: Prison Reform Trust, 1998), p. 3.

119   The National Archives (hereafter TNA), HO 383/151, Margaret Miller Smith, 'After-care Grendon and other Psychiatric Units in the Prison Service: Duties of Psychiatric Social Worker', 4 December 1967.

120   TNA, HO 383/151, Memorandum, Dr W. J. Gray to Dr I. G. W. Pickering, Prisons Head Office, 4 December 1967.

121   *Ibid.*, Memorandum Dr W. J. Gray to Director of Prison Medical Services, Home Office, re: Boys' Borstal and Young Persons' Medical After-care Services, 11 December 1967.

122   *Ibid.*, R. H. Beeson, 'Proposal that a Psychiatric Social Worker at Grendon Prison should do After-care Work in London', 23 February 1968.

123   *Ibid.*, W. Hague, Grendon Underwood, Toynbee Hall follow-up After-care Clinic, 2 October 1969.

124   *Ibid.*, Interim Report on the Grendon Flat, 1971.

125   BRC, TOY/SPE/1, *Annual Report, 1968*, p. 37.

126   *Ibid.*, *Annual Report, 1969*, p. 29; *Toynbee Report, 1970*, p. 24.

127   *Ibid.*, *Toynbee Report, 1970*, p. 23.

128   *Ibid.*, *1972*, pp. 21–2.

129   TNA, HO 383/151, Interim Report on the Grendon Flat, 1971.

130   BRC, TOY/SPE/1, *Toynbee Hall Report, 1971*, p. 28.

131   *Ibid.*, *1973*, p. 22.

132   TNA, HO 383/151, Memo, L., P. Wright to Weiler, 28 March 1973.

133   BRC, TOY/SPE/1, *Annual Report, 1968*, p. 37.

134 Lambeth Archives (hereafter LAD), IV183/5/7, NACRO Bail/Aftercare Hostel, LMH and NACRO, 'Community Placement Project: Proposal for Bail and Aftercare Accommodation', p. 4.

135 LAD, IV183/5/7, Letter, E Knapman, Inner London Probation and After Care Service (ILPACS), to David Rhys, LMHS, 21 December 1972.

136 *Ibid.*, Attachment to letter, E. Knapman to David Rhys, LMHS, 21 December 1972, 'ILPACS Information: Community Service by Offenders'.

137 *Ibid.*, Letter to Members, *c.* 1975.

138 *Ibid.*, Letter, Beryl Wells to Keith, 11 April 1975; letter, P. Jean Cameron to A. E. J. Butterworth, 12 May 1975.

139 A. Paterson, *Legal Aid as a Social Service* (London: Cobden Trust, 1971), p. 7.

140 B. Abel-Smith and R. Stevens, *Lawyers and the Courts: A Sociological Study of the English Legal System, 1750–1965* (London: Heinemann, 1967), p. 327; see also Abel-Smith and Stevens, *In Search of Justice: Society and the Legal System* (London: Allen Lane, 1968), *passim.*

141 D. H. Hene, *A Simple Explanation of the Legal Aid Scheme* (London: *Daily Express* Legal Guides, 1951), p. 5.

142 Paterson, *Legal Aid as a Social Service*, p. 22.

143 R. I. Morgan, 'The introduction of civil legal aid in England and Wales', *Twentieth Century British History* 5:1 (1994), p. 38.

144 Abel-Smith and Stevens, *Lawyers and the Courts* and *In Search of Justice*.

145 R. Egerton, *Legal Aid* (London: Kegan Paul Trench Trubner, 1945).

146 Paterson, *Legal Aid as a Social Service*.

147 Morgan, 'The Introduction of civil legal aid in England and Wales'.

148 D. Leat, 'The rise and role of the poor man's lawyer', *British Journal of Law and Society* 2:2 (1975).

149 Paterson, *Legal Aid as a Social Service*.

150 J. Mervyn Jones, *Free Legal Advice in England and Wales* (Oxford: Slatter & Rose, 1940).

151 J. Richards, *Inform, Advise and Support: Fifty Years of the Citizens' Advice Bureau* (Cambridge: Lutterworth, 1989).

152 Paterson, *Legal Aid as a Social Service*, p. 11.

153 *Ibid.*, p. 11.

154 Morgan, 'The Introduction of civil legal aid in England and Wales', p. 42.

155 *Ibid.*, p. 44.

156 *Ibid.*, p. 49.

157 *Ibid.*, p. 48.

158 *Ibid.*, p. 51.

159 *Ibid.*, p. 56; Paterson, *Legal Aid as a Social Service*, p. 12.

160 Paterson, *Legal Aid as a Social Service*, p. 13.

161 Morgan, 'The introduction of civil legal aid in England and Wales', p. 63.

162 Abel-Smith and Stevens, *Lawyers and the Courts*, p. 319.

163 Morgan, 'The introduction of civil legal aid in England and Wales', pp. 44, 45–7.

164 E. J. Cohn and R. Egerton, *A Guide to Legal Aid for the Poor* (London: Stevens, 1947), p. 13.
165 *Ibid.*, p. 15.
166 *Ibid.*, pp. 17–18.
167 Morgan, 'The introduction of civil legal aid in England and Wales', p. 74.
168 Paterson, *Legal Aid as a Social Service*, p. 14.
169 Abel-Smith and Stevens, *In Search of Justice*, p. 163.
170 Paterson, *Legal Aid as a Social Service*, p. 24.
171 *Ibid.*, p. 25; also M. McCarthy, *Campaigning for the Poor: CPAG And the Politics of Welfare* (Beckenham: Croom Helm, 1986); C. Harlow and R. Rawlings, *Pressure through Law* (London: Routledge, 1992).
172 Richards, *Inform, Advise and Support*, p. 1; Abel-Smith and Stevens, *Lawyers and the Courts*, p. 316.
173 Abel-Smith and Stevens, *Lawyers and the Courts*, p. 329.
174 Egerton, *Legal Aid*, pp. 29–30.
175 Oxford House, *The Oxford House in Bethnal Green, 1884–1948* (London: Brakell, 1948), p. 103.
176 Pimlott, *Toynbee Hall*, p. 116.
177 Egerton, *Legal Aid*, p. 27.
178 Jones, *Free Legal Advice in England and Wales*, p. 13.
179 *Ibid.*, p. 5.
180 *Ibid.*, p. 18.
181 *Ibid.*, p. 9.
182 Hene, *A Simple Explanation of the Legal Aid Scheme*, p. 5.
183 D. H. Hene, *The State is at your Service from Birth to Old Age* (London: *Daily Express* Legal Guides, 1952), p. 6.
184 *Ibid.*, 7.
185 Harlow and Rawlings, *Pressure through Law*, 22.
186 Department for Constitutional Affairs, *A Fairer Deal for Legal Aid*, Cm 6591 (London: HMSO, 2005), p. 6.
187 R. Pattenden, *English Criminal Appeals, 1844–1994: Appeals against Conviction and Sentence* (Oxford: Oxford University Press, 1996); Pimlott, *Toynbee Hall*, p. 246.
188 B. D. Vernon, *Ellen Wilkinson, 1891–1947* (London: Croom Helm, 1982), p. 149; Pimlott, *Toynbee Hall*, p. 240.
189 BRC, TOY/SPE/1, *Annual Report, 1935–1938*.
190 Vernon, *Ellen Wilkinson*, p. 148.
191 *Ibid.*, pp. 149–50.
192 BRC, TOY/SPE/1, *Report, 1962–1963*, p. 17.
193 Richards, *Inform, Advise and Support*, p. 2.
194 Jones, *Free Legal Advice in England and Wales*, p. 9.
195 BRC, TOY/SPE/1, *Report, 1962–1963*, p. 14.
196 *Ibid.*, *Toynbee Hall Report, 1970*, p. 20.
197 *Ibid.*, *Annual Report, 1967*, p. 32.
198 *Ibid.*, *Annual Report*, p. 31.

199 *Ibid., Toynbee Hall Report, 1973*, p. 15.
200 *Ibid., Toynbee Hall Report, 1974*, pp. 12–13.
201 *Ibid., Annual Report, 1968; Toynbee Hall Report, 1973*, p. 15; *Annual Report, 1968*, p. 37.
202 *Ibid., Annual Report, 1968; Annual Report, 1969*, p. 24; *Annual Report, 1968*, p. 54.
203 *Ibid., Annual Report, 1969*, p. 24.
204 *Ibid., Toynbee Hall Report, 1971*, p. 25.
205 *Ibid., Toynbee Hall Report, 1973*, p. 15.
206 *Ibid., Toynbee Hall Report, 1976*, Citizens' Advice Bureau insert.
207 *Ibid., Toynbee Hall Report, 1975*, p. 8.
208 Newham Rights Centre, *Newham Rights Centre: Two Years' Work, 1975–1977* (London: Newham Rights Centre, 1977), p. 6.

6

Changing communities:
the East End, migration and racism

This chapter will explore the ways in which the settlement movement and its associates dealt with immigrant communities, and in particular their responses to the changing nature of race relations in the twentieth century. It will begin by looking at the responses of the settlement movement and the Council of Citizens of East London (CCEL), which was based at Toynbee Hall, to the challenges posed by the British Union of Fascists (BUF) to the Whitechapel Jewish community in the 1930s and 1940s, before examining the work of the CCEL's descendant, the Council of Citizens of Tower Hamlets (CCTH), to the needs of the Bangladeshi community and the attacks on them by the National Front in the course of the 1970s.

The relationship of the settlement movement to minority ethnic groups is often an overlooked one, despite the fact that its location in impoverished areas often located it by default in areas of high immigration. The focus of this chapter will largely be on the East End. Toynbee Hall's immediate neighbourhood was predominantly Jewish in 1918 and, by the end of our period, Bengali.[1] As Tony Kushner has argued, the Whitechapel area occupies a special place in immigrant and minority history for being so exceptional in its diversity,[2] being first home to the Huguenots, then East European Jews and then the Bengalis, along with Chinese, Irish and Somali communities. But, alongside its representation as a place of tolerance and understanding, the Whitechapel area witnessed some of the most violent episodes of intolerance in British history, notably the 'Battle of Cable Street' in 1936 and the Brick Lane episodes of 1978.[3]

Although race and ethnicity are one of the major lines of enquiry in sociological and anthropological studies, they remain under-researched areas in the field of contemporary history. Tony Kushner's work on the historical development of the Jewish community, from his study of Jewish and non-Jewish relations in the East End and official responses to antisemitism to his work on the Battle of Cable Street are key texts,[4] providing an anthropological perspective on the operation of Jewish East End society that adds to the wealth of autobiography and memoirs. Although many East End autobiographies tend towards childhood nostalgia, those of Joe Jacobs and Phil Piratin on the far left of the political spectrum and erstwhile BUF member Arthur Harding directly consider the themes of this chapter.[5] Morris Beckman's superb memoir, *The 43 Group*,[6] explores the development of this anti-fascist group, which along with Jacobs' and Piratin's memoirs, is complemented by Dave Renton's work on the growth and development of anti-fascist and anti-racist groups from the inter-war period through to the 1980s and 1990s,[7] whilst Thomas Linehan has examined the functioning of the BUF in Stoke Newington and Hackney in the 1930s.[8] There is furthermore a substantial literature on the history of black and Asian communities in Britain, of which there is space to mention but a few especially relevant cases: Caroline Adams's *Across Seven Seas*, oral histories carried out with pioneering members of the East End Bangladeshi community;[9] John Eade's more recent work on the political development of the same;[10] Pnina Werbner's work on the Manchester Pakistani community;[11] Avtar Brah's work on the processes of migration;[12] and, last but not least, Paul Gilroy's seminal work on black Britain, *There ain't no Black in the Union Jack*.[13]

There is a dichotomy in the literature on anti-fascism between those groups who were more 'active' in their tactics and those who opted for more peaceful or passive approaches. It is the former group who have attracted more historical attention, and our understanding of these organisations from the perspectives of their activists is relatively good. But there is still a need to look critically at those organisations whose work was perhaps less immediately exciting, especially where these were driven by middle-aged, middle-class people rather than young radicals. These 'establishment' groups require our attention: they may have had appeal for different parts of victimised communities or drawn their support from other social groups; likewise, they often had better links with the police and authorities. This chapter will examine the role of these less well known groups, and assess their place within the broader field of anti-fascism and anti-racism in the twentieth century.

The East End and the fascists

The British fascist movement found a ready home in East London, largely as a result of white British resentment and fear of East European Jewish migration. Although the Jewish and Gentile communities existed alongside each other, often discretely, with little contact,[14] the various campaigns for what would be the Aliens Act of 1905 were well supported in the East End. As early as 1900 Stepney returned Major Evans-Gordon, the founder of the anti-immigration British Brothers' League, as its Conservative MP. [15] Attitudes towards the Jewish community were complex: on the one hand, organisations such as Toynbee Hall would actively seek to work on behalf of the Jewish community yet felt aggrieved if the Jewish community preferred recourse to its own organisations. This was one of the motivations for the settlement to move farther east during the First World War in order to reach the white working-class men it felt were not benefiting from the same educational and welfare provision.[16] Likewise Basil Henriques, the warden of the Jewish Bernhard Baron Settlement and an assimilated Sephardic Jew, was upset by Henrietta Barnett's comment that he should go to Palestine[17] yet was deeply unhappy at the unwillingness of some of his East End co-religionists to abandon Yiddish.[18] The underlying discourse behind all these debates and campaigns was one of 'Englishness', of fears of the degeneration of the 'English' in east London and in Britain as a whole, of the apparent differences between the 'English' and the Jewish community, of the attitudes of the assimilated and newer arrivals.[19]

Antisemitism and anti-immigrant sentiments continued into the inter-war period, but were given new impetus by the development of Oswald Mosley's British Union of Fascists. Mosley's political career began when he was elected Unionist MP for Harrow in Middlesex in 1918, before crossing the floor of the House over the use of the Black and Tans by Lloyd George in Ireland. Mosley remained an Independent until finding a home, for a time, in the Labour Party, although he fell out with it catastrophically over the handling of the economic depression of the later 1920s and 1930s. After his expulsion from the Labour Party, Mosley founded his New Party in 1931, the forerunner of his next project, the British Union of Fascists of 1932.[20]

As the New Party and the British Union of Fascists found their anti-communist and antisemitic feet, so they found a home in the 'white' areas of the East End adjacent to Jewish districts or where Jews were beginning to move in.[21] In the 1930s BUF candidates for LCC elections were canvassing in Bethnal Green, Hoxton, Shoreditch and Haggerston, all areas immediately to the north of the more Jewish Whitechapel.[22] The BUF ran a branch and speakers in the Hackney area from 1933 onwards.[23] As its membership grew it developed its portfolio of antisemitic activities to include both physical and verbal harassment and provocation.[24] By the late 1930s many members of the Jewish community in the Hackney and other northern areas were scared to leave their homes, especially at night, for fear of attacks and abuse.[25] Provocation was not, however, limited to those Jews living outside Whitechapel. BUF members and sympathisers also attempted to create havoc in the Whitechapel 'ghetto', most notoriously at the 'Battle of Cable Street' on 4 October 1936.

The Battle of Cable Street has come to assume a privileged status in the history of the East End, as communists, anarchists and trade unionists, and Jew and Gentile alike, joined forces to prevent Mosley and the BUF from marching down Cable Street and hence through the heart of the Jewish East End.[26] The repulsion of the march and its Metropolitan Police support was a particular victory for those members of the community who had suffered or who had seen friends and neighbours suffer at the hands of the BUF and their sympathisers. The battle was also a symbol of community defiance and solidarity, particularly for young east Londoners, who were alienated from mainstream politics and who felt that the police and other bodies were not interested in their plight. But the case of the Battle of Cable Streets highlights another historical problem, namely the division in attitudes as to how the fascists could be combated. Whilst the young and the left advocated more active approaches, bodies such as the settlements and the British Board of Deputies preferred to maintain calm, and to proverbially turn the other cheek. Whichever course may prove to be the wiser, this marks a significant fault line in the development of community or race relations from the 1930s onwards.

It was in the turmoil surrounding the Battle of Cable Street that the Council of Citizens of East London (CCEL) was founded at Toynbee Hall in 1936. The CCEL was ostensibly charged with developing harmonious community race relations, yet in its early days it was often involved in political matters, namely checking the growth of the Communist Party. In this way, the CCEL and particularly its chair, J. J. Mallon, was part of a larger discourse on the antagonistic relationship of the Labour Party to the Communist Party of Great Britain. As we have seen elsewhere, Mallon was a long-standing member of the Labour Party, having joined the Independent Labour Party in 1903, and he unsuccessfully stood for election as MP in 1918, 1922 and 1923.[27] Mallon maintained his links through his membership of the Romney Street group,[28] as well as through various projects such as serving on Ramsay MacDonald's Economic Advisory Council and as secretary to Labour's campaign for public control of the liquor trade.[29] Mallon was also close to Herbert Morrison, the Labour MP for South Hackney, from 1935,[30] and a notorious Labour Party witch hunter.[31]

7 'Toynbee Hall and the Jewish community', leaflet produced by the
Council of Citizens of East London

In a letter to the editor of the *Manchester Guardian* in October 1936[32]
Mallon wrote of how the turmoil was directly related to the growth
of communism and fascism in Europe as the two came to the streets
of London and engaged in battle with each other. Mallon believed that
the communists, hungry for new members, were happy to accept Jews
in order to swell their ranks – assuming, perhaps, that other groups
did not want to attract them as members. He also thought that the

fascists were plotting to drive the Jewish community to the Communist Party, in order to further build upon 'the dislike that traditional England feels for Communism', thereby discrediting both groups in the process. Yet Mallon's friend Basil Henriques appeared to be more perceptive in his attitude to youth and communism. As Mallon recounted in this letter, Henriques believed that the Jewish community had little choice but to organise itself and resist the fascists, else be labelled cowards – and, as Henriques pointed out in his autobiography, the communists were the only people seen to be attacking the fascists.[33] But for Mallon and his colleagues at CCEL there was little virtue in forming paramilitary groups to combat the fascists, as 'that way madness lies. The way of safety lies in quietude. Our refrain should be "refrain".'[34] The main achievement of the CCEL before the Second World War was to secure, with Herbert Morrison, the passing of the Public Order Act of 1936, which seriously curtailed the BUF's freedom to march and organise intimidating events.[35] Yet whilst the Act made provision to tackle the fascists it also created a mechanism through which left-wing activists could be and were prosecuted, especially in the 1940s.

BUF members and those of sympathetic organisations were interned during the Second World War but resumed their activities as the 'Union Movement' after 1945. The League of British ex-Servicemen and Women was formed in 1944, and began to draw support through their holding of antisemitic meetings at Speakers' Corner. In 1946 Oswald Mosley felt confident enough to announce in a *News Chronicle* article that his experience of the war had served only to strengthen his beliefs.[36] By February 1946 there were fourteen identifiable fascist groups on the streets of London,[37] including the main group, Mosley's Union Movement. As before the war, activities included selling newspapers and standing on street corners spouting antisemitic abuse. Dealing with the resurgence of fascism took two approaches. On the one hand, the Board of Deputies revived its Jewish Defence Committee, aiming as before the war for peaceable, democratically driven solutions. On the other hand, frustrated ex-Jewish service people were attracted first to the Association of Jewish ex-Servicemen and then to the more militant 43 Group.[38] The younger members of the Jewish community, in particular, were angry at the apparent legality of fascist activities, and furious with the often preferential treatment given to the fascists by the Metropolitan Police. To many it seemed as though their efforts during the war had been pointless. Although neither of these groups was in any way formally attached to the Communist Party, the communists were also closely involved in providing an active response to the fascists, and particularly in filling an ideological void left by the now governing Labour Party.[39]

The CCEL clearly aligned itself with the position of the Board of Deputies and the Labour governments of 1945–51 in adopting a peaceable approach.[40] In the post-war period the CCEL saw its role as being first non-political and second as being educational. The 'non-political' aspect of its role was a problematic characteristic of its work in the later 1940s. The CCEL abhorred certain elements of the Union Movement's policies but condoned others. As Hallam Tennyson, the first secretary of the post-war CCEL, wrote in his report for 1949, 'We are not as a Council concerned with Fascism because of its total-itarian political ideas or its advocacy of a corporate state, but with its use of antisemitism.'[41] The Council, as mentioned earlier, was anti-communist. Mallon's distrust of communism continued into the 1940s. At a CCEL committee meeting in October 1949 he drew attention to conversations he had had with Herbert Morrison about publicising antisemitism in the Soviet Union as a means of trying to discourage East End Jews from joining the Communist Party.[42] This became a pet project for Mallon. A month later he was in discussion with Percy Cudlipp, editor of the *Daily Herald*. Mallon told Cudlipp that he and Morrison were of the opinion that the communists were using the Jewish community for political gain, and needed to be discredited in order to weaken any alliance between them. Mallon suggested that Cudlipp should engage a writer to write a pungent article on the matter, as he thought the piece 'would be very warmly welcomed by many Jews who have a sense of responsibility and regret very much the attachment to Communism of the younger members of their community'.[43] Mallon was referring to those members of the Jewish community who were assimi-lated or middle-class, often both, and who, as Dave Renton has pointed out, tended to live farther away from the flashpoints of violence in Whitechapel and Hackney. These were also the same people with whom the anti-communist Board of Deputies had a greater affinity.[44]

Although a separate body from the settlement, the executive com-mittee membership of the CCEL was closely tied to Toynbee Hall, which was the case through to the 1970s. For example, throughout the later 1940s and early 1950s Mallon was chairman, with his sub-warden, F. C. McNulty, acting as treasurer, and a former sub-warden, Lionel Ellis, also a committee member. Edith Ramsay was on the committee, as were the Reverend Dr James Parkes, the Reverend D. W. Booth and the Reverend W. Simpson, with Canon T. J. Fitzgerald as vice-chair and Hallam Tennyson as secretary. Mallon had been a member of the short-lived and powerless Aliens Deportation Advisory Committee at the Home Office,[45] whilst Parkes and Simpson were involved with the Council of Christians and Jews, founded in 1942.[46] Tennyson was notable as the grandson of Alfred Tennyson, the Victorian poet, and for turning his back on his privileged upbringing to undertake social work in the East End (including a stint as a member of the communists) before later joining the BBC.[47] But not one of the committee was Jewish. The appointment of a Jewish member was suggested at the executive committee meeting of 6 October 1949 but rejected on the grounds that:

> Nothing would be so fatal to a constructive development of our work than that members from any community should be included simply because they were representative. The effectiveness of our present body was due to its concern rather than its representative character.[48]

This was a curious attitude to adopt when London had such an array of suitably qualified Jewish people to choose from – including fellow local settlement organisers Miriam Moses and Basil Henriques. But this attitude revealed much about the committee's self-perception: it was concerned to speak on the community's behalf, but not necessarily to allow the community to speak to it in proactive ways. It also suggested that being 'representative' was not synonymous with appropriate or judicious concern. This detached attitude would become a serious flaw some thirty years later, when the National Front began its attacks on the Bangladeshi community.

In the meantime the CCEL began to develop itself as a watchdog body, although, as the following discussion will demonstrate, the emphasis was more on 'watch' than on 'dog'. In 1949, following a brutal attack on two Jewish Dalston teenagers, Mallon was contacted by Sidney Salomon, executive officer of the Jewish Defence Committee,[49] first on account of his contacts in east London and second through his background in licensing law and practice.[50] Salomon had received reports of the Ridley Arms in Dalston being used as a centre for fascist activities – including visits by Oswald Mosley.[51] Mallon contacted the owner of the pub, Colonel Buxton of the brewers Truman Hanbury Buxton, and was assured that the pub was not being used in such a manner, and appeared content to leave the matter there.[52] However, Salomon was able to present evidence from an informant[53] who had infiltrated a fascist meeting at the pub which included as a highlight a visit from Mosley himself. Salomon and his informants had found that local belief was such that 'Sir Oswald Mosley is the owner of this pub as it is the Fascist HQ in the area, and as such is boycotted by all other than Fascist supporters'.[54] Here Mallon's involvement appeared to wane, but as the Ridley Arms, along with the Green Gate in Bethnal Green and the Rose and Crown in Dalston, continued to be known as Mosleyite strongholds, they failed to prevent the pubs being used in that way.[55]

The teachers' committee of the CCEL also reported incidents to the executive committee for consideration. In 1954 it was noted that there had been an increasing number of Mosleyite meetings in Bethnal Green, including one at a local secondary school. Anti-Jewish slogans had been chalked across the district, whilst the Communist Party's local headquarters and neighbouring houses had been vandalised. Although A. I. Polack, then secretary of the CCEL, didn't feel that the activity was serious, the committee felt that it was worth reporting.[56] Despite similar reports from an American researcher working in Bethnal Green to Mallon, the consensus was to watch and wait.[57] Yet many other groups – AJEX and the 43 Group, for example – did not feel that watching and waiting was an appropriate solution. Oswald Mosley continued to stand for election in various districts, including North Kensington in 1959, each time whipping up the Union Movement and racist sentiment. The CCEL appeared to be overly concerned in this period with the democratic rights of the fascists and not enough, perhaps, with the upset it caused many Londoners.

Educating east London

'Educational activity' was an important part of the CCEL's self-defined role. The Council had an extensive programme of day conferences for schoolchildren. But sometimes the attempts to rationally discuss questions of race turned sour. A teacher at Cephas School noted that a pre-conference discussion had disintegrated into virulent racism, although he felt that during and after the conference 'some modification of their prejudices had taken place'.[58] School was an arena in which young white people could encounter young people of other races. Although getting to know children from different backgrounds through school was always possible, school was also a place to which children and young people brought and repeated the views of their parents. Teachers were often powerless to implement anti-racist policies if the headmaster or governors blocked them, or were faced with overwhelming prejudice. The teachers' committee was successful, however, in providing a space for these teachers to meet, to share their problems and successes in dealing with racism and promoting anti-racism in their schools.

From the 1950s onwards, the CCEL produced a series of 'bulletins' that could be used as a teaching resource in schools or distributed through youth clubs. *Our East London* emphasised the collective input of all immigrant groups, from the Huguenots to the newest communities, to the particular culture of east London. The series was relatively successful in terms of producing attractive documents that were popular with schools.[59] However, the 1958 version of the leaflets did not let historical accuracy get in the way of a good story. Kevin McDonnell, a finishing PhD student of medieval London history at Queen Mary College at the time,[60] read the texts with great disappointment, finding many errors.[61] With some editing the earlier leaflets were republished as a single volume entitled *Our East London*.[62] Whatever the series' faults, it was nevertheless a well meaning attempt to develop an early 'history from below' approach to engaging schoolchildren and their families with the idea of a composite and complex East End identity. The series was accompanied by a touring exhibition, produced by Hallam Tennyson in 1950. The exhibition boards addressed the themes of the booklets in more visual form, whilst attenders were able to handle a range of items, some produced by members of youth clubs and school groups.[63]

The CCEL also held lectures and seminars aimed at adults with speakers from different religions that aimed to demystify and compare practices which were often aimed at social workers and teachers. But the CCEL's approach to tackling the ignorance that accompanied racist behaviour was limited in its scope. It had little idea of how to reach the 'unclubbables', the 'unattached' – those adults and young people who were not part of larger or unionised workplaces, who did not go to regular religious services or to clubs or classes. Instead, as Mallon outlined, they approached the citizens of east London through mediating agencies, through teachers, social workers and the clergy, through clubs and social organisations.[64] The settlements were using their old methods of reaching out to people who were more than likely to be half-way to conversion by definition of being a club member, a problem they had frequently encountered in their attempts to rescue young people from delinquency through youth clubs. But the problem was not easily solved. The question of effective anti-racist outreach was revisited by the Greater London Council with its 'Let's kick racism out of town' poster campaign of the 1980s, as Paul Gilroy has described. Whilst the GLC had the powers and the means to ensure that its billboards were visible across the metropolis, their message was not one that necessarily presented an image of the black community as empowered and equal.[65] Likewise, the Swann report of 1985 argued that schools had an important role to play in changing racialised views and behaviour, that racism in schools as well as in broader society disadvantaged children from particular communities, and that the school curriculum should embrace multicultural teaching.[66] On the other hand, as Paul Gilroy has argued, less formal groups such as Rock against Racism were far more successful. Rock against Racism used youth and pop culture to speak the language of young people and to treat the issues they dealt with daily, and to create a supportive community for the building and maintenance of anti-racist ideology.[67] But Rock against Racism and related bodies such as the Anti-Nazi League were run by and aimed at younger people; it is questionable whether a group such as the CCEL could have developed a similar programme, even had it been willing to adopt the same methods.

Basil Dearden's *Sapphire*

Basil Dearden's feature film *Sapphire* (1959) attempted to examine the problems of racism in post-war Britain. The eponymous Sapphire was a murdered young female student whom the police had initially assumed to be white. With the arrival of her brother, Dr Robbins, it becomes clear that Sapphire was black. This 'discovery' highlights the prejudices of the police and the community that had spurned her, and how this had led to her being killed to prevent her giving birth to a child of mixed heritage.[68] In October 1958 the film makers allegedly sought permission to shoot a riot scene for the film in Notting Hill, barely two months after the race riots in the area. The riot scenes were promptly condemned by the Association of Cinematograph Television and Allied Technicians in the *Times*. The secretary of the Association, G. H. Elvin, wrote that 'the decision to do the shooting in the Notting Hill area [was] tactless. There was no need . . . for it, either, since films these days were often made in one place though they were taking place in another.' J. Arthur Rank believed that the film, which was based on a fictional story, would not cause any problems. The Rank publicity manager wrote, 'If they did not shoot a film in the location they got hundreds of letters from people complaining of deception.' The Rank Organisation also argued in the article that Dearden's film would be 'extremely intelligent', as had his treatment of the police in *The Blue Lamp*. The *Times* journalist also approached the Home Office for comment, but the Home Office denied that the film was in any way its responsibility.[69]

The news article attracted the attention of the CCEL, and at a meeting on 15 October 1958 it resolved to take action by contacting the mayor of Kensington. In a letter to the mayor, A. N. E. McHaffie, A. E. Morgan (now chair) wrote of the CCEL's apprehension that the filming or any related disturbances might exacerbate already delicate relations in the East End. The CCEL solicited the mayor's opinion of the film, and whether he planned to take any action in his borough.[70] In reply the mayor stated that he believed the film 'would be in thoroughly bad taste', and that he would prepare a joint letter with the mayors of neighbouring boroughs to present to the Rank Organisation.[71] Within days McHaffie had enlisted the support of the mayors of Hammersmith, Paddington and Marylebone. Their letter to the film company strongly attacked the idea of riot scenes being filmed:

> We cannot conceive of a topic or film more undesirable at the present time and if the press reports are correct that it is proposed to shoot the film in North Kensington, this, in our view, verges on the irresponsible as no act is more likely to cause a fresh outbreak of violence in that area. Feelings in the locality continue to run high and the whole situation is extremely tense.

The mayors also indicated to the Rank Organisation that copies of their letter had been forwarded to the British Board of Film Censors in addition to the Home Office, and in personal correspondence exhorted the Council of Citizens to also write to the film company.[72] In addition to sending his own letter to the Rank Organisation, Morgan penned another letter to R. A. Butler, the Home Secretary, asking him to prevent this 'most miscalculated project' being made'.[73]

The British Board of Film Censors wrote to Morgan pointing out that it was not within its powers to prevent Rank from filming the material.[74] John H. Davis, the managing director of the Rank Organisation, replied to Morgan that the company had already reviewed its decision to film in Notting Hill, as it was both 'inappropriate and in fact unnecessary to the making of the film'. Davis drew attention to the fact that the film was being made by Michael Ralph and Basil Dearden, the producer and director respectively of the renowned police drama *The Blue Lamp*, and argued that the two men were 'conscious of their civic as well as their commercial duties'. Davis contended that the filming of *Sapphire* was coincidental with the riots, the script having been in production for some time: 'it would be quite wrong to assume that the Notting Hill riots were the mainspring of our desire to make a film of this nature'.[75]

A week later, Morgan replied to the Rank Organisation. He concurred that it was the *Times* article that had prompted the CCEL to action, but said he was pleased on behalf of his colleagues that the filming would not go ahead, and that the film had not been planned on the back of the riots. Yet Morgan was still uneasy with the question of making a film about race relations at all. He wrote, 'I am not wholly convinced of the wisdom of reviving what is at least seemingly dormant.'[76] Morgan then wrote to the mayor of Kensington, congratulating him on his victory in preventing the filming from taking place,[77] before forwarding the correspondence to Polack for his records. In Polack's view 'even if the film is now produced, it is unlikely to have the unfortunate effects we first envisaged'.[78]

But the optimism seems misplaced and naive at best. The Council had in no way succeeded in preventing Rank from filming provocative scenes for *Sapphire* either in a studio or elsewhere. After all, race riots in the 1940s and 1950s were by no means confined to London – the Notting Hill riots were paralleled by riots in Nottingham.[79] The CCEL's view appears to have been that the simulacrum of a riot as seen with cameras, crew and extras by passers-by on the streets or on the screen of a cinema would be the means by which ordinary Londoners might be provoked into violence. What the Council did not discuss was the question of why young white people should riot in the first place: how their fears of and attitudes to Caribbean migrants developed, how prejudice was inflamed into violence and then how these problems could be addressed. They did not question why a film of fictional content should need to have a 'riot' section in order to deal with themes of race. The overriding concern of the Council did not appear to be for members of the London Caribbean community or their views on the proposed filming of *Sapphire* in their neighbourhood, but rather that whatever malevolent forces had prompted the riots should remain dormant – and therefore unaddressed. The incident also demonstrated the Council's inherent paternalism in believing that it knew what was best for community relations, and its desire to impose its views on the film industry and broader society.

Researching the 'race problem'

Although the response of the CCEL to *Sapphire* did not display an intense interest in the deeper roots of the 'race problem', the CCEL was still keen to investigate the nature of immigration in their neighbourhood. One of its responses was to commission Richard Hauser to work on the issue, although the CCEL's interest waned as the costs of the project rose.

The Reverend A. H. Apps of Trinity Church in Mile End had contacted Morgan and the Council of Citizens with an enquiry about vice in the Stepney area, particularly with regard to what he felt to be brewing resentment of black 'pimps' and more general discontent over housing.[80] Richard Hauser, of the Institute for Group Studies, had previously been in contact with the Council of Christians and Jews on a related note.[81] Hauser and his wife, Hephzibah Menuhin Hauser, the pianist sister of Yehudi Menuhin, had met in Australia and on their return to Britain founded the Institute for Group Studies, which aimed to investigate the needs of school leavers, the mentally ill, homo-sexuals and ethnic minorities. In 1958 the Hausers had been hard at work in the Notting Hill area, having trained some twenty community liaison officers, most of whom came from minority ethnic backgrounds. The Hausers were also experimenting with housing co-operative pro-jects, and trying to engage local 'Teddy boys', the young white men at the epicentre of the race riots. To try to promote good race relations in the area, the Institute had sponsored a children's Christmas party for both black and white at Holland Park school, the first comprehens-ive in London.[82]

Hauser had originally been in contact with the Council in relation to his liaison officer project. The Council's interest in the project was dampened somewhat when Dr Israel Feldman pointed out that the expenditure was now likely to exceed £1,200, a far greater amount than they had expected, and they had already granted Hauser £360 in respect of his project. Hauser was present at the meeting and suggested that it might be particularly helpful to him if the Council were to lend its support to his appeals for funding to other bodies. The Council refused, although it did agree to lend support on an individual basis.[83] An attach-ment to the minutes of this meeting reveal that before Hauser arrived at the meeting Feldman had presented a report on the Survey of Race Relations in East London that Hauser and the Institute had been work-ing on. Feldman revealed that Hauser's original bid had been for £200, eventually raised to £363 as costs rose, and the Council defrayed this. Hauser's new plan requested £1,200 to £1,500 for the purposes of paying an LCC teacher on secondment, a Mr Braithwaite, to work on the project (at £65 per month), along with five liaison workers (£5 each per month) and to cover office expenses of £12 per month. Although Hauser and his wife were actively seeking funding elsewhere, the Council demurred. Whilst Polack and others supported Hauser's work, the committee was nevertheless divided, with some members opposed to the scheme in any form.[84]

Hauser presented an interim report on his survey of black com-munities in east London in March 1958. It aimed to uncover 'a) Both attitude and opinion of coloured people b) The attitude and opinions of "Native" English people toward coloured people'. The study used investigators of both white and non-white backgrounds, and smaller comparative studies were simultaneously undertaken in Islington, Brixton and Fulham. The survey was divided into a qualitative survey, with data drawn from such professionals as social workers, teachers and health officers, and a quantitative survey, with those 'involved in the problems personally (white and coloured)'. From it the Hausers hoped to be able to make statements about the United Kingdom as a whole.[85]

The preliminary findings demonstrated that housing was the 'sorest point' in inter-community relations, especially as tenants were afraid to complain about their landlords. White respondents were afraid of finding themselves isolated among black neighbours, often claimed that the black community bought up 'cheap houses and over-[crowded] them'[86] and accused black people of 'hanging about'. Black respondents, on the other hand, were regarded by the Hausers as having an 'inferiority complex', lesser educational qualifications, professional and vocational standards and skills, a lack of organisation and self-help mechanisms, as well as a 'sense of isolation (four years here and never been in an Englishman's home)'. Black women came in for especial scrutiny and, unlike black men, were noted as having a 'special problem owing to preparation required for a different climate and social condition'. The report suggested that white women were the most hostile to the new arrivals, and also that the West Indian families were themselves to blame for increasing racist attitudes by aggravating pressure on housing and 'because of different manners'. It also noted that black women had to go out to work to support their husbands, but that they 'often refuse[d] domestic service as they consider it undignified. This leaves only factory work which is bad for family.' Finally, the interim report concluded, the black community was typical of a 'depressed minority anywhere'.[87]

The Hausers' findings were not as progressive as they may have thought. Their questionnaire was formed through engagement with popular imperialist discourses, hence the questions they asked and the conclusions they reached were contiguous with that. Whilst the Hausers noted tensions over housing, they did not, at least in this document, hint that they might more fully explore the question of slum landlords, or of the anecdotal unwillingness of white landlords to let rooms or flats to black tenants. Although Peter Rachman's corrupt reign in Notting Hill would not be exposed for another four years, a variety of sources demonstrate that black tenants had immense difficulty in finding affordable lodgings, and often had to accept what they could find, regardless of its quality. In this context, buying up cheap housing was a survival strategy. As Roger Ballard has demonstrated in the context of Asian migrants, buying cheap housing was a means of protecting meagre resources, especially when male migrants were trying to save and to send as much money to relatives at home as possible.[88] The concept of an 'inferiority' complex was an attempt to label the black community, and it was not substantiated as to how the Hausers reached their conclusion. The claim that the black migrants had inferior qualifications and skills was, again, nonsensical, based on the idea that schools and universities in the Commonwealth must be anything less than their British counterparts – although the British had successfully transplanted their own model of education to the empire, and the majority of imperial grammar school children took the same Oxford and Cambridge A-level syllabus as 'home' students. As for the question of lack of organisation, this was a common perception of white anti-racist community workers, who tended to see groups formed around restaurants or cafés as inherently corrupt, or found fault with 'unprofessional' organisation – as will be discussed later.

The findings presented by the Hausers on the question of black women were even more biased. 'Needing' to adapt to the climate was hardly an exclusively female issue, as the opening chapters of Sam Selvon's *The Lonely Londoners* (1956) suggests.[89] With high unemployment in Jamaica and other parts of the West Indies as the push factor encouraging people to move to Britain to escape poverty, buying suitable winter clothes beforehand – if they were available – was not a reasonable use of resources. But the 'coldness' of the weather served two metonymic purposes, indicating a lack of welcome, but also, as Mary Chamberlain has found, an indication of the destruction of previous, imperialist assumptions about the 'motherland'.[90] Working to make up deficits in the husband's income was hardly a problem unique to black women, and their lack of enthusiasm for domestic service was shared by large numbers of white working-class women. But if white girls and women no longer wanted to go into domestic service, this may suggest that there was an assumption on the part of the Hausers and others that their place should be taken by black girls and women. In essence, the Hausers' project did nothing other than confirm views held by the white majority, and at this stage at least, did not challenge those perceptions.

The Race Relations Acts and the Bengali community in east London

Not relating to the needs of the local community in a meaningful way was a problem faced by many settlements, especially if in the post-war period their neighbourhood demographics changed. This was particularly the case at Toynbee Hall, where the local community evolved from being predominantly Jewish to predominantly Bengali in around twenty years. This had a particular impact upon the settlement's work in terms of community race relations. The positioning of the settlement in relation to the local community also had an impact upon its connections with local community groups.

The first Bangladeshi community organisations grew out of the networks of Lascar seamen who had found themselves in east London having arrived in the docks.[91] Lascar seamen became a more common sight in British ports after 1780, when they were able to join voyages past the Cape of Good Hope.[92] Following government pressure to concern itself with the welfare of the Lascars, the East India Company opened a home for destitute sailors in Hackney, on the outskirts of early nineteenth-century London,[93] before the Strangers' Home for Asiatics, Africans and South Sea Islanders was opened in the West India Docks in 1857.[94] Larger numbers of Indian seamen were recruited during the expansion of steam shipping, as they were believed by the shipping companies to be better able to cope with the boiler rooms,[95] as well as accepting lower pay and conditions than British sailors.[96] Some 3,427 seamen of Indian origin serving in the merchant navy were killed during the First World War, with a further 1,200 taken prisoner,[97] and thousands served again in the Second World War on the North Atlantic.[98] Although there were British-run hostels like the Strangers' Home, the first instance of a network of Bengali seamen has been traced back to the early 1920s. Some sailors had settled in London after the First World War, and were visited by seamen on shore leave, before being joined by more settlers in the 1930s. Seamen found their way to Aldgate, where a Mr Munshi ran a lodging house and Ayub Ali ran the Shah Jalal restaurant in Commercial Street. These two establishments formed a safe hub for runaway sailors to gravitate to as well as to access help with writing letters and dealing with paperwork.[99]

Thus the origins of Bangladeshi community politics lay in networks of younger males setting themselves up in London. Groups of friends created and congregated around cafés to enjoy home cooking, or the closest approximation to it in wartime London. Cafégoers who spoke English would read and write letters for their friends.[100] The first formal organisations to develop were Muslim burial societies, which were pioneered by Haji Taslim Ali, *imam* at the East London Mosque from 1956. Although the mosque formed a focal point for the growing community, the Pakistan Welfare Association was established in 1952 to support its welfare needs.[101] When the British had granted independence to India in 1947 the country was split according to religious divisions – Hindu India and Muslim Pakistan, the latter in turn divided into West and East Pakistan. The Bengali community became citizens of East Pakistan, although their capital was located in West Pakistan. During the course of the 1950s the East Pakistanis found themselves at a disadvantage to the West Pakistanis.[102] Early tensions centred upon the introduction of Urdu, the main language of West Pakistan, as the official language of East Pakistan. The first mutterings of dissent came from students at the University of Dhaka, who were obliged to learn and write essays in another language.[103] The language question proved to be an enduring fault line between East and West Pakistan, and a galvanising factor for the East Pakistanis. The shooting of the Language Martyrs, students protesting over the introduction of Urdu, on 21 February 1952 mustered support for the Awami League and the United Front, which came to power in a land-slide victory in 1954. The West Pakistani government saw this election result as a threat, and launched a military *coup*.[104] These events had a direct impact upon the Bengali community in the United Kingdom, especially when the leader of the United Front sought exile in London.[105] The Pakistan High Commission began to refuse to issue passports to Bengalis wishing to travel to the United Kingdom to live and work, yet at the same time granted travel visas to people from West Pakistan whose lives had been disrupted by Partition to move to Bradford to work in the textile industry.[106]

Although the passport issue was resolved in 1956, relations between West and East Pakistan shaped the nature of early Bengali community politics in London. The Pakistan Welfare Association, as it was known before 1971, was concerned with campaigning for the rights of Bengalis, as support was not always readily forthcoming from the Pakistan High Commission. It was also dominated by a group of men who were gradually joined by their wives and children. Networking through friends or kinship groups was essential for survival in Britain, and then as a means of consolidating the community's position.[107] This method of community organisation shaped such initiatives as the Immigrants' Advice Bureau (IAB).

The following discussion will look at the relationship between the IAB and the Council of Citizens and Toynbee Hall. This relationship illuminates the ways in which grass-roots organisations could spring up in 1960s east London, but also how their relations with established charities such as Toynbee Hall could be problematic. Such difficulties were the root of later tension, wherein grass-roots activists distrusted their colleagues at the settlements, often believing that the settlements and their related bodies were ill equipped to deal with the emergent needs of the Bengali community or that they were paternalistic. As with other initiatives, such as the Workers' Education Centre at Toynbee Hall, which provided English classes,[108] the IAB grew out of the Pakistani Welfare Association networks of the early 1960s, and specifically from a gambling club, the Commonwealth Club.[109] One of the founder members, Nawab Ali, recounted the difficulties of dealing with paperwork in English, and that an organic solution had grown out of friends who could speak and read English interpreting letters and drafting suitable correspondence. This inspired them to consider formalising and extending such work through an advice centre.[110]

The IAB working group established premises for its centre in Hanbury Street, Whitechapel, and proposed to run the advice centre along the lines of the Citizens' Advice Bureaux. By December 1967 they were ready to open the centre, and invited a number of local dignitaries, including Peter Shore, the MP for Stepney.[111] At this point a campaign emanating from Toynbee Hall to thwart the IAB came to light. The community relations officer at the Council of Citizens of Tower Hamlets, which was then based at the settlement, appeared to be at the centre of this campaign. On learning that Shore planned to attend the meeting, the officer phoned Shore's office to protest, arguing that the group who had founded it had 'associations with gambling and owe the GLC money in respect of previous ventures in the field'.[112] A Bashir Uddin wrote to Shore claiming that, despite the IAB's desire to help immigrants, its aim was instead to profit from them.[113] Nevertheless, Shore attended the event and inaugurated the centre. In his speech he noted that Britain relied on the work of voluntary agencies to tackle new social problems, and highlighted the work of the National Committee for Commonwealth Immigrants and the CCTH in this regard. But Shore also pointed to the need to continue to extend work against discrimination further – such as through the IAB and other initiatives working together.[114]

This did not satisfy the CCTH. A letter from the community relations officer to Shore indicated uncertainty and competition between a group purporting to be the IAB and the Ghar Se Ghar Tower Hamlets Asian Advice Project. The officer also suggested that Subid Ali and others had lied about having support from the Pakistani High Commission for their project, and that Subid Ali and Amar Bose (an English teacher at Toynbee Hall) had likewise been petitioning the CCTH for support. Amar Bose later challenged the CCTH, asking for the annual general meeting of 1967 to be filmed by a visiting film company as part of a protest against the lack of Asians sitting on the

CCTH liaison committee. Bose and a Mr Arshidullah presented the AGM with a petition of 274 signatures requesting their membership of the CCTH executive committee. The officer stated that 'many uninvited Pakistanis did appear but obviously did not understand the proceedings and no demonstration took place'. She finally reported that Abdul Malik had brought her an invitation to the launch event but had evaded her questions about its organisation. Following this incident, she phoned the Pakistan High Commission, which denied knowledge of the group. The officer attached a confidential addendum on the opening of the centre to her letter, in which the correspondent noted that Alderman John Orwell told her that the IAB would affiliate to the CCTH. The correspondent was upset that the LBTH had not corresponded with them on the matter, as the 'agent of the Local Authority', and was perturbed when Orwell displayed lack of concern over the East London Mosque or the Pakistan Welfare Association having knowledge of the IAB, or about the IAB being 'purely a money making venture'. In the report Subid Ali was believed to have expressed the view that 'no one in this area understood the ways of Pakistanis. There was a language barrier and he felt that Pakistanis should help their own people.'[115] The IAB functioned successfully until the mid-1970s, when it was subsumed within the general Toynbee Hall Citizens' Advice Bureau due to lack of funding.[116] The community relations officer's anxieties, which seem to have focused largely on a group being able to organise itself without her expertise, were unfounded. The IAB was a project that provided a much needed service to the community, but it had problems with settlement staff who were not always as cognisant as they might be of others' needs, and who attempted to shoehorn them into particular ways of working.

As the 1960s progressed, the CCEL changed its aims. It retained its interest in working as a watchdog body and, to an extent, in educating the local population. The Race Relations Act 1965 introduced the Race Relations Board, and with it a series of local boards to act as conciliators in disputes.[117] The CCEL was consequently reformed as the Council of Citizens of Tower Hamlets (CCTH), first as a local board in respect of the 1965 Act, and as a 'community relations council' following the 1968 Act.[118] It evolved from being concerned with the protection of the Jewish community and became more involved with the issues around new Commonwealth immigration. Race was at the forefront of the political agenda in the 1960s as groups such as the Campaign against Racial Discrimination (also based at Toynbee Hall) drew the government's attention to the deficiencies of the Race Relations Acts, and Enoch Powell spoke infamously of 'rivers of blood'. By the late 1960s the CCTH appointed a community relations officer whose job was to undertake conciliation work but also to develop partnerships between local voluntary organisations.

Whilst the CCTH did a relatively good job of encouraging charities and organisations in the new London Borough of Tower Hamlets to join the Council as members, it was not as successful in developing networks with ethnic minority community groups. By 1970 the CCEL counted the majority of local organisations and group as members, but it was strangely slow to develop full working links with the League of Overseas Pakistanis and the Pakistani Welfare Association, although it worked hard to improve relations between the Metropolitan Police and the local Asian community.[119] This was somewhat surprising given that 1970 was a year of particular violence in the area, with regular 'skinhead' attacks on the Bangladeshi community. Two London Chest Hospital staff members were viciously attacked in April 1970, prompting a group of around 200 East Pakistanis to form a vigilante association to help protect themselves and their community.[120]

What was becoming increasingly clear was that, as in 1936, groups such as the CCEL or CCTH were not felt to be totally useful by local immigrant communities. Whilst a total of sixty-five individual complaints were made in 1970 to the CCTH,[121] the inability of the Council and the police to prevent attacks and far right harassment did not inspire confidence among members of the Bangladeshi community. In the same year, a CCTH detached youth worker found that local youth club provision did not on the whole appeal to young Bengalis, who preferred to go to the West End or to the cinema for entertainment if funds allowed. Those who remained at home felt bored and vulnerable, the latter especially after the skinhead attacks.[122] Whilst the skinhead attacks subsided, tension simmered and occasionally boiled over into violent attacks, especially in the case of Bengali families housed outside the Spitalfields area. In the immediate run-up to the murder of Altab Ali and the Brick Lane to Downing Street march, tension had been stirred up by large groups of white youngsters rampaging through Brick Lane on 26 April 1978 and again in June.[123] The latter was exacerbated by the GLC 'ghetto' scandal, which implied that the GLC was to create a Bengali 'ghetto' in Spitalfields.[124] In the eyes of local activists such as the Reverend Kenneth Leech the CCTH was a redundant if well funded body in terms of dealing with the tensions of 1978, whilst Caroline Adams of the Avenues Unlimited youth group saw the Anti-racist Committee of Asians in East London, founded in 1976, as a far more effective body and its role in 1978 as marking the 'coming of age' of the Bengali community.[125]

Toynbee Hall was interested in the Bengali community up to a point, although the Council of Citizens of Tower Hamlets was seen as a redundant body by the late 1970s. Initiatives like the Bengali Health Advisory Service of the same period were somewhat more popular, and Donald Chesworth, warden from 1977 onwards, would support a number of more successful projects in the course of the 1980s. But Bengali community groups had grown up successfully despite or without the help of the settlement.

Conclusion

Following the activities of the CCEL and the CCTH is one of the means by which we can unpack the complexity of relations between the new Bangladeshi community and existing state and voluntary welfare organisations. There are parallels between the Bengali and Jewish communities, and it is important that such historical linkages are fully explored. Yet we should avoid the tendency to see immigration and assimilation in the East End in linear terms, with the Huguenots being seamlessly replaced by the Jewish community, and in turn by the Bengali community. What this chapter has shown is that, although well meaning, groups such as the CCTH risked being out of touch with the new communities around them, the CCEL and the CCTH ultimately failed in an area in which they had long seen themselves as experts. They were often paternalistic, and not always able or willing to accept that their expertise could fall short of what was required.

Notes

1 Note that 'Pakistani' or 'East Pakistani' are used interchangeably with Bangladeshi/Bengali in this chapter, reflecting the changing status of the country. After Partition in 1947, the Muslim areas of India formed part of West and East Pakistan. East Pakistan – present-day Bangladesh – was separated from West Pakistan by several thousand miles, and tensions soon emerged over the union. In 1971 East and West Pakistan went to war, with the result that East Pakistan split from its Western counterpart and became Bangladesh. 'Coloured' is used only when directly quoted from contemporary sources.

2 T. Kushner, 'Jew and non-Jew in the East End of London: towards an anthropology of 'everyday' relations', in G. Alderman and C. Holmes (eds) *Outsiders and Outcasts: Essays in Honour of William J. Fishman* (London: Duckworth, 1993), pp. 32–3.

3 *Ibid.*

4   *Ibid.* and Kushner, 'Ambivalence or antisemitism? Christian attitudes and responses in Britain to the crisis of European Jewry during the Second World War', *Holocaust and Genocide Studies* 5:2 (1990); T. Kushner and N. Valman, *Remembering Cable Street: Fascism and Anti-fascism in British Society* (London: Valentine Mitchell, 1999).

5   J. Jacobs, *Out of the Ghetto: My Youth in the East End. Communism and Fascism, 1913–1939* (London: Janet Simon, 1978); P. Piratin, *Our Flag stays Red* (London: Lawrence & Wishart, 1980); R. Samuel, *East End Underworld: Chapters in the Life of Arthur Harding* (London: Routledge, 1981).

6   M. Beckman, *The 43 Group* (London: Centreprise, 1993).

7   D. Renton, *Fascism, Anti-fascism and Britain in the 1940s* (Basingstoke: Palgrave, 2000); *When We Touched the Sky: The Anti-Nazi League, 1977–1981* (Cheltenham: New Clarion Press, 2006).

8   T. P. Linehan, 'The British Union of Fascists in Hackney and Stoke Newington, 1933–1940', in Alderman and Holmes, *Outsiders and Outcasts.*

9   C. Adams, *Across Seven Seas and Thirteen Rivers: Life Stories of Pioneer Sylhetti Settlers in Britain* (London: THAP, 1987).

10   J. Eade, *The Politics of Community: The Bangladeshi Community in East London* (Aldershot: Avebury, 1989); *Placing London: From Imperial Capital to Global City* (Oxford: Berghahn, 2000); J. Eade *et al.* (eds) *Tales of Three Generations of Bengalis in Britain: Oral History and Socio-cultural Heritage Project* (London: Nimrul Committee and CRONEM, 2006).

11   P. Werbner, *Imagined Diasporas among Manchester Muslims: The Public Performance of Pakistani Transnational Identity Politics* (Oxford: James Currey, 2002).

12   A. Brah, *Cartographies of Diaspora: Contesting Identities* (London: Routledge, 1996).

13   P. Gilroy, *There ain't no Black in the Union Jack: The Cultural Politics of Race and Nation* (London: Routledge, 2002).

14   See Jacobs, *Out of the Ghetto*, esp. p. 29.

15   K. Leech, *Brick Lane, 1978: The Events and their Significance*, 2nd edn (London: Stepney Books, 1994), p. 6.

16   Toynbee Hall, *Toynbee Hall Annual Report, 1916–1917, 1917–1918, 1918–1919* (London: Toynbee Hall, 1919), pp. 9–10.

17   B. L. Q. Henriques, *The Indiscretions of a Warden* (London: Methuen, 1937), p. 95.

18   *Ibid.*, p. 91.

19   See D. Feldman, 'The importance of being English: Jewish immigration and the decay of liberal England', in D. Feldman and G. Stedman Jones (eds) *Metropolis. London: Histories and Representations since 1800* (London: Routledge, 1989).

20   R. Skidelsky, 'Mosley, Sir Oswald Ernald, sixth baronet (1896–1980)', in H. C. G. Matthew and B. Harrison (eds) *Oxford Dictionary of National Biography* (Oxford: Oxford University Press, 2004); ed. L. Goldman, January 2007.

21 Linehan, 'The British Union of Fascists in Hackney and Stoke Newington'.
22 Leech, *Brick Lane, 1978*, p. 6.
23 Linehan, 'The British Union of Fascists in Hackney and Stoke Newington', p. 140.
24 *Ibid.*, p. 141.
25 Beckman, *The 43 Group*, pp. 8–9.
26 Kushner, 'Jew and non-Jew in the East End', pp. 46–7.
27 A. Briggs, 'Mallon, James Joseph (1874–1961)', in Matthew and Harrison, *Oxford Dictionary of National Biography*.
28 J. M. Lee, 'The Romney Street group: its origins and influence, 1916–1922', *Twentieth Century British History* 18:1 (2007).
29 Briggs, 'Mallon, James Joseph (1874–1961)'.
30 B. Donoughue and G. W. Jones, *Herbert Morrison: Portrait of a Politician* (London: Weidenfeld & Nicolson, 1973), p. 219.
31 *Ibid.*, pp. 226–7.
32 Barnett Research Centre at Toynbee Hall (hereafter BRC), TOY/EXT/10/2, Letter, J. J. Mallon to the editor of the *Manchester Guardian*, 20 October 1936.
33 Henriques, *The Indiscretions of a Warden*, p. 97.
34 BRC, TOY/EXT/10/2, Letter, J. J. Mallon to the editor of the *Manchester Guardian*, 20 October 1936.
35 BRC, TOY/EXT/10/1, J. J. Mallon and Harold Nicolson, 'Understanding our Neighbours: Prejudice and Democracy', *c.* 1949.
36 Beckman, *The 43 Group*, pp. 11–12.
37 *Ibid.*, p. 14.
38 *Ibid.*, pp. 15–17.
39 Renton, *Fascism, Anti-fascism and Britain in the 1940s*, pp. 5, 36.
40 *Ibid.*, p. 36, pp. 72–5 on Labour, pp. 90–1 on the Board of Deputies.
41 BRC, TOY/EXT/10/5, CCEL, Report 3, Work since the Executive Committee in March, 13 June 1949.
42 *Ibid.*, CCEL Executive Committee, Minutes, 6 October 1949.
43 *Ibid.*, Letter, J. J. Mallon to P. Cudlipp, *Daily Herald*, 18 November 1949.
44 Renton, *Fascism, Anti-fascism and Britain in the 1940s*, p. 90.
45 BRC, TOY/SPE/2/2/13, *Toynbee Hall and the Jewish Community*, *c.* 1936; L. London, *Whitehall and the Jews, 1933–1948: British Immigration Policy, Jewish Refugees and the Holocaust* (Cambridge: Cambridge University Press, 2000); R. Cohen, *Migration and its Enemies: Global Capital, Migrant Labour and the Nation State* (London: Ashgate, 2006).
46 Kushner, 'Ambivalence or antisemitism?'
47 A. Pleasance, 'Obituary: Hallam Tennyson', *Guardian*, 6 January 2006, p. 38.
48 BRC, TOY/EXT/10/5, CCEL Executive Committee, Minutes, 6 October 1949.
49 *Ibid.*, Letter, Sidney Salomon to J. J. Mallon, 12 May 1949.
50 Briggs, 'Mallon, James Joseph (1874–1961)'.

51 BRC, TOY/EXT/10/5, Letter, Sidney Salomon to J. J. Mallon, 12 May 1949.
52 *Ibid.*, Copy letter, Mallon to Salomon, 26 May 1949, and copy letter, Mallon to Salomon, 7 June 1949.
53 Jewish Defence Committee informants/observers often co-operated with Special Branch by infiltrating Union Movement branches and other fascist groups: Renton, *Fascism, Anti-Fascism and Britain in the 1940s*, p. 91.
54 BRC, TOY/EXT/10/5, Letter, Salomon to Mallon, 15 June 1949, with enclosure, 'Mosley Social, May 1st 1949'.
55 Renton, *Fascism, Anti-fascism and Britain in the 1940s*, p. 35.
56 BRC, TOY/EXT/10/5, Letter, A. I. Polack to Mallon, 4 March 1954.
57 *Ibid.*, Copy letter, Mallon to Polack, 15 March 1954, and Minutes of CCEL Schools Committee, 19 January 1954.
58 BRC, TOY/EXT/10/4, CCEL Schools Committee, Report on the meeting at Dame Colet House, 5 February 1962.
59 BRC, TOY/EXT/10/6, Letter, Polack to A. E. Morgan, 28 February 1958.
60 K. G. T. McDonnell, 'The Economic and Social Structure of the Parishes of Bromley, Hackney, Stepney and Whitechapel from the Thirteenth to the Sixteenth Century' (PhD dissertation, Queen Mary, University of London, 1958–59).
61 BRC, TOY/EXT/10/6, Attachment to letter, Polack to A. E. Morgan, 28 February 1958.
62 BRC, TOY/EXT/10/18, Council of Citizens of East London, *Our East London: A Study in Diversity* (London: CCEL, 1963).
63 BRC, TOY/EXT/10/21, Mobile exhibition flyer.
64 BRC, TOY/EXT/10/1, J. J. Mallon, 'Understanding our Neighbours: Prejudice and Democracy', *c.* 1949.
65 Gilroy, *There ain't no Black in the Union Jack*, pp. 181–2.
66 Education of Children from Ethnic Minority Groups, Committee of Inquiry, *Education for All: Report of the Committee of Enquiry into the Education of Children from Ethnic Minority Backgrounds*, Cmnd 9453 (London: HMSO, 1985), pp. 767–9.
67 Gilroy, *There ain't no Black in the Union Jack*, pp. 156–8, 164–9.
68 See R. Durgnat, 'Two "social problem" films: *Sapphire* and *Victim*', in A. Burton, T. O'Sullivan and P. Wells (eds) *Liberal Directions: Basil Dearden and Postwar British Film Culture* (Trowbridge: Flicks, 1997).
69 BRC, TOY/EXT/10/8, 'Tactless to film in Notting Hill: union's protest', *The Times*, 11 October 1958, p. 3.
70 *Ibid.*, Letter, A. E. Morgan to A. N. E. McHaffie, Mayor of Kensington, 16 October 1958.
71 BRC, TOY/EXT/10/8, Letter, McHaffie to Morgan, 18 October 1958.
72 *Ibid.*, Copy letter, McHaffie, J. F. F. Heaks, Mayor of Hammersmith, A. W. Carruthers, Mayor of Paddington, A. D. H. Plummer, Mayor of Marylebone, to the Secretary of the Rank Organisation, 21 October 1958; Letter, S. R. Kellett, Secretary to the Mayor of Kensington, to Morgan, 23 October 1958.

73 *Ibid.*, Copy letter, Morgan to R. A. Butler, 24 October 1958.
74 *Ibid.*, Letter, John Trevelyan, Secretary, British Board of Film Censors, to Morgan, 28 October 1958.
75 *Ibid.*, Letter, John H. Davis to Morgan, 30 October 1958.
76 *Ibid.*, Copy letter, Morgan to Davis, 6 November 1958.
77 *Ibid.*, Copy letter, Morgan to McHaffie, 10 November 1958.
78 *Ibid.*, Letter, Polack to Morgan, 13 November 1958.
79 M. Dresser, *Black and White on the Buses: The 1963 Colour Bar Dispute in Bristol* (Bristol: Bristol Broadsides, 1986), p. 10.
80 BRC, TOY/EXT/10/8, Letter, Apps to Morgan, 12 September 1958.
81 *Ibid.*, Letter, Polack to Morgan, 17 September 1958.
82 'For white and coloured children: a party with a purpose', *The Times*, 24 December 1958, p. 4.
83 BRC, TOY/EXT/10/8, CCEL Executive Committee meeting, 6 July 1958.
84 *Ibid.*
85 BRC TOY/EXT/10/8, Richard Hauser for the Centre for Group Studies, Interim report to A. E. Morgan, Chairman of the Committee of Citizens of East London, 13 March 1958, p. 1.
86 *Ibid.*, p. 2.
87 *Ibid.*, p. 3.
88 R. Ballard, 'Introduction: The Emergence of Desh Pardesh', in R. Ballard (ed.) *Desh Pardesh: The South Asian Presence in Britain*, ed. Roger Ballard (London: Hurst, 1994) pp. 14–17.
89 S. Selvon, *The Lonely Londoners* (London: Allan Wingate, 1956).
90 M. Chamberlain, *Narratives of Exile and Return* (New Brunswick NJ: Transaction, 2005).
91 See Adams, *Across Seven Seas*.
92 R. Visram, *Ayahs, Lascars and Princes: Indians in Britain, 1700–1947* (London: Pluto, 1986), p. 34.
93 *Ibid.*, p. 39; Adams, *Across Seven Seas*, p. 20.
94 Visram, *Ayahs, Lascars and Princes*, p. 49.
95 Adams, *Across Seven Seas*, p. 21.
96 *Ibid.*, p. 24.
97 *Ibid.*, p. 23.
98 *Ibid.*, pp. 33–4.
99 *Ibid.*, pp. 39–43.
100 *Ibid.*, pp. 46–8.
101 *Ibid.*, p. 55; M. A. Asghar, *Bangladeshi Community Organisations in East London* (London: Bangla Heritage, 1996), p. 123.
102 Eade *et al.*, *Tales of Three Generations of Bengalis in Britain: Oral History and Socio-cultural Heritage Project*, p. 16.
103 *Ibid.*, p. 15.
104 Adams, *Across Seven Seas*, p. 55.
105 *Ibid.*, p. 57.
106 *Ibid.*, p. 59.

107 K. Gardner and A. Shukur, ' "I'm Bengali, I'm Asian, and I'm living here": the changing identity of British Bengalis', p. 151; Ballard, 'Introduction. The emergence of Desh Pardesh', pp. 11–13, both in Ballard, *Desh Pardesh.*

108 TOY/SPE/1, *Annual Report, 1965*, p. 4.

109 Adams, *Across Seven Seas*, pp. 85–6.

110 *Ibid.*, p. 88.

111 British Library of Political and Economic Science, London School of Economics (hereafter BLPES), Peter Shore Papers, 19/34, Constituency affairs: Immigrants' Advice Bureau.

112 *Ibid.*, 19/34, Memorandum, R. Dines to Peter Shore, 19 December 1967.

113 *Ibid.*, 19/34, Letter, Bashir Uddin to Peter Shore, 15 December 1967.

114 *Ibid.*, 19/34, Copy letter, Peter Shore to CCTH Community Relations Officer, 21 December 1967.

115 *Ibid.*, 19/34, Letter, CCTH Community Relations Officer to Peter Shore, 5 January 1968, and Addendum – Confidential, 20 December 1967.

116 *Ibid.*, 19/34, CAB (Specialists in Immigrant Affairs), 48 Hanbury Street, fifth year anniversary, report by E. Akin Olulode, Adviser and Organiser, 1973.

117 Commission for Racial Equality (2005), 'Forty Years of Law against Racial Discrimination', www.cre.gov.uk/40years/act_one.html (accessed 9 June 2007).

118 *Ibid.*

119 BLPES, Peter Shore Papers, 19/68, Council of Citizens of Tower Hamlets, Report of the Community Relations Officer at the annual general meeting, 9 July 1970, pp. 4–5.

120 *Ibid.*, 19/62, 'Tempers rise about P***-bashing', *Hackney Gazette*, 10 April 1970; 'Pakistanis volunteer to be vigilantes', *East London Advertiser*, 24 April 1970.

121 *Ibid.*, 19/68, Council of Citizens of Tower Hamlets, Report of the Community Relations Officer at the annual general meeting, 9 July 1970, p. 11.

122 *Ibid.*, 19/66, *CCTH News*, October–November 1970, pp. 5–7.

123 Leech, *Brick Lane, 1978*, pp. 7, 9.

124 *Ibid.*, p. 13.

125 *Ibid.*, pp. 20, 22.

Conclusion

This study has traced the changes and continuities in the university settlement movement from the end of the First World War through to the late 1970s, looking at a range of settlement activities: work to promote health and well-being for all age groups; youth clubs; work with the juvenile courts; free legal advice and advocacy; and attempts to develop anti-racist work. It also considered the ways in which life at the settlements changed between 1918 and 1950, particularly in regard to the ways in which women from working-class and lower middle-class backgrounds became involved with settlements.

The book has looked at the settlement movement during a time of immense change in the nature of the relationship between the state, charities and individuals as a whole. In 1918 charities, including the settlements, were involved in the provision of certain personal social services – such as health care for women – yet by 1939 the expansion of local authority powers in particular and a desire not to needlessly duplicate certain activities led to the withdrawal of settlements from that type of work. This pattern was accompanied by the increased tendency of settlements to tailor their work to the availability of funding by the early 1920s. Funding continued to dictate the nature of work by the settlements from this period through to the 1970s and beyond. In the inter-war period their work was characterised by the development of fund raising for specific projects or areas of work, with paid staff employed to do the work over a set period of time and a lessening emphasis on volunteers. These trends continued into the post-war period, being negotiated again by the areas covered by national and local government, and the availability of funds to undertake projects. Although the settlements and other charities saw themselves as innovators in social welfare, these experiments, however valuable, were ultimately vulnerable where the state and major funders were unwilling to take on the responsibility of funding them.

Settlement leaders were keen to embrace local and national government, and to attempt to use settlement expertise to drive the welfare
mix in their locality or area of interest. Thus CTWS and Mansfield House
were involved first in the provision of health care for women and
children in the West Ham area, and then later in campaigning with
the South West Ham Health Society to ensure that gaps in health provision were filled. Research work, such as that led by Toynbee Hall,
could bring the question of the health of the poor to the attention of
politicians, but ultimately others were more successful in leading
such debates. This work – as providers of health care or as advocates
for working-class communities – changed drastically with the advent
of the National Health Service and the developing role of local
authorities. The settlements sought out and were sought out by new
client groups, those whose needs were not being fully met by the NHS,
such as families with disabled children who required moral support
above and beyond what was offered by the state. Experiments with
boarding schools for evacuees had resonance with such activities as
the Children's Country Holiday Fund, work with older people and
later with therapeutic communities. In terms of health, the Second World
War and the NHS of 1948 onwards had a massive impact upon the
work of these charities. Settlements remained in the welfare mix, but
were providers of services in addition to mainstream care or worked
to improve the well-being of such groups as the elderly. Their efforts
were far surpassed by the local authority, yet their importance lay in
providing top-up services to their local communities, if not at borough
level.

Boys' and girls' clubs, such a staple of settlement life before the
Second World War, underwent many changes from the 1960s. During
the war they had a vital role to play in providing those in the Forces
with another means of keeping in touch with life at home, as well
as with regular entertainment and news. Boys' clubs in particular
were tied up with notions of citizenship and healthful manliness, and
the war accelerated such ideas and associations. Girls' clubs were a
means of helping girls to become 'good' home makers and mothers
of the future, although from the 1950s onwards they were more likely
to evolve into mixed clubs providing 'social' activities rather than a
diet of training activities. But whether or not clubs were segregated
by gender or were purely 'social' places rather than offering access to
sport or adult education, it was essential for the local community to
feel it had some ownership of the activities. The club – be it for young
people or for the elderly – or, similarly, an adult education class had
to be a resource that met the needs and wants of the community. The

settlements were not always successful in judging when it was best to speak for the community and when to listen to them, but this lesson was often learned when communities rejected or subverted particular activities. Similar imperatives operated in the development of anti-racist work. Settlement leaders thought that they were offering the best solution to the problem of fascism in the East End, but they often failed to empathise with the frustrations of young Jewish people and to strike a chord with them. Likewise, work with the Bangladeshi community focused on trying to impose the norms of British charitable and committee work upon such groups as the Immigrants' Advice Bureau rather than adopting different strategies to help the group develop a successful service. Again, the response of the Council of Citizens of Tower Hamlets to the resurgence of racism in the 1970s did not impress or encourage young Bangladeshi people. Settlements could not impose themselves upon communities – they had to learn what it was people wanted, and then to provide a means of doing or enabling this. Barnett's notion that the settlement resident should be a leader of the community held little weight before the Second World War; it held less afterwards.

Legal work in all its manifestations was more successful. Work with the juvenile courts before the early 1950s merged such voluntary provision as boys' clubs, hostels and services for families with state legal mechanisms. Those with voluntary expertise – such as Henriques and Lady Cynthia Colville – used this to innovatively shape the delivery of youth justice and welfare. But as the 'old guard' retired from both settlements and the magistracy, new directions were taken. Following the expansion of the state in terms of the provision of local authority care for children and young people, the establishment of the Youth Service and the extension and expansion of secondary schooling, the settlements turned their attention to those who were not adequately provided for: adult ex-prisoners. Settlements such as Toynbee Hall, Blackfriars and Lady Margaret Hall were concerned that those leaving prison were not given adequate support to reintegrate into mainstream society, and thus the settlements experimented with befriending, outpost flats and bail hostels. These were bold, innovative projects that had much in common with the therapeutic community model, but failed to attract sufficient resources and funding. But not all working-class Londoners had difficulty with the criminal law – one of the most enduring and important areas of settlement work was the provision of free legal advice and advocacy. Although this was an important area of work before the Second World War, it became even more so in the course of the 1960s and 1970s. Problems with landlords and employers remained major areas of complaint, but the expansion and increasing complexity of the welfare state meant that many people were bewildered by dealings with bureaucrats.

The settlements between 1918 and 1979 retained their original focus on working with their local communities, but what changed was the manner in which this was achieved. The 1960s and 1970s in particular saw a flurry of new activities and approaches, which both anticipated and responded to lacks in welfare state provision. If settlements were to survive the post-welfare state world they needed to be able to adapt to changing local needs and national imperatives, balancing the emergent needs of a community in the midst of post-war rebuilding with the changes brought in by the various reports, White Papers and Acts of Parliament of the 1960s and 1970s. On some occasions – as with the Grendon outpost – the settlements were able to set up a project that was innovative, but it did not follow that they would be able to get the state to take up or fund the work. In this way the dynamic between the settlements and all levels of the state was much the same as before the Second World War, if the nature of the welfare mix was radically different. And at all times, in this period, the settlements had to be able to provide something that their local community wanted and needed – if they lost sight of their community, their efforts floundered. Between 1918 and 1979 the settlements continued to act as a buffer between the private individual and the worst effects of poverty and social inequality in a continually dynamic and protean mixed economy of welfare.

Appendix

The diversification of settlement income: Toynbee Hall, 1920–45

The following tables demonstrate the diversification of settlement income and the rise of specialist or project staff in the period 1920–45. Table A1 illustrates the rise in paid staff and the diversification of their roles, despite the impact of the Second World War. Table A2 shows how traditional forms of settlement income – subscriptions from individual donors or 'associates' – became secondary to large donors, such as those mentioned in Table A3, who made major contributions to the Jubilee Fund to build the theatre and teaching block (1935–38).

Table A1 Expenditure on staff pay (£)

Staff	1920	1926	1930	1938	1945
Secretary and clerks' salaries	163	322	316	471	607
Wages of domestic staff	482	999	1,020	1,096	1,003
Warden's salary	100	500	500	500	527
Sub-warden's salary	0	300	172	348	0
Registrar and teachers	0	0	495	1,090	239
Research worker	0	0	0	0	139
Music scholarship teachers	0	0	0	0	85
Registrar (previously with teachers	0	0	0	0	137
Total	745	2,121	2,503	3,505	2,737

Appendix

Table A2 Sources of income

Source	1920	1926	1930	1938	1940	1945
Associates	538	109	152	118	112	94
Subscriptions and donations	506	1,033	684	1,685	196	16,196
Societies	263	200	149	99	0	0
Rents	116	699	0	0	0	0
Residents' rents	2,547	2,927	0	0	0	0
London County Council grants	568	0	800	1,027	0	2,900
Student fees	46	0	201	597	0	0
Board of Education grant	31	0	0	0	0	0
Subscriptions from Cambridge	0	0	9	4	0	0
Subscriptions from Oxford	0	0	37	13	0	0

Sources: Data from *Toynbee Hall Annual Report, 1919–1920*; *Toynbee Hall 1884–1925: Fortieth Annual Report, 1926*; *Toynbee Hall Annual Report, 1929, 1930*; *Toynbee Hall Report, 1935–1938*; *Toynbee Hall Report, 1938–1946*.

Table A3 Jubilee Fund: major donors (£)

Donor	Donation	% of total
Carnegie Trust	10,000	37.8759185
London Parochial	10,000	37.8759185
Pilgrim Trust	6,000	22.7255511
Goldsmiths' Company	250	0.94689796
United Dominions Trust	52	0.19695478
Ironmongers' Company	50	0.18937959
Thames Police Court	20	0.07575184
London Commercial Club	20	0.07575184
Historical Association	10	0.03787592
Total	26,402	100

Sources: Data from *Toynbee Hall Annual Report, 1919–1920*; *Toynbee Hall 1884–1925: Fortieth Annual Report, 1926*; *Toynbee Hall Annual Report, 1929, 1930*; *Toynbee Hall Report, 1935–1938, 1938–1946*.

Bibliography

Primary sources

Barnett Research Centre at Toynbee Hall
TOY/CEN/2/2/6, Nutrition research.
TOY/CEN/7/5, Doris Greening.
TOY/CEN/8/5, Park House.
TOY/DEP/3/3, Toynbee Hall Old People's Welfare Service.
TOY/DEP/9/4, Stepney Children's Fund.
TOY/DEP/10, Special Families Centre.
TOY/DEP/11/2, Family Centre.
TOY/EXT/10, Citizens of East London/Tower Hamlets, *c.* 1936 onwards.
TOY/SPE, Annual Reports of Toynbee Hall, 1918–79.

British Film Institute
Lee, J. dir. *Children on Trial* (United Kingdom: Crown Film Unit, 1946).

British Library of Political and Economic Science, London School of Economics
Papers of Peter Shore: 19/10; 19/34; 19/62; 19/66; 19/68; 19/79.

Hackney Archives
Hoxton Café Project, Annual Reports.

Lambeth Archives Department
IV183, Papers of Lady Margaret Hall Settlement.
IV183/3/1, Wages Book.
IV183/3/2, Correspondence, including job descriptions and applications for domestic employees, 1930–52.
IV183/5/1, Children's Country Holiday Fund.
IV183/5/7, NACRO Bail/Aftercare Hostel.

London Metropolitan Archives
A/KE/250/7, King's Hospital Fund for London, Invalid and Crippled Children's Society Hospital, formerly Canning Town Women's Settlement Hospital, 1898–1929.

LMA/4040, Children's Country Holiday Fund.
PS/IJ/O/019, PS/IJ/O/027, PS/IJ/O/028, PS/IJ/O/058, PS/IJ/O/070, Inner London Juvenile Court, 1930–50.

National Archives
HO 383/151, HM Prison, Grendon.

NSPCC Library
The Child's Guardian.

National Sound Archive, British Library
Tony Lynes, interviewed by Niamh Dillon, Pioneers in Social Welfare and Charitable Work Series, F16969. London: National Sound Archive, 2005.
Elizabeth Hoodless, interviewed by Louise Brody, Pioneers in Social Welfare and Charitable Work Series, F18454. London: National Sound Archive, 2006.

Newham Local Studies and Archives
Papers of Daisy Parsons.
Canning Town Women's Settlement, Executive Committee, minutes, 1891–1939.
27/1, Fairbairn House Standing Committee, 1945–46.
27/2, Fairbairn House Standing Committee, October 1943 to July 1945.
34/1, Fairbairn House, wartime correspondence.
2/81, Fairbairn House, papers and correspondence.
2/83, Mansfield House, Warden's Letter.
Mansfield House Hospital Letter Society, minute book.
Mansfield House Magazine.
Mansfield House Men's and Boys' Club, address books, 1906–10.
South West Ham Children's Welfare Society, minutes, 1948–60.
South West Ham Health Society, minutes, 1918–52.

Royal London Hospital Archives and Museum
Dr Spence Galbraith, Personal Papers, 'An Invalid and Crippled Children's Hospital', MS loose sheet.

Women's Library
5/WUS, Women's University/Blackfriars Settlement.
5WUS/1/J/1/b12–21 FL609, St Mary's Girls' Clubs, Workers' Sub-committee, 1925–27.
5/WUS/142/, Blackfriars Scheme.

Worshipful Company of Goldsmiths Library
Committee book, 1937–41.
Court book, 1936–42.

Film and television

Dearden, B. dir. *Sapphire* (United Kingdom: Artna Films, 1959).

Wyler, W. dir. *Mrs Miniver* (United States: MGM Studios, 1942).

ITN Source. 'Miss Earhart', footage of visit to Toynbee Hall, 25 June 1928, British Pathé BP25062873621.

ITN Source. 'King and Queen in the East End: Their Majesties visit famous Toynbee Hall Social Centre, and the Queen's Hospital for Children', 28 November 1938, British Pathé BGX407232377.

Published primary sources

Addams, J. *Twenty Years at Hull-House*, ed. J. Hurt. Urbana IL: Prairie State and University of Illinois Press, 1990. Reprint, 1910.

Alden, P. 'Settlements in relation to local administration', in *University and Social Settlements*, ed. W. Reason, 27–44. London: Methuen, 1898.

Atherley Jones, L. A., and H. H. L. Bellot. *The Law of Children and Young Persons (in Relation to Penal Offences), including the Children Act, 1908*. London: Butterworth, 1909.

Barnett, H. *Canon Barnett: His Life, Work and Friends*, 2 vols. London: John Murray, 1918.

Barnett House. *London Children in War-time Oxford: A Study of Social and Educational Results of Evacuation*. London: Oxford University Press, 1947.

Barnett, S. A. 'University settlements'. *Nineteenth Century*, December 1895, 1015–24.

Barnett, S. A. 'Charity versus outdoor poor relief'. *Nineteenth Century*, November 1899, 818–26.

Barnett, S. A. 'The ideal city', in *The Ideal City*, ed. H. E. Meller, 55–66. Leicester: Leicester University Press, 1979.

Beveridge, W. *Voluntary Action: A Report on Methods of Social Advance*. London: Allen & Unwin, 1948.

Birmingham, M. *You Can Help Me*. London: Collins, 1974.

Braithwaite, W. J. *Lloyd George's Ambulance Wagon, being the Memoirs of William J. Braithwaite, 1911–1912*. London: Chivers, 1970.

Brew, J. M. *In the Service of Youth: A Practical Manual of Work among Adolescents*. London: Faber & Faber, 1943.

British Association of Residential Settlements. *The British Association of Residential Settlements: Report, 1935–1938*. London: British Association of Residential Settlements, 1938.

British Association of Residential Settlements. *Residential Settlements: A Survey*. London: British Association of Residential Settlements, 1951.

British Hospitals Association. *The Hospitals Year-Book, 1947*. London: British Hospitals Association, 1947.

British Hospitals Association. *The Hospitals Year-Book, 1948*. London: British Hospitals Association, 1948.

Brittain, V. 'Is sane mad and mad sane? Myths of the family', *The Times*, Saturday 2 October 1972, 12.

Burdett's. *Burdett's Hospitals and Charities*. London: Faber & Gwyer, 1928.

Butterworth, J. *Clubland*. London: Epworth Press, 1932.

Canning Town Women's Settlement. 'A settlement hospital', in *University and Social Settlements*, ed. W. Reason, 160–1. London: Methuen, 1898.

Carr-Saunders, A. M., H. Mannheim and E. C. Rhodes. *Young Offenders: An Enquiry into Juvenile Delinquency*. Cambridge: Cambridge University Press, 1942.

Catchpool, E. St John. *Candles in the Darkness*. London: Bannisdale, 1966.

Children's Country Holidays Fund. *Children's Country Holidays Fund: What It's All About, How You Can Help*. London: Children's Country Holidays Fund, 1981.

Children's Country Holidays Fund. *Will there be a Holiday for him this Year?* London: Children's Country Holidays Fund, 1981.

Clutton-Brock, G. 'Homes, hostels, lodgings' 2, 'A. G. Clutton Brock, Principal Probation Officer for the Metropolitan Area'. *Probation Journal* 3:2 (1938): 23–4.

Edgar, D. *Mary Barnes*. London: Methuen, 1979.

'Editorial'. *Probation Journal* 8:3 (1939): 115.

Education of Children from Ethnic Minority Groups, Committee of Inquiry, *Education for All: Report of the Committee of Enquiry into the Education of Children from Ethnic Minority Backgrounds*, Cmnd 9453. London: HMSO, 1985.

Egerton, R. *Legal Aid*. London: Kegan Paul Trench Trubner, 1945.

Engels, F. *The Condition of the Working Class in England*, trans. W. O. Henderson and W. H. Chaloner. Oxford: Blackwell, 1971.

'For white and coloured children: a party with a purpose', *The Times*, 24 December 1958, 4.

Gavin, H. *Sanitary Ramblings, being Sketches and Illustrations of Bethnal Green, a Type of the Condition of the Metropolis and other Large Towns*. London: Frank Cass, 1971.

Grant, C. E. *Work and Clo' Fund*. London: Clara E. Grant, 1905.

Grant, C. E. *Farthing Bundles*. London: Fern Street Settlement, 1935.

Grant, C. E. *From 'Me' to 'We': Forty Years on Bow Common*. London: Fern Street Settlement, 1940.

Greenwood, A. 'Blind-alley labour', *Economic Journal*, 22 (1912): 309–14.

Harvey, T. E. *A London Boy's Saturday*. Bournville: St George Press, 1906.

Hene, D. H. *A Simple Explanation of the Legal Aid Scheme*. London: *Daily Express* Legal Guides, 1951.

Hene, D. H. *The State is at your Service from Birth to Old Age*. London: *Daily Express* Legal Guides, 1952.

Henriques, B. L. Q. *Club Leadership*. London: Humphrey Milford, 1933.

Henriques, B. L. Q. *The Indiscretions of a Warden*. London: Methuen, 1937.

Henriques, B. L. Q. *The Indiscretions of a Magistrate: Thoughts on the Work of the Juvenile Court*. London: Non-fiction Book Club, 1950.

Henriques, B. L. Q. *Fratres: Club Boys in Uniform*. London: Secker & Warburg, 1951.

Holden, H. M., *The Hoxton Café Project: Report on Seven Years' Work*. Leicester: Youth Service Information Centre, 1972.

Hutchins, B. L., and J. J. Mallon. *Women in Modern Industry, with a Chapter (Women's Wages in the Wage Consensus of 1906) contributed by J. J. Mallon*. London: Bell, 1915.

Isaacs, S., ed., *The Cambridge Evacuation Survey: A Wartime Study in Social Welfare and Education*. London: Methuen, 1941.

Jackson, C. 'The Children's Country Holidays Fund and the settlements', in *The Universities and the Social Problem: An Account of the University Settlements in East London*, ed. J. M. Knapp, 87–105. London: Rivington Percival, 1895.

Jephcott, P. *Clubs for Girls: Notes for New Helpers at Clubs*. London: Faber & Faber, 1943.

Jephcott, P. *Rising Twenty: Notes on some Ordinary Girls*. London: Faber & Faber, 1943.

Jones, J. M. *Free Legal Advice in England and Wales*. Oxford: Slatter & Rose, 1940.

Kingsley Hall and Children's House. *Report, 1943–1934*. London: Kingsley Hall and Children's House, 1944.

Knapp, J. M., ed., *The Universities and the Social Problem: An Account of the University Settlements in East London*. London: Rivington Percival, 1895.

Llewellyn Smith, H. *The Borderland between Public and Voluntary Action in the Social Services*, Barnett House Papers. London: Oxford University Press, 1937.

M'Gonigle, G. C. M. 'Poverty, nutrition and public health: an investigation into some of the results of moving a slum population to modern dwellings', *Proceedings of the Royal Society of Medicine* 26:6 (1933): 677–87.

Manchester University Settlement. *Ancoats: A Study of a Clearance Area. Report of a Survey Made in 1937–1938*. Manchester: Manchester University Settlement, 1945.

Markham, V. *May Tennant: A Portrait*. London: Falcon, 1949.

Mary Ward Settlement. *Annual Report for the Year ended 31st August 1959*. London: Mary Ward Settlement, 1959.

Ministry of Health. *Report on Conditions in Reception Areas, by a Committee under the Chairmanship of Mr Geoffrey Shakespeare, MP*. London: HMSO, 1941.

Ministry of Health. *Hostels for 'Difficult' Children: A Survey of Experience under the Evacuation Scheme*. London: HMSO, 1944.

Morgan, A. E. *The Needs of Youth: A Report made to the King George's Jubilee Trust Fund*. London: Oxford University Press, 1939.

Morgan, A. E. *The Young Citizen*. Harmondsworth: Penguin, 1943.

Newham Rights Centre. *Newham Rights Centre: Two Years' Work, 1975–1977*. London: Newham Rights Centre, 1977.

Oxford House. *The Oxford House in Bethnal Green, 1884–1948*. London: Brakell, 1948.

Oxford House Country Schools. *Citizens in Readiness, being an Account of the Oxford House Country Schools*. London: Brakell, 1945.

Padley, R., and M. Cole, eds. *Evacuation Survey: A Report to the Fabian Society*. London: Routledge, 1940.

Paterson, A. *Across the Bridges, or, Life by the South London Riverside*. London: Edward Arnold, 1911.

Paterson, A. *Legal Aid as a Social Service*. London: Cobden Trust, 1971.

Philadelphia Association. *Philadelphia Association Report*. London: Philadelphia Association, 1969.

Picht, W. *Toynbee Hall and the English Settlement Movement*, trans. L. A. Cowell. London: Bell, 1914.

Port of London Authority Amateur Boxing Club. *Port of London Boxing Championships, 1977*. London: Port of London Authority Amateur Boxing Club, 1977.

Report of the Committee on Scottish Health Services, Cmnd 5204. Edinburgh: HMSO, 1936.

Report of the Royal Commission on Population, Cmnd 7695. London: HMSO, 1949.

Rowntree, B. S. *The Human Needs of Labour*. London: Longmans Green, 1938.

Selvon, S. *The Lonely Londoners*. London: Allan Wingate, 1956.

Sewell, Margaret, and Eleanor G. Powell. 'Women's settlements in England', in *University and Social Settlements*, ed. W. Reason, 89–100. London: Methuen, 1898.

Sherwell, A. 'Settlements and the labour movement', in *University and Social Settlements*, ed. W. Reason, 115–36. London: Methuen, 1898.

'Sir Ian Horobin on indecency charges'. *The Times*, Wednesday 16 May 1962, 9.

'Sir Ian Horobin sentenced to four years' imprisonment'. *The Times*, Wednesday 18 July 1962, 9.

'Sir Ian Horobin'. *The Times*, Thursday 8 July 1976, 18.

Smith, F. 'The nation's schools', in *A Century of Municipal Progress, 1835–1935*, ed. H. Laski, W. I. Jennings and W. Robson, 219–43. London: Allen & Unwin, 1935.

Society of Friends. *Hostels for Old People*. London: Friends' Relief Service, 1945.

St Hilda's East. *Annual Report, 1956–1957*. London: St Hilda's East, 1957.

St Hilda's East. *Annual Report, 1961–1962*. London: St Hilda's East, 1962.

Tribe, R. 'Results of treatment at the Poplar School clinic'. *School Hygiene* 2:5 (1911): 252–8.

Urwick, E. J., ed. *Studies of Boy Life in our Cities*. London: Dent, 1904.

Secondary sources

Books and articles

Abel-Smith, B. *The History of the Nursing Profession*. London: Heinemann, 1975.

Abel-Smith, B., and R. Stevens. *Lawyers and the Courts: A Sociological Study of the English Legal System, 1750–1965*. London: Heinemann, 1967.

Abel-Smith, B., and R. Stevens. *In Search of Justice: Society and the Legal System*. London: Allen Lane, 1968.

Abel-Smith, B., and P. Townsend. *The Poor and the Poorest: A New Analysis of the Ministry of Labour's 'Family Expenditure Surveys' of 1953–1954 and 1960.* London: Bell, 1965.

Adams, C. *Across Seven Seas and Thirteen Rivers: Life Stories of Pioneer Sylhetti Settlers in Britain.* London: THAP, 1987.

Aitken, W. F. *Canon Barnett, Warden of Toynbee Hall: His Mission and its Relation to Social Movements.* London: Partridge, 1902.

Alderman, G., and C. Holmes, eds. *Outsiders and Outcasts: Essays in Honour of William J. Fishman.* London: Duckworth, 1993.

Asghar, M. A. *Bangladeshi Community Organisations in East London.* London: Bangla Heritage, 1996.

Ashworth, M. *Oxford House in Bethnal Green, 1884–1984.* London: Oxford House, 1984.

Bailey, P. *Leisure and Class in Victorian England: Rational Recreation and the Contest for Control, 1830–1885.* London: Methuen, 1987.

Bailey, V. *Delinquency and Citizenship: Reclaiming the Young Offender, 1914–1948.* Oxford: Clarendon Press, 1987.

Ballard, R. 'Introduction. The Emergence of Desh Pardesh', in *Desh Pardesh: The South Asian Presence in Britain,* ed. R. Ballard, 1–34. London: Hurst, 1994.

Barbuto, D. M. *American Settlement Houses and Progressive Social Reform: An Encyclopedia of the American Settlement Movement.* Phoenix AZ: Oryx, 1999.

Barbuto, D. M. *The American Settlement Movement: A Bibliography.* Westport CT: Greenwood, 1999.

Barker, R. *Children of the Benares: A War Crime and its Victims.* London: Grafton, 1990.

Barnes, M., and J. Berke. *Mary Barnes: Two Accounts of a Journey through Madness.* Harmondsworth: Penguin, 1973.

Barrett, G. *Blackfriars Settlement: A Short History.* London: Blackfriars Settlement, 1985.

Beauman, K. B. *Women and the Settlement Movement.* London: Radcliffe, 1996.

Beckman, M. *The 43 Group.* London: Centreprise, 1993.

Beer, R., and C. A. Pickard. *Eighty Years on Bow Common.* London: Fern Street Settlement, 1987.

Behlmer, G. *Friends of the Family: The English Home and its Guardians.* Stanford CA: Stanford University Press, 1998.

Berridge, V., 'Health and medicine', in *The Cambridge Social History of Britain, 1750–1950* III, *Social Agencies and Institutions,* ed. F. M. L. Thompson, 171–242, Cambridge: Cambridge University Press, 1990.

Bilson, G. *The Guest Children: The Story of British Child Evacuees sent to Canada during World War II.* Saskatoon: Fifth House, 1988.

Blair, R. 'Jackson, Sir Cyril (1863–1924)', in *Oxford Dictionary of National Biography,* ed. H. C. G. Matthew and B. Harrison. Oxford: Oxford University Press, 2004.

Bochel, D. *Probation and After-care: Its Development in England and Wales.* Edinburgh: Scottish Academic Press, 1976.

Bourdieu, P. *Outline of a Theory of Practice*, trans. R. Nice. Cambridge: Cambridge University Press, 1977.

Bowlby, J. *Attachment and Loss*. London: Hogarth Press, 1969.

Bradley, K. M. *Bringing People Together: Bede House Association, Bermondsey and Rotherhithe, 1938–2003*. London: Bede House Association, 2004.

Bradley, K. M. 'Creating local elites: the university settlement movement, national elites and citizenship in east London, 1884–1940', in *In Control of the City: Local Elites and the Dynamics of Urban Politics, 1800–1960*, ed. S. Couperus, C. Smit and D. J. Wolffram, 81–92. Leeuven: Peeters, 2007.

Bradley, K. M. 'Juvenile delinquency, the juvenile courts and the settlement movement, 1908–1950: Basil Henriques and Toynbee Hall', *Twentieth Century British History* (2007). Advance access publication 13 December 2007, doi: 10.1093/tcbh/hwm038.

Brah, A. *Cartographies of Diaspora: Contesting Identities*. London: Routledge, 1996.

Bressey, C. 'Invisible presence: the whitening of the black community in the historical imagination of British archives'. *Archivaria* 61 (2006): 47–61.

Briggs, A. 'Mallon, James Joseph (1874–1961)', in *Oxford Dictionary of National Biography*, ed. H. C. G. Matthew and B. Harrison. Oxford: Oxford University Press, 2004.

Briggs, A., and A. Macartney. *Toynbee Hall: The First Hundred Years*. London: Routledge, 1984.

Brodie, M. 'Benn, Sir John Williams, First Baronet (1850–1922)', in *Oxford Dictionary of National Biography*, ed. H. C. G. Matthew and B. Harrison. Oxford: Oxford University Press, 2004.

Bruce, M. *The Coming of the Welfare State*. London: Batsford, 1961.

Burton, A., T. O'Sullivan and P. Wells (eds). *Liberal Directions: Basil Dearden and Postwar British Film Culture*. Trowbridge: Flicks, 1997.

Calder, A. *The Myth of the Blitz*. London: Pimlico, 1992.

Chamberlain, M. *Narratives of Exile and Return*. New Brunswick NJ: Transaction, 2005.

Cherry, S. 'Before the National Health Service: financing the voluntary hospitals, 1900–1939'. *Economic History Review* 50:2 (1997): 305–26.

Clapp, E. J. 'The Chicago Juvenile Court Movement in the 1890s', Leicester: Centre for Urban History, University of Leicester, 1995. www.le.ac.uk/hi/teaching/papers/clapp1.html.

Cohen, R. *Migration and its Enemies: Global Capital, Migrant Labour and the Nation State*. London: Ashgate, 2006.

Cohn, E. J., and R. Egerton. *A Guide to Legal Aid for the Poor*. London: Stevens, 1947.

Collins, M. *Modern Love: An Intimate History of Men and Women in Twentieth Century Britain*. London: Atlantic, 2003.

Commission for Racial Equality (2005) 'Forty Years of Law against Racial Discrimination'. www.cre.gov.uk/40years/act_one.html and www.cre.gov.uk/40years/act_two.html (accessed 9 June 2007).

Cooper, R. 'What we take for granted', in *Between Psychotherapy and Philosophy: Essays from the Philadelphia Association*, ed. P. Gordon and R. Mayo, 1–16. London: Whurr, 2004.

Cooter, R. ed. *In the Name of the Child: Health and Welfare, 1880–1940*. London: Routledge, 1992.

Cordery, S. *British Friendly Societies, 1750–1914*. Basingstoke: Palgrave, 2003.

Cox, P. *Gender, Justice and Welfare: Bad Girls in Britain, 1900–1950*. Basingstoke: Palgrave, 2003.

Crosby, T. L. *The Impact of Civilian Evacuation in the Second World War*. London: Croom Helm, 1986.

Crowther, A. *British Social Policy, 1914–1939*. Basingstoke: Macmillan, 1988.

Cullen, E. *Grendon and Future Therapeutic Communities in Prison*. London: Prison Reform Trust, 1998.

Cunningham, H. *Leisure in the Industrial Revolution, 1780–1880*. London: Croom Helm, 1980.

Cunningham, H. *Children and Childhood in Western Society since 1500*. London: Longman, 1995.

Curthoys, M. C., and T. Wales, 'Alden, Sir Percy (1865–1944)', in *Oxford Dictionary of National Biography*, ed. H. C. G. Matthew and B. Harrison. Oxford: Oxford University Press, 2004.

Curtis, H., and M. Sanderson. *The Unsung Sixties: Memoirs of Social Innovation*. London: Whiting & Birch, 2004.

Darley, G. *Octavia Hill: A Life*. London: Constable, 1990.

Daunt, M. *By Peaceful Means: The Story of Time and Talents, 1887–1987*. London: Time and Talents Association, 1989.

Davies, A. 'The police and the people: gambling in Salford, 1900–1939'. *Historical Journal* 34: 1 (1991): 87–115.

Davies, A. *Leisure, Gender and Poverty: Working-class Culture in Manchester and Salford, 1900–1939*. Buckingham: Open University Press, 1992.

Davies, A. ' "These viragoes are no less cruel than the lads": young women, gangs and violence in late Victorian Manchester and Salford'. *British Journal of Criminology* 39:1 (1999): 72–89.

Davies, J. S., and M. Freeman. 'Education for citizenship: the Joseph Rowntree Charitable Trust and the Educational Settlement movement'. *History of Education* 32:3 (2003): 303–18.

Davin, A. 'Imperialism and motherhood'. *History Workshop Journal* 5:1 (1978): 9–65.

Davin, A. 'Community, life-cycle, diaspora: a daughter's view', in *Communities of Women: Historical Perspectives*, ed. B. Brookes and D. Page, 13–26. Dunedin NZ: University of Otago Press, 2002.

Davis Smith, J., C. Rochester and R. Hedley, eds. *An Introduction to the Voluntary Sector*. London: Routledge, 1995.

Deakin, N. *In Search of Civil Society*. Basingstoke: Palgrave, 2001.

Dench, G., K. Gavron, and M. D. Young. *The New East End: Kinship, Race and Conflict*. London: Profile, 2006.

Department for Constitutional Affairs. *A Fairer Deal for Legal Aid*, Cm 6591. London: HMSO, 2005.

Donoughue, B., and G. W. Jones. *Herbert Morrison: Portrait of a Politician*. London: Weidenfeld & Nicolson, 1973.

Dresser, M. *Black and White on the Buses: The 1963 Colour Bar Dispute in Bristol*. Bristol: Bristol Broadsides, 1986.

Durgnat, R. 'Two "social problem" films: *Sapphire* and *Victim*', in *Liberal Directions: Basil Dearden and Postwar British Film Culture*, ed. A. Burton, T. O'Sullivan and P. Wells, 59–88. Trowbridge: Flicks, 1997.

Eade, J. *The Politics of Community: The Bangladeshi Community in East London*. Aldershot: Avebury, 1989.

Eade, J. *Placing London: From Imperial Capital to Global City*. Oxford: Berghahn, 2000.

Eade, J., A. A. Ullah, J. Iqbal and M. Hey, eds. *Tales of Three Generations of Bengalis in Britain: Oral History and Socio-cultural Heritage Project*. London: Nimrul Committee and CRONEM, 2006.

Feldman, D. 'The importance of being English: Jewish immigration and the decay of liberal England', in *Metropolis. London: Histories and Representations since 1800*, ed. D. Feldman and G. Stedman Jones, 56–84. London: Routledge, 1989.

Feldman, D., and G. Stedman Jones, *Metropolis. London: Histories and Representations since 1800*. London: Routledge, 1989.

Field, F. *Back to the Thirties for the Poor? A Report on the Living Standards of the Poor in 1975*. London: Child Poverty Action Group, 1975.

Finlayson, G. 'A moving frontier: voluntarism and the state in British social welfare, 1911–1949'. *Twentieth Century British History* 1:2 (1990): 183–206.

Fishman, W. J. *East End, 1888: A Year in a London Borough among the Labouring Poor*. London: Duckworth, 1988.

Flegel, M. 'Changing faces: the NSPCC and the use of photography in the construction of cruelty to children', *Victorian Periodicals Review* 39:1 (2006): 1–20.

Fowler, D. *The First Teenagers: The Lifestyle of Young Wage-earners in Interwar Britain*. London: Woburn Press, 1995.

Fraser, D. *The Evolution of the British Welfare State: A History of Social Policy since the Industrial Revolution*. Basingstoke: Palgrave, 2003.

Freeman, M. ' "No finer school than a settlement": the development of the educational settlement movement'. *History of Education* 31:3 (2002): 245–62.

Freeman, M. 'The provincial social survey in Edwardian Britain'. *Historical Research* 75 (2002): 73–89.

Freeman, M. 'The magic lantern and the cinema: adult schools, educational settlements and secularisation in Britain, *c*. 1900–1950', *Quaker Studies*, 11 (2007): 192–203.

Gardiner, A. G. *John Benn and the Progressive Movement*. London: Dent, 1925.

Gardner, K., and A. Shukur. '"I'm Bengali, I'm Asian, and I'm living here": the changing identity of British Bengalis', in *Desh Pardesh: The South Asian Presence in Britain*, ed. R. Ballard, 142–64. London: Hurst, 1994.

Garrard, J. *Democratisation in Britain: Elites, Civil Society and Reform since 1800*. Basingstoke: Palgrave, 2002.

Garry, R. C., and D. F. Smith. 'Cathcart, Edward Provan (1877–1954)', in *Oxford Dictionary of National Biography*, ed. H. C. G. Matthew and B. Harrison. Oxford: Oxford University Press, 2004.

Gilbert, B. B. *The Evolution of National Insurance in Great Britain: The Origins of the Welfare State*. London: Michael Joseph, 1966.

Gilroy, P. *'There ain't no Black in the Union Jack': The Cultural Politics of Race and Nation*. London: Routledge, 2002.

Glasby, J. *Poverty and Opportunity: One Hundred Years of the Birmingham Settlement*. Studley: Brewin, 1999.

Gordon, P., and R. Mayo, eds. *Between Psychotherapy and Philosophy: Essays from the Philadelphia Association*. London: Whurr, 2004.

Gorsky, M. *Patterns of Philanthropy: Charity and Society in Nineteenth Century Bristol*. Woodbridge: Boydell & Brewer, 1999.

Gorsky, M., and J. Mohan. 'London's voluntary hospitals in the inter-war period: growth, transformation, or crisis?' *Nonprofit and Voluntary Sector Quarterly* 30:2 (2001): 247–75.

Gorsky, M., J. Mohan and M. Powell. 'The financial health of voluntary hospitals in inter-war Britain'. *Economic History Review* 55:3 (2002): 533–57.

Grant, W. *Pressure Groups, Politics and Democracy in Britain*. New York: Harvester, 1995.

Green, D. G., *Reinventing Civil Society: The Rediscovery of Welfare without Politics*. London: IEA, 1993.

Griffin, C. *Representations of Youth: The Study of Youth and Adolescence in Britain and America*. London: Polity Press, 1993.

Habermas, J. *The Structural Transformation of the Public Sphere: An Inquiry into a Category of Bourgeois Society*, trans. T. Burger and F. Lawrence. Cambridge: Cambridge University Press, 1989.

Hardy, A. *Health and Medicine in Britain since 1860*. Basingstoke: Palgrave, 2001.

Harlow, C., and R. Rawlings. *Pressure through Law* London: Routledge, 1992.

Harris, B. *The Origins of the British Welfare State: Society, State and Social Welfare in England and Wales, 1800–1945*. Basingstoke: Palgrave, 2004.

Harris, J. *Private Lives, Public Spirit: Britain, 1870–1914*. London: Penguin, 1993.

Harris, J. 'Beveridge, William Henry, Baron Beveridge (1879–1963)', in *Oxford Dictionary of National Biography*, ed. H. C. G. Matthew and Brian Harrison. Oxford: Oxford University Press, 2004.

Harris, J. M., and D. Oppenheimer. *Into the Arms of Strangers: Stories of the Kindertransport*. London: Bloomsbury, 2000.

Harris, K. *Attlee*. London: Weidenfeld & Nicolson, 1982.

Hayward, P. *Children into Exile: The Story of the Evacuation of School Children from Hellfire Corner in the Second World War*. Dover: Buckland, 1997.

Heller, M. 'The National Insurance Acts 1911–1947, the Approved Societies and the Prudential Assurance Company'. *Twentieth Century British History* 19:1 (2008): 1–28.

Hendrick, H. *Images of Youth: Age, Class and the Male Youth Problem, 1880–1920.* Oxford: Clarendon Press, 1990.

Hendrick, H. *Child Welfare: England, 1872–1989.* London: Routledge, 1994.

Hilton, T. *John Ruskin.* London: Yale University Press, 2002.

Hobbs, D. *Doing the Business: Entrepreneurship, the Working Class and Detectives in the East End of London.* Oxford: Oxford University Press, 1989.

Hollis, P. *Ladies Elect: Women in English Local Government, 1865–1914.* Oxford: Clarendon Press, 1987.

Hood, R., and E. Joyce. 'Three generations: oral testimonies on crime and social change in London's East End'. *British Journal of Criminology* 39:1 (1999): 136–60.

Inglis, R. *The Children's War: Evacuation, 1939–1945.* London: Collins, 1989.

Jackson, L. A. 'Care or Control? The Metropolitan Women Police and child welfare, 1919–1969'. *Historical Journal* 46:3 (2003): 623–48.

Jacobs, J. *The Death and Life of Great American Cities.* New York: Random House, 1961.

Jacobs, J. *Out of the Ghetto: My Youth in the East End, Communism and Fascism, 1913–1939.* London: Janet Simon, 1978.

Jarvis, F. V. *Advise, Assist and Befriend: A History of the Probation and After-care Service.* London: National Association of Probation Officers, 1972.

Jeffs, T. 'Changing their ways: youth work and "underclass" theory', in *Youth, the Underclass and Social Exclusion,* ed. R. McDonald, 153–66. London: Routledge, 1997.

Jennings, H. *University Settlement Bristol: Sixty Years of Change, 1911–1971.* Bristol: University Settlement Bristol Community Association, 1971.

John, A. V. 'Macarthur, Mary Reid (1880–1921)', in *Oxford Dictionary of National Biography,* ed. H. C. G. Matthew and B. Harrison. Oxford: Oxford University Press, 2004.

J. Sainsbury PLC. 'Our History', www.j-sainsbury.co.uk/index.asp?pageid= 188&caseid=interwar#interwar (viewed 16 January 2008).

Kadish, A. 'Toynbee, Arnold (1852–1883)', in *Oxford Dictionary of National Biography,* ed. H. C. G. Matthew and B. Harrison. Oxford: Oxford University Press, 2004.

Kadish, S. 'Moses, Miriam (1884–1965)', in *Oxford Dictionary of National Biography,* ed. H. C. G. Matthew and B. Harrison. Oxford: Oxford University Press, 2004.

Kennedy, A. 'The settlement heritage', in *National Conference of Social Work,* ed. International Federation of Settlements: International Federation of Settlements, 1953.

Kendall, J. *The Voluntary Sector: Comparative Perspectives in the UK.* London: Routledge, 2003.

Kendall, J., and M. Knapp. *The Voluntary Sector in the United Kingdom.* Manchester: Manchester University Press, 1996.

Kendall, J., and M. Knapp. 'The United Kingdom', in *Defining the Nonprofit Sector: A Cross-national Analysis*, ed. L. M. Salamon and H. K. Anheier, 249–79. Manchester: Manchester University Press, 1997.

Ker, I. 'Newman, John Henry (1801–1890)', in *Oxford Dictionary of National Biography*, ed. H. C. G. Matthew, B. Harrison and L. Goldman. Oxford: Oxford University Press, 2004 and 2007.

Kotowicz, Z., R. D. *Laing and the Paths of Anti-Psychiatry*. London: Routledge, 1997.

Koven, S. 'From rough lads to hooligans: boy life, national culture and social reform', in *Nationalisms and Sexualities*, ed. A. Parker, M. Russo, D. Sommer and P. Yaeger, 365–89. London: Routledge, 1991.

Koven, S. 'Henrietta Barnett, 1851–1936: the (auto)biography of a late Victorian marriage', in *After the Victorians: Private Conscience and Public Duty in Modern Britain. Essays in Memory of John Clive*, ed. P. Mandler, S. Pedersen and J. Clive, 31–53. London, New York: Routledge, 1994.

Koven, S. 'Barnett, Dame Henrietta Octavia Weston (1851–1936)', in *Oxford Dictionary of National Biography*, ed. H. C. G. Matthew and B. Harrison. Oxford: Oxford University Press, 2004.

Koven, S. 'Barnett, Samuel Augustus (1844–1913)', in *Oxford Dictionary of National Biography*, ed. H. C. G. Matthew and B. Harrison. Oxford: Oxford University Press, 2004.

Koven, S. *Slumming: Sexual and Social Politics in Victorian London*. Princeton NJ: Princeton University Press, 2005.

Koven, S., and S. Michel. 'Womanly duties: maternalist politics and the origins of welfare states in France, Germany, Great Britain and the United States, 1870–1939'. *American Historical Review* 95:4 (1990): 1076–108.

Koven, S., and S. Michel. *Mothers of a New World: Maternalist Politics and the Origins of Welfare States*. New York: Routledge, 1993.

Kushner, T. 'Ambivalence or antisemitism? Christian attitudes and responses in Britain to the crisis of European Jewry during the Second World War'. *Holocaust and Genocide Studies* 5:2 (1990): 175–89.

Kushner, T. 'Jew and non-Jew in the East End of London: towards an anthropology of everyday relations', in *Outsiders and Outcasts: Essays in Honour of William J. Fishman*, ed. G. Alderman and C. Holmes, 32–52. London: Duckworth, 1993.

Kushner, T., and N. Valman. *Remembering Cable Street: Fascism and anti-Fascism in British Society*. London: Valentine Mitchell, 1999.

Lady Margaret Hall Settlement. 'Summary: Brief History of the Settlement since 1887', www.lmhs.org.uk/about.php (accessed 2 August 2007).

Leat, D. 'The rise and role of the Poor Man's Lawyer'. *British Journal of Law and Society* 2:2 (1975): 166–81.

Lee, J. M. 'The Romney Street group: its origins and influence, 1916–1922'. *Twentieth Century British History* 18:1 (2007): 106–28.

Leech, K. *Brick Lane, 1978: The Events and their Significance*, 2nd edn. London: Stepney Books, 1994.

Lewis, J. *Women and Social Action in Victorian and Edwardian England.* London: Edward Elgar, 1991.

Lewis, J. *The Voluntary Sector, the State and Social Work in Britain: The Charity Organisation Society/Family Welfare Association since 1869.* London: Edward Elgar, 1995.

Lewis, J. 'The voluntary sector and the state in twentieth-century Britain', in *Welfare Policy in Britain: The Road from 1945*, ed. H. Fawcett and R. Lowe, 52–68. Basingstoke: Macmillan, 1999.

Linehan, T. P. 'The British Union of Fascists in Hackney and Stoke Newington, 1933–1940', in *Outsiders and Outcasts: Essays in Honour of William J. Fishman*, ed. G. Alderman and C. Holmes, 136–66. London: Duckworth, 1993.

Loewe, L. L. *Basil Henriques: A Portrait, based on his Diaries, Letters and Speeches and collated by his Widow, Rose Henriques.* London: Routledge & Kegan Paul, 1976.

Logan, A. ' "A suitable person for suitable cases": the gendering of juvenile courts in England, c. 1910–1939'. *Twentieth Century British History* 16:2 (2005): 129–45.

London, L. *Whitehall and the Jews, 1933–1948: British Immigration Policy, Jewish Refugees and the Holocaust.* Cambridge: Cambridge University Press, 2000.

Lowe, R. 'The Second World War, consensus and the foundation of the welfare state', *Twentieth Century British History* 1:2 (1990): 152–82.

Lowe, R. *The Welfare State in Britain since 1945.* Basingstoke: Palgrave, 2005.

Macadam, E. *The New Philanthropy: A Study of the Relations between the Statutory and Voluntary Services.* London: Allen & Unwin, 1934.

Malleier, E. *Jüdische Frauen in Wien 1816–1938. Wohlfahrt, Mädchenbildung, Frauenarbeit.* Vienna: Mandelbaum, 2003.

Malleier, E. *Das Ottakringer Settlement. Zur Geschichte eines frühen internationalen Sozialprojekts.* Vienna: Verband der Wiener Volksbildung, 2005.

Malleier, E. 'Making the world a better place: welfare and politics, welfare as politics? Activities of Jewish women in Vienna before 1938'. *Aschkenas* 16:1 (2007): 261–8.

Mallon, J. J., and E. Lascelles. *Poverty Today and Yesterday.* London: Student Christian Movement Press, 1930.

Marks, L. V. ' "They're magicians." Midwives, doctors and hospitals: women's experiences of childbirth in east London and Woolwich in the inter-war years'. *Oral History* 23:1 (1995): 46–53.

Marks, L. V. *Metropolitan Maternity: Maternal and Infant Welfare Services in early Twentieth Century London.* Amsterdam: Rodopi, 1996.

Marshall, T. H. 'Citizenship and social class', in *Citizenship and Social Class*, ed. T. Bottomore and T. H. Marshall, 3–51. London: Pluto, 1992.

Marshall, T. H., and T. Bottomore, eds. *Citizenship and Social Class.* London: Pluto, 1992.

Marwick, A. *Britain in the Century of Total War: War, Peace and Social Change, 1900–1967.* Harmondsworth: Penguin, 1970.

McCabe, S. 'Henriques, Sir Basil Lucas Quixano (1890–1961)', in *Oxford Dictionary of National Biography*, ed. H. C. G. Matthew and B. Harrison. Oxford: Oxford University Press, 2004.

McCarthy, F. *William Morris: A Life for our Time*. London: Faber, 1994.

McCarthy, M. *Campaigning for the Poor: CPAG and the Politics of Welfare*. Beckenham: Croom Helm, 1986.

McKibbin, R. *Classes and Cultures: England, 1918–1951*. Oxford: Oxford University Press, 1998.

McLaurin, S. 'M'Gonigle, George Cuthbert Mura (1889–1939)', in *Oxford Dictionary of National Biography*, ed. H. C. G. Matthew and B. Harrison. Oxford: Oxford University Press, 2004.

McLeod, H. *Class and Religion in the late Victorian City*. London: Croom Helm, 1974.

McLeod, H. *Religion and the Working Class in Nineteenth Century Britain*. London: Macmillan, 1984.

McLeod, H. *The Religious Crises of the 1960s*. Oxford: Oxford University Press, 2007.

McNamee, G. H. 'The origins of the Cook County Juvenile Court', in *A Noble Social Experiment? The First 100 Years of the Cook County Juvenile Court, 1899–1999*, ed. G. H. McNamee, 14–23. Chicago: Chicago Bar Association with the Children's Court Centennial Committee, 1999.

McNamee, G. H., ed. *A Noble Social Experiment? The First 100 Years of the Cook County Juvenile Court, 1899–1999*, Chicago: Chicago Bar Association with the Children's Court Centennial Committee, 1999.

Means, R., and R. Smith. *From Poor Law to Community Care: The Development of Welfare Services for Elderly People, 1939–1971*. Bristol: Policy Press, 1998.

Means, R., H. Morbey and R. Smith. *From Community Care to Market Care? The Development of Welfare Services for Older People*. Bristol: Policy Press, 2002.

Meller, H. E. *Leisure and the Changing City, 1870–1914*. London: Routledge & Kegan Paul, 1976.

Meller, H. E., ed. *The Ideal City*. Leicester: Leicester University Press, 1979.

Menzies, J., ed. *Children of the Doomed Voyage*. Chichester: Wiley, 2005.

Meyer-Kelly, M., and M. D. Kandiah. ' "The poor get poorer under Labour": the validity and effect of CPAG's campaign in 1970'. Paper presented at the ICBH Witness Seminar, 2003.

Mingay, G. E., ed. *The Rural Idyll*. London: Routledge, 1989.

Morgan, R. I. 'The introduction of civil legal aid in England and Wales, 1914–1949'. *Twentieth Century British History* 5:1 (1994): 38–76.

Murdoch, L. *Imagined Orphans: Poor Families, Child Welfare, and Contested Citizenship in London*. New Brunswick NJ: Rutgers University Press, 2006.

NACRO. 'Frequently Asked Questions', www.nacro.org.uk/mediacentre/FAQ.htm.

Osgerby, B. *Youth in Britain since 1945*. Oxford: Blackwell, 1998.

Owen, D. *English Philanthropy, 1660–1960*. London: Oxford University Press, 1965.

Parker, J. *Citizenship, Work and Welfare: Searching for the Good Society*. Basingstoke: Macmillan, 1998.

Parsloe, P. *The Work of the Probation and After-care Officer*. London: Routledge & Kegan Paul, 1967.

Parsons, M., and Penny, S. *The Evacuation: The True Story*. Peterborough: DSM, 1999.

Pattenden, R. *English Criminal Appeals, 1844–1994: Appeals against Conviction and Sentence*. Oxford: Oxford University Press, 1996.

Pearce, R. *Attlee*. London: Longman, 1997.

Phelps, E. S., ed. *Altruism, Morality and Economic Theory*. New York: Russell Sage Foundation, 1975.

Pimlott, J. A. R. *Toynbee Hall: Fifty Years of Social Reform*. London: Dent, 1935.

Piratin, P. *Our Flag stays Red*. London: Lawrence & Wishart, 1980.

Pleasance, A. 'Obituary: Hallam Tennyson', *Guardian*, Friday 6 January 2006, 38.

Powell, W. W., ed. *The Nonprofit Sector: A Research Handbook*. New Haven CT: Yale University Press, 1987.

Prochaska, F. K. *Women and Philanthropy in Nineteenth Century England*. Oxford: Clarendon Press, 1980.

Prochaska, F. K. *The Voluntary Impulse: Philanthropy in Modern Britain*, London: Faber & Faber, 1988.

Prochaska, F. K. 'Philanthropy', in *The Cambridge Social History of Britain, 1750–1950*, ed. F. M. L. Thompson, 357–93. Cambridge: Cambridge University Press, 1990.

Prochaska, F. K. *Philanthropy and the Hospitals of London: The King's Fund, 1897–1990*. Oxford: Clarendon Press, 1992.

Prochaska, F. K. *Christianity and Social Service in Modern Britain: The Disinherited Spirit*. Oxford: Oxford University Press, 2006.

Putnam, R. *Bowling Alone: The Collapse and Revival of American Community*. New York: Simon & Schuster, 2000.

Rainer Society. 'Our history', www.raineronline.org/gen/m1_i3_ourhistory. aspx.

Reason, W., ed. *University and Social Settlements*. London: Methuen, 1898.

Renton, D. *Fascism, anti-Fascism and Britain in the 1940s*. Basingstoke: Palgrave, 2000.

Renton, D. *When we Touched the Sky: The Anti-Nazi League, 1977–1981*. Cheltenham: New Clarion Press, 2006.

Reynolds, K. D. 'Colville (*née* Crewe-Milnes) Lady (Helen) Cynthia (1884–1968)', in *Oxford Dictionary of National Biography*, ed. H. C. G. Matthew and B. Harrison. Oxford: Oxford University Press, 2004.

Richards, J. *Inform, Advise and Support: Fifty Years of the Citizens' Advice Bureau*. Cambridge: Lutterworth, 1989.

Roberts, M. J. D., *Making English Morals: Voluntary Association and Moral Reform in England, 1787–1886*. Cambridge: Cambridge University Press, 2004.

Rock, P. 'Rules, boundaries and the courts: some problems in the neo-Durkheimian sociology of deviance'. *British Journal of Sociology* 49:4 (1998): 586–601.

Rooff, M. *Voluntary Societies and Social Policy*. London: Routledge & Kegan Paul, 1957.

Rooff, M. *A Hundred Years of Family Welfare: A study of the Family Welfare Association (formerly Charity Organisation Society), 1869–1969*. London: Michael Joseph, 1972.

Rose, J. *The Intellectual Life of the British Working Classes*. New Haven CT: Yale University Press, 2001.

Rose, M. E., and A. Woods. *Everything Went on at the Round House: A Hundred Years of the Manchester University Settlement*. Manchester: Manchester University Press, 1995.

Salamon, L. M. 'Partners in public service: the scope and theory of government–nonprofit relations', in *The Nonprofit Sector: A Research Handbook*, ed. W. W. Powell, 99–117. New Haven CT: Yale University Press, 1987.

Salamon, L. M., and H. K. Anheier. 'The challenge of definition: thirteen realities in search of a concept', in *Defining the Nonprofit Sector: A Cross-national Analysis*, ed. L. M. Salamon and H. K. Anheier, 11–28. Manchester: Manchester University Press, 1997.

Salamon, L. M., and H. K. Anheier, eds. *Defining the Nonprofit Sector: A Cross-national Analysis*. Manchester: Manchester University Press, 1997.

Samuel, R. *East End Underworld: Chapters in the Life of Arthur Harding*. London: Routledge, 1981.

Scotland, N. *Squires in the Slums: Settlements and Mission Settlements in late Victorian Britain*. London: I. B. Tauris, 2007.

Sennett, R. *Respect in an Age of Inequality*. Harmondsworth: Penguin, 2003.

Sheard, J. 'From Lady Bountiful to active citizen: volunteering and the voluntary sector', in *An Introduction to the Voluntary Sector*, ed. J. Davis Smith, C. Rochester and R. Hedley, 114–27. London: Routledge, 1995.

Sokoloff, B. *Edith and Stepney. The Life of Edith Ramsay: Sixty Years of Education, Politics and Social Change*. London: Stepney Books, 1987.

Spring Rice, M. *Working-class Wives: Their Health and Conditions*. London: Virago, 1981.

Stamp, T. *Stamp Album*. London: Bloomsbury, 1987.

Steedman, C. *Childhood, Culture and Class in Britain: Margaret McMillan, 1860–1931*. London: Virago, 1990.

Steedman, C. 'Margaret Macmillan, 1860–1931', in *Oxford Dictionary of National Biography*, ed. H. C. G. Matthew and B. Harrison. Oxford: Oxford University Press, 2004.

Sutherland, G. 'Education', in *The Cambridge Social History of Britain, 1750–1950* III, *Social Agencies and Institutions*, ed. F. M. L. Thompson, 119–69. Cambridge: Cambridge University Press, 1990.

Sutherland, J. *Mrs Humphrey Ward: Eminent Victorian, Pre-eminent Edwardian*. Oxford: Clarendon Press, 1990.

Sutherland, J. 'Ward, Mary Augusta (Mrs Humphry Ward) (1851–1920)', in *Oxford Dictionary of National Biography*, ed. H. C. G. Matthew and B. Harrison. Oxford: Oxford University Press, 2004.

Taylor-Gooby, P., and J. Zinn, eds. *Risk in Social Science*. Oxford: Oxford University Press, 2006.

Thane, P. 'Government and society in England and Wales', in *The Cambridge Social History of Britain, 1750–1950*, ed. F. M. L. Thompson, 1–61. Cambridge: Cambridge University Press, 1990.

Thane, P. 'Women in the British Labour Party and the construction of state welfare, 1906–1939', in *Mothers of a New World: Maternalist Politics and the Origins of Welfare States*, ed. S. Koven and S. Michel, 343–77. New York: Routledge, 1993.

Thane, P. *Foundations of the Welfare State*, 2nd edn. London: Longman, 1996.

Thane, P., ed. *The Long History of Old Age*. London: Thames & Hudson, 2005.

'Times obituary: John Profumo'. *The Times*, www.timesonline.co.uk/tol/news/uk/article739657.ece.

Titmuss, R. M. *Problems of Social Policy*. London: HMSO and Longmans Green, 1950.

Todd, S. 'Poverty and aspiration: young women's entry to employment in inter-war England'. *Twentieth Century British History* 15:2 (2004): 119–42.

Townsend, P. *The Family Life of Old People: An Inquiry in East London*. abridged edn. Harmondsworth: Penguin, 1970.

Townsend, P. *Poverty in the United Kingdom: A Survey of Household Resources and Standards of Living*. Harmondsworth: Penguin, 1979.

Townsend, P., ed. *The Concept of Poverty: Working Papers on Methods of Investigation and Life-styles of the Poor in Different Countries*. London: Heinemann, 1970.

Townsend, P., A. Sinfield, B. Kahan, P. Mittler, H. Rose, M. Meacher, J. Agate, T. Lynes and D. Bull, eds. *The Fifth Social Service: A Critical Analysis of the Seebohm Proposals*. London: Fabian Society, 1970.

Treble, R. 'The Victorian picture of the country', in *The Rural Idyll*, ed. G. E. Mingay, 50–60. London: Routledge, 1989.

Trolander, J. 'Microfilm review. Archives of the settlement movement, the National Federation of Settlements and successors, 1899–1958'. *Journal of American History* 79: 4 (1993): 1699–700.

Vanstone, M. *Supervising Offenders in the Community: A History of Probation Theory and Practice*. Aldershot: Ashgate, 2004.

Vernon, B. D. *Ellen Wilkinson, 1891–1947*. London: Croom Helm, 1982.

Vicinus, M. *Independent Women: Work and Community for Single Women, 1850–1920*. London: Virago, 1985.

Vincent, A. 'Green, Thomas Hill (1836–1882)', in *Oxford Dictionary of National Biography*, ed. H. C. G. Matthew and B. Harrison. Oxford: Oxford University Press, 2004.

Visram, R. *Ayahs, Lascars and Princes: Indians in Britain, 1700–1947*. London: Pluto, 1986.

Waddington, K. *Charity and the London Hospitals, 1850–1898*. Woodbridge: Boydell & Brewer, 2000.

Wales, T. 'Parsons (*née* Millo), Marguerite Lena (Daisy) (1890–1957)', in *Oxford Dictionary of National Biography*, ed. H. C. G. Matthew and B. Harrison. Oxford: Oxford University Press, 2004.

Walkowitz, J. R. *City of Dreadful Delight: Narratives of Sexual Danger in late Victorian London*. London: Virago, 2000.

Walvin, J. *Leisure and Society, 1830–1950*. London: Longman, 1978.

Watkin, A. E., and C. Clark. 'Baron, Bernhard (1850–1929)', in *Oxford Dictionary of National Biography*, ed. H. C. G. Matthew and B. Harrison. Oxford: Oxford University Press, 2004.

Webster, C. 'Healthy or hungry thirties?' *History Workshop Journal* 13:1 (1982): 110–29.

Webster, C. 'Conflict and consensus: explaining the British health service'. *Twentieth Century British History*, 1:2 (1990): 115–51.

Werbner, P. *Imagined Diasporas among Manchester Muslims: The Public Performance of Pakistani Transnational Identity Politics*. Oxford: James Currey, 2002.

Weisbrod, B. A. 'Toward a theory of the voluntary nonprofit sector in a three-sector economy', in *Altruism, Morality and Economic Theory*, ed. E. S. Phelps, 171–96. New York: Russell Sage Foundation, 1975.

Weisbrod, B. A. *The Voluntary Nonprofit Sector: An Economic Analysis*. Lexington MA: Lexington Books, 1977.

Weisbrod, B. A. *The Nonprofit Economy*. Cambridge MA: Harvard University Press, 1988.

White, J. *Rothschild Buildings: Life in an East End Tenement Block, 1887–1920*. London: Routledge & Kegan Paul, 1980.

White, J. *The Worst Street in North London: Campbell Bunk, Islington between the Wars*. London: Routledge and Kegan Paul, 1986.

White, J. *London in the Nineteenth Century: 'a human awful wonder of God'*. London: Jonathan Cape, 2007.

Whitehead, P., and R. Statham. *The History of Probation: Politics, Power and Cultural Change, 1876–2005*. Crayford: Shaw, 2006.

Whiting, R. C. 'Attlee, Clement Richard (1883–1967)', in *Oxford Dictionary of National Biography*, ed. H. C. G. Matthew and B. Harrison. Oxford: Oxford University Press, 2004.

Wills, A. 'Delinquency, masculinity and citizenship in England, 1950–1970'. *Past and Present*, 187 (2005): 157–85.

Winnicott, C., R. Shepherd and M. Davis, eds. *D. W. Winnicott: Deprivation and Delinquency*. London: Tavistock, 1984.

Winnicott, D. W. 'Children's hostels in war and peace', in *D. W. Winnicott: Deprivation and Delinquency*, ed. C. Winnicott, R. Shepherd and M. Davis, 73–7. London: Tavistock, 1984.

Winnicott, D. W., and C. Britton. 'Residential management as treatment for difficult children', in *D. W. Winnicott: Deprivation and Delinquency*, ed. Clare Winnicott, Ray Shepherd and Madeleine Davis, 54–72. London: Tavistock, 1984.

Winter, J. M. 'Infant mortality, maternal mortality and public health in
    Britain in the 1930s'. *Journal of European Economic History* 8:2 (1979):
    439–62.
Women's University Settlement. *Annual Report, 1956–1957*. London: Women's
    University Settlement, 1957.
Young, M., and P. Willmott. *Family and Kinship in East London*, rev. edn.
    Harmondsworth: Penguin, 1962.

Unpublished theses
Abel, E. K. 'Canon Barnett and the First Thirty Years of Toynbee Hall', PhD
    dissertation, Queen Mary, University of London, 1969.
Bradley, K. M. 'Poverty and Philanthropy in East London, 1918–1959: The
    University Settlements and the Urban Working Classes', PhD dissertation,
    Institute of Historical Research, University of London, 2006.
Glessner, R. 'Hosts of the *Kindertransport*: The Role of the Nation, the
    Organisation and the Individual', MA dissertation, Institute of Historical
    Research, University of London, 2007.
Harrow, J. 'The Development of the University Settlements in England,
    1884–1939', PhD dissertation, London School of Economics, University of
    London, 1987.
Koven, S. D. 'Culture and Poverty: The London Settlement House
    Movement, 1870–1914', PhD dissertation, Harvard University, 1987.
McDonnell, K. G. T. 'The Economic and Social Structure of the Parishes of
    Bromley, Hackney, Stepney and Whitechapel from the Thirteenth to the
    Sixteenth Century', PhD dissertation, Queen Mary, University of London,
    1958–59.
Meyer-Kelly, M. L. 'The Child Poverty Action Group, 1965–1974: The Origins
    and Effectiveness of a Single Issue Pressure Group', PhD dissertation,
    University of Bristol, 2001.
Rusby, J. S. M. 'Childhood Temporary Separation: Long-term Effects of War-
    time Evacuation in World War II', PhD dissertation, Birkbeck, University
    of London, 2006.

Other Web resources (as at June 2008)
British Association of Settlements and Social Action Centres, www.bassac.
    org.uk
Evacuees Reunion Association, www.evacuees.org.uk
International Federation of Settlements, www.ifsnetwork.org

Index

Ingram Content Group UK Ltd.
Milton Keynes UK
UKHW041334230323
419051UK00003B/198